MULTITHREADING FOR VISUAL EFFECTS

MULTITHREADING for VISUAL EFFECTS

Martin Watt • Erwin Coumans • George ElKoura • Ronald Henderson
Manuel Kraemer • Jeff Lait • James Reinders

CRC Press
Taylor & Francis Group
Boca Raton London New York

CRC Press is an imprint of the
Taylor & Francis Group, an **informa** business

CRC Press
Taylor & Francis Group
6000 Broken Sound Parkway NW, Suite 300
Boca Raton, FL 33487-2742

© 2015 by Taylor & Francis Group, LLC
CRC Press is an imprint of Taylor & Francis Group, an Informa business

No claim to original U.S. Government works

Printed on acid-free paper
Version Date: 20140618

International Standard Book Number-13: 978-1-4822-4356-7 (Hardback)

Visit the Taylor & Francis Web site at
http://www.taylorandfrancis.com

and the CRC Press Web site at
http://www.crcpress.com

Multithreading applications is hard, but for today's performance—critical codes, an absolute necessity. This book shows how the latest parallel-programming technology can simplify the daunting challenge of producing fast and reliable software for multicore processors. Although the instructive case studies are drawn from visual effects applications, the authors cover the gamut of issues that developers face when parallelizing legacy applications from any domain.

**Charles Leiserson, MIT Computer Science
and Artificial Intelligence Laboratory**

Multithreading graphics algorithms is a new and exciting area of research. It is crucial to computer graphics. This book will prove invaluable to researchers and practitioners alike. Indeed, it will have a strong impact on movie visual effects and games.

Jos Stam, Senior Principal Research Scientist, Autodesk, Inc.

Visual effects programming is undergoing a renaissance as high-end video game effects technology approaches the state-of-the-art defined by blockbuster Hollywood movies, empowered by the capabilities of multi-Teraflop GPU hardware. A wealth of graphics algorithms are now graduating into the realm of real-time rendering, yet today's programmers face a formidable challenge in structuring these algorithms to take full advantage of today's multicore CPU architectures and deliver on their potential.

This book, the collaborative result of many industry luminaries, wonderfully bridges the gap between the theory of multithreading and the practice of multithreading in advanced graphical applications. Join them on this journey to bring real-time visual effects technology to the next level!

Tim Sweeney, CEO and Founder of Epic Games

Contents

Preface   xiii

Acknowledgments   xv

Authors   xvii

List of Figures   xix

List of Tables   xxiii

1 Introduction and Overview   1
James Reinders
1.1 Introduction 1
1.2 Overview of Case Studies 2
1.3 Motivation 3
    1.3.1 Quickly Increasing Clock Speeds Ended by 2005 3
    1.3.2 The Move to Multicore 4
    1.3.3 SIMD Is Parallelism Too 6
    1.3.4 Highly Threaded Hardware 7
1.4 Program in Tasks, Not Threads 7
1.5 Value of Abstraction 8
1.6 Scaling and Vectorization 9
1.7 Advancing Programming Languages for Parallel Programming 10
    1.7.1 Abstraction 10
    1.7.2 Parallel Programming Needs 10
    1.7.3 Relaxed Sequential Semantics 11
1.8 Parallel Programming in C and C++ 11
    1.8.1 Brief Survey of Key Parallelism Options 12
       1.8.1.1 TBB 12
       1.8.1.2 Cilk Plus 12
       1.8.1.3 OpenMP 12
       1.8.1.4 OpenCL 13
       1.8.1.5 GPU Specific Models 13
    1.8.2 More on TBB: Intel Threading Building Blocks 13
       1.8.2.1 Parallel for: parallel_for(...) 14
       1.8.2.2 Parallel Reductions: parallel_reduce 15
       1.8.2.3 Parallel Invocation of Functions: parallel_invoke 16
       1.8.2.4 Learning More about TBB 16
1.9 Data Movement and Layout 16
1.10 Summary 17
1.11 Additional Reading 18

2 Houdini: Multithreading Existing Software **19**

Jeff Lait

2.1 What Is Houdini? 19
2.2 Rewrite or Refactor 21
    2.2.1 Cleaning Statics 22
    2.2.2 Threading the Simple Cases 27
2.3 Patterns 30
    2.3.1 Always Be Reentrant 30
    2.3.2 Never Lock 31
    2.3.3 Atomics Are Slow 31
    2.3.4 Never Blindly Thread 32
    2.3.5 Command Line Control 33
    2.3.6 Constant Memory versus Number of Cores 33
    2.3.7 Memory Allocation 34
2.4 Copy on Write 34
    2.4.1 Const Correctness 35
    2.4.2 Reader/Writer Locks 35
    2.4.3 Ownership Is Important 36
    2.4.4 Sole Ownership Is a Writer Lock 37
    2.4.5 Failure Modes of This System 38
2.5 Dependencies 40
    2.5.1 Task Locks 41
    2.5.2 Mantra 43
2.6 OpenCL 44

3 The Presto Execution System: Designing for Multithreading **47**

George ElKoura

3.1 Introduction 48
    3.1.1 A Note about Interactivity 48
3.2 Presto 49
    3.2.1 Presto Objects 50
    3.2.2 Rigging in Presto 51
    3.2.3 Animation in Presto 52
3.3 Presto's Execution System 52
    3.3.1 Phases of Execution 53
        3.3.1.1 Compilation 53
        3.3.1.2 Scheduling 54
        3.3.1.3 Evaluation 54
    3.3.2 Engine Architecture 54
        3.3.2.1 Network 55
        3.3.2.2 Schedulers 55
        3.3.2.3 Data Managers 56
        3.3.2.4 Executors 56
        3.3.2.5 Engine Architecture and Multithreading 56
3.4 User Extensions 57
    3.4.1 Dependencies Declared *a Priori* 57
    3.4.2 Client Callbacks Are Static Functions 57
    3.4.3 Presto Singletons Are Protected 58
    3.4.4 Iterators 58
    3.4.5 And Then There's Python 58
        3.4.5.1 Global Interpreter Lock 58

　　　　　3.4.5.2　Performance 59
　3.5　Memory Access Patterns 59
　3.6　Flexibility to Experiment 60
　　　3.6.1　Modular Design 60
　　　3.6.2　Targeting Other Platforms 60
　3.7　Multithreading Strategies 61
　　　3.7.1　Per-Node Multithreading 61
　　　3.7.2　Per-Branch Multithreading 62
　　　3.7.3　Per-Model Multithreading 62
　　　3.7.4　Per-Frame Multithreading 64
　3.8　Background Execution 64
　　　3.8.1　User Interaction 65
　　　3.8.2　Frame Scheduling 65
　　　3.8.3　Interruption 66
　　　3.8.4　Constant Data 67
　　　3.8.5　Problematic Data Structures 67
　3.9　Other Multithreading Strategies 69
　　　3.9.1　Strip Mining 69
　　　3.9.2　Predictive Computations 70
　3.10　Debugging and Profiling Tools 70
　3.11　Summary 71

4　LibEE: Parallel Evaluation of Character Rigs　　　　　　　　73
Martin Watt
　4.1　Introduction 74
　4.2　Motivation 76
　4.3　Specific Requirements for Character Animation 76
　　　4.3.1　Animation Graph Goals 77
　　　4.3.2　Animation Graph Features 77
　　　　　4.3.2.1　Few Unique Traversed Paths through Graph 77
　　　　　4.3.2.2　Animation Rigs Have Implicit Parallelism 78
　　　　　4.3.2.3　Expensive Nodes Which Can Be Internally Parallel 78
　　　4.3.3　Animation Graph Constraints 78
　　　　　4.3.3.1　No Graph Editing 78
　　　　　4.3.3.2　No Scripting Languages in Operators 78
　4.4　Graph 79
　　　4.4.1　Threading Engine 79
　　　4.4.2　Graph Evaluation Mechanism 80
　4.5　Threadsafety 80
　　　4.5.1　Node Threadsafety 81
　　　　　4.5.1.1　API Layer 81
　　　　　4.5.1.2　Parallel Unit Tests 81
　　　　　4.5.1.3　Threading Checker Tools 82
　　　　　4.5.1.4　Compiler Flags 82
　　　　　4.5.1.5　LD_PRELOAD 83
　　　　　4.5.1.6　The Kill Switch 84
　　　4.5.2　Graph Threadsafety 84
　4.6　Scalability: Software Considerations 85
　　　4.6.1　Authoring Parallel Loops 86
　　　4.6.2　Overthreading 87
　　　4.6.3　Threading Fatigue 87

	4.6.4	Thread-Friendly Memory Allocators	88
	4.6.5	Oversubscription Due to Multiple Threading Models	88
	4.6.6	Cache Reuse—Chains of Nodes	89
	4.6.7	Cache Reuse—Scheduling Nodes to Maximize Sharing	89
	4.6.8	Task Priorities	89
	4.6.9	Graph Partitioning	89
	4.6.10	Other Processes Running on System	91
	4.6.11	The Memory Wall	91
	4.6.12	Failed Approaches Discussion	91
4.7	Scalability: Hardware Considerations		92
	4.7.1	CPU Power Modes	92
	4.7.2	Turbo Clock	92
	4.7.3	NUMA	92
	4.7.4	Hyperthreading	93
	4.7.5	CPU Affinity	94
	4.7.6	Many-Core Architectures	94
4.8	Production Considerations		95
	4.8.1	Character Systems Restructure	96
	4.8.2	No More Scripted Nodes	96
	4.8.3	Optimizing for Maximum Parallelism	96
4.9	Threading Visualization Tool		97
4.10	Rig Optimization Case Studies		100
	4.10.1	Case Study 1: Quadruped Critical Path Optimization	100
	4.10.2	Case Study 2: Hair Solver	100
	4.10.3	Case Study 3: Free Clothes!	100
4.11	Overall Performance Results		104
4.12	Limits of Scalability		104
4.13	Summary		106

5 Fluids: Simulation on the CPU   111

Ronald Henderson

5.1	Motivation			111
5.2	Programming Models			112
	5.2.1	Everything You Need to Get Started		114
	5.2.2	Example: Over		114
	5.2.3	Example: Dot Product		115
	5.2.4	Example: Maximum Absolute Value		117
	5.2.5	Platform Considerations		118
	5.2.6	Performance		119
5.3	Fluid Simulation			120
	5.3.1	Data Structures		120
	5.3.2	Smoke, Fire, and Explosions		122
		5.3.2.1	Advection Solvers	124
		5.3.2.2	Elliptic Solvers	126
	5.3.3	Liquids		128
		5.3.3.1	Parallel Point Rasterization	132
5.4	Summary			136

6   Bullet Physics: Simulation with OpenCL   **137**
Erwin Coumans
   6.1   Introduction 138
         6.1.1   Rigid Body Dynamics Simulation 138
         6.1.2   Refactoring before the Full Rewrite 139
   6.2   Rewriting from Scratch Using OpenCL 140
         6.2.1   Brief OpenCL Introduction 140
         6.2.2   Exploiting the GPU 142
         6.2.3   Dealing with Branchy Code/Thread Divergence 143
         6.2.4   Serializing Data to Contiguous Memory 144
         6.2.5   Sharing CPU and GPU Code 144
         6.2.6   Precompiled Kernel Caching 145
   6.3   GPU Spatial Acceleration Structures 145
         6.3.1   Reference All Pairs Overlap Test 146
         6.3.2   Uniform Grid 147
         6.3.3   Parallel 1-Axis Sort and Sweep 148
         6.3.4   Parallel 3-Axis Sweep and Prune 149
         6.3.5   Hybrid Approaches 150
         6.3.6   Static Local Space AABB Tree 150
   6.4   GPU Contact Point Generation 151
         6.4.1   Collision Shape Representation 151
         6.4.2   Convex 3D Height Field Using Cube Maps 152
         6.4.3   Separating Axis Test 153
         6.4.4   Sutherland Hodgeman Clipping 153
         6.4.5   Minkowski Portal Refinement 154
         6.4.6   Contact Reduction 154
   6.5   GPU Constraint Solving 155
         6.5.1   Equations of Motion 155
         6.5.2   Contact and Friction Constraint Setup 155
         6.5.3   Parallel Projected Gauss-Seidel Method 156
         6.5.4   Batch Creation and Two-Stage Batching 157
         6.5.5   Non-Contact Constraints 159
         6.5.6   GPU Deterministic Simulation 159
         6.5.7   Conclusion and Future Work 159

7   OpenSubdiv: Interoperating GPU Compute and Drawing   **163**
Manuel Kraemer
   7.1   Representing Shapes 164
         7.1.1   Why Fast Subdivision? 165
         7.1.2   Legacy 165
         7.1.3   OpenSubdiv 166
   7.2   The Control Cage 166
         7.2.1   Patches and Arbitrary Topology 166
         7.2.2   Topological Data Structures 167
         7.2.3   Manifold Surfaces 167
         7.2.4   The Limit Surface 168
   7.3   Uniform Subdivision 169
         7.3.1   Implementing Subdivision Schemata 169
   7.4   Serializing the Mesh Representation 170
         7.4.1   Case Study: Subdividing a Pyramid 170
         7.4.2   Generating Indexing Tables 170

      7.4.3   Preparing for Parallel Execution 172
7.5   Transition from Multicores to Many-Cores. 173
      7.5.1   Streaming Multiprocessors and SIMT 173
      7.5.2   Practical Implementation with OpenCL 174
7.6   Reducing Branching Divergence 175
      7.6.1   Sorting Vertices by Type 176
      7.6.2   Further Vertex Sorting 176
7.7   Optimization Trade-Offs 179
      7.7.1   Alternative Strategy: NVIDIA Dynamic Parallelism 179
      7.7.2   Alternative Strategy: Vertex Stencils 180
      7.7.3   Memory Bottlenecks 181
7.8   Evaluating Our Progress 182
7.9   Fundamental Limitations of Uniform Subdivision 183
      7.9.1   Exponential Growth 184
      7.9.2   Geometric Fidelity 184
      7.9.3   Animating Subdivision Surfaces 185
      7.9.4   Better, Faster, Different 185
7.10 Feature-Adaptive Subdivision 186
      7.10.1 GPU Hardware Tessellation 186
      7.10.2 Catmull-Clark Terminology 187
      7.10.3 Bi-Cubic Patch Representation 188
      7.10.4 Feature-Adaptive Subdivision 189
7.11 Implementing the GPU Rendering Engine 190
      7.11.1 Bi-Cubic Bspline Patches with GLSL 191
          7.11.1.1 Handling Surface Boundaries 192
          7.11.1.2 Handling Patch Transitions 193
          7.11.1.3 "End" Patches 194
      7.11.2 Mitigating Drawing Overheads 196
7.12 Texturing 197
      7.12.1 Displacement Mapping 198
7.13 Conclusion 199

Bibliography   **203**

Index   **209**

Preface

In 2013, Martin Watt assembled us together, a group of software engineers and researchers, to give a SIGGRAPH course on the use of multithreading techniques in the visual effects industry. The course was first presented at the 2013 SIGGRAPH conference in Anaheim, California. We were all excited to share our experience of writing and optimizing high performance software for a computationally demanding field. We discovered that there was a lot we could learn from each other and from others. We wanted to continue sharing our experiences: the pitfalls we ran into, the solutions we adopted, and our successes and failures. This book was born out of this desire.

As the "free lunch" of faster software was ending and as hardware manufacturers turned to increasing the number of cores from increasing their speed, the computational power required by the visual effects community kept growing. We wanted faster and richer renders, faster and more accurate simulations, faster and higher fidelity iterations on our work. How do you harness the power of the new architectures to squeeze more seconds out of your simulation? Or more milliseconds out of your interactive 3D application? These are some of the questions we struggle with.

The approach we have taken in this book is to present case studies that describe how we have used multithreading techniques to achieve better performance. We each present the problems we ran into and how we solved them. Some of the case studies target solutions for shaving milliseconds, while others are aimed at optimizing longer running tasks. Some of the case studies concentrate on multithreading techniques for modern CPU architectures, while others focus on massive parallelism using GPUs. Some of the case studies are of open source projects, so you can download and try out these techniques for yourself and see how well they work. The breadth of topics and approaches should give you an idea of the diverse solutions that currently exist for solving the performance problems we face.

We have not attempted exhaustive coverage of all the different threading technologies, or all possible areas of visual effects, since that would result in an unmanageably large book. Thus, the fact that a specific threading approach is not covered in this book should not be taken as an indication that we consider it less useful, merely that it was not the approach chosen by the specific authors to solve the specific problems they faced. We hope that the descriptions of the problem areas and approaches taken in this series of case studies should be sufficient to allow the reader to map the ideas presented onto their specific combination of problem domain and preferred threading technology. Multithreading is challenging and difficult to get right, and we hope that by sharing both our successes and our failures in the messy real-world application area of production software, we can inspire and encourage others to follow a similar path.

There is a Web site at `http://www.multithreadingandvfx.org`, which was created for the original SIGGRAPH 2013 course, and remains live. We will post material relevant to this book on that site, and would also welcome feedback, opinions, and dialog with others.

We hope we can all learn from our diverse experiences as we tackle the difficult but necessary challenges of parallel programming for our industry.

Martin Watt
Erwin Coumans
George ElKoura
Ron Henderson
Manuel Kraemer
Jeff Lait
James Reinders

Acknowledgments

Martin Watt wishes to thank Lincoln Wallen and Jeff Wike for support for the ambitious project of reworking our character evaluation system, the entire Rigging and Animation RnD team at DreamWorks Animation, and the invaluable contributions from Intel engineers including in particular Mark Hampton and Alex Wells.

Erwin Coumans wishes to thank Takahiro Harada for his research and discussions about GPU and physics simulation, Raja Koduri and Jason Yang at AMD, and Dominic Mallinson and Yoshimichi Kitaya at Sony for supporting open source, and all contributors and users of the Bullet Physics SDK.

George ElKoura wishes to thank Ed Catmull, Steve May, Guido Quaroni, Adam Woodbury, Dirk Van Gelder, Florian Sauer, Aaron Luk, Andrew Butts, Florian Zitzelsberger, Pixar's entire Software R&D group, and all the Pixar artists who always inspire us to build better tools.

Ron Henderson wishes to thank Ken Museth, Nafees Bin Zafar, Mihai Alden, David Hill, Peter Cucka, and the many FX artists at DreamWorks Animation who have contributed feedback, testing, advice, and inspiring imagery during the development of our simulation tools. Thanks also to DreamWorks studio management for their continuing support of research and development.

Manuel Kraemer wishes to thank Charles Loop, Matthias Nießner, Tony DeRose, and Mark Meyer: OpenSubdiv would not exist without your pioneering research; Dirk Van Gelder, David Yu, Takahito Tejima, and Julian Fong, the Pixar engineers who have contributed to the implementation, and Bill Polson, Guido Quaroni, Steve May, and Ed Catmull for supporting our first steps along the arduous open-source path.

Jeff Lait wishes to thank Edward Lam for leading the way in our multithreading of Houdini; and all the developers at Side Effects Software who have contributed to this quest over the decade.

James Reinders wishes to thank the numerous customers who have provided feedback and inspiration for Intel products, in particular Martin Watt and the DreamWorks team, the team at Pixar, all the Intel engineers working on Intel tools and libraries, and those working on the Intel MIC architecture products. Reinders is especially grateful for the support and encouragement received from Susan Meredith, Andrew Reinders, Kim Colosimo, Kunjan Raval, Charles Winstead, Jim Jeffers, David Mackay, Michael McCool, Joe Curley, Herb Hinstroff, Arch Robison, and Greg Stoner.

All the authors wish to thank the publisher (Rick Adams, executive editor; Linda Leggio, our project editor; and Joselyn Banks-Kyle, our project coordinator of Taylor & Francis).

Authors

Martin Watt is a principal engineer at DreamWorks Animation where he has spent 5 years working on a ground-up replacement for the existing in-house animation tool. Prior to that he worked at Autodesk and Alias in Toronto, Canada, as a senior developer and software architect on Maya, working initially on modeling tools, then focusing on performance optimization and multithreading across the codebase. He has a PhD in astrophysics from the University of Birmingham in the United Kingdom.

Erwin Coumans is a principal engineer at AMD, where he is responsible for real-time physics simulation research and development for film and game productions. His work is used by game companies such as Disney Interactive Studios and Rockstar Games, and film studios such as Sony Pictures Imageworks and DreamWorks Animation. After his study of computer science at Eindhoven University, he has been involved in collision detection and physics simulation research for Guerrilla Games in the Netherlands, Havok in Ireland, and Sony Computer Entertainment U.S. R&D. Coumans is the main author of the open source Bullet Physics library at `http://bulletphysics.org`.

George ElKoura is a lead engineer at Pixar Animation Studios. He has 14 years of animation industry experience, first as an engineer at Side Effects Software, working on Houdini, and later joining Pixar where he has been for the past 7 years. At Pixar, his current responsibilities include leading a small team of engineers to deliver high performance proprietary animation software to artists.

Ron Henderson is a director of R&D at DreamWorks Animation where he is responsible for developing visual effects, simulation, and rendering tools. In 2014, he received a Technical Achievement Academy Award for Flux, a general purpose fluid simulation system used for effects such as dust, smoke, fire, and explosions in recent films such as *Rise of the Guardians, Puss in Boots, Megamind*, and *The Croods*. Prior to joining DreamWorks in 2002, he was a senior scientist at Caltech working on efficient techniques for simulating fluid turbulence on massively parallel computers. He has a PhD in mechanical and aerospace engineering from Princeton University, where he wrote his first distributed simulation framework for the Intel i860 Hypercube.

Manuel Kraemer is a graphics software engineer at Pixar Animation Studios. Prior to that he worked as a technical director at Disney Feature Animation, Double Negative, and the BBC. He is currently working on OpenSubdiv, the open source subdivision surface API.

Jeff Lait is a senior mathematician at Side Effects Software where he has worked on Houdini since version 1.0. He has contributed to geometry processing, rigid body solvers, and fluid simulations. He has also had the "joy" of working with many architectures over the years: SGI, Alpha, x86, Itanium, PS2, and PS3; and is still waiting for the system that solves more problems than it causes.

James Reinders is a director at Intel and their parallel programming evangelist. Reinders is currently involved in multiple efforts at Intel to bring parallel programming models to the industry including for the Intel MIC architecture. He is a senior engineer who joined Intel Corporation in 1989 and has contributed to projects including the world's first TeraFLOP/s supercomputer (ASCI Red) and the world's first TeraFLOP/s microprocessor (Intel® Xeon Phi™ Coprocessor, code named Knights Corner). Reinders is an author of books on *VTune*™ (Intel® Press, 2005), *Threading Building Blocks* (O'Reilly Media, 2007), *Structured Parallel Programming* (Morgan Kaufmann, 2012), and *Intel Xeon Phi Coprocessor High Performance Programming* (Morgan Kaufmann, 2013).

List of Figures

1.1 Growth of processor clock rates over time (plotted on a log scale). 4
1.2 Moore's Law continues! (plotted on a log scale). 5
1.3 Cores and hardware threads per processor (plotted on a log scale). 6
1.4 Width of largest data (plotted on a log scale). 7
1.5 Highly scalable coprocessor versus a standard high-end processor. 8
1.6 AoS versus SoA. 17

2.1 Screenshot of a simulation running in Houdini. 20

3.1 Screenshot of a session in Presto, Pixar's proprietary animation system.
Presto provides an integrated environment that supports rigging and animation workflows, among others. The editors shown here (the spline editor
and the spreadsheet editor) are commonly used for animation. This chapter describes Presto's execution system, which is responsible for posing the
characters and other such computations at interactive rates. 49
3.2 High-level view of where the execution system libraries fit in the overall
system. 50
3.3 Objects used to build a scene graph in Presto. 51
3.4 The components of the execution system's architecture. 55
3.5 Per-node multithreading. 62
3.6 Per-branch multithreading. 63
3.7 Per-model multithreading. 63
3.8 Per-frame multithreading. 64

4.1 Animator working interactively on a character in Premo. 74
4.2 Detail from a still frame from the DreamWorks movie *How to Train Your
Dragon 2.* 75
4.3 A typical hero character graph. 77
4.4 Tasks plotted against processor ID for a 12 core system. 90
4.5 Scalability dropoff with four socket systems compared with two socket systems for a single hero character workload. 93
4.6 Hyperthreading performance impact. 94
4.7 Evaluation of a character graph over a range of frames on four cores. . . . 95
4.8 The threading visualization tool enables riggers to investigate bottlenecks
within the graph. 98
4.9 Mode to compare two profiles to check benefits of optimizations. 99
4.10 Example showing the process for optimizing a quadruped character. 101
4.11 The top profile shows the initial hair system implementation. 102
4.12 The top graph shows a character with motion and deformation systems, the
bottom graph shows the addition of rigged clothing. 103
4.13 A demonstration of different levels of parallelism in a graph evaluation on
a 12 core machine. 105

4.14 Evaluation of a single frame of animation for eight independent hero characters on a 32 core machine. 107
4.15 Multiple graph evaluations for 100 frames of playback. 108
4.16 Multiple graph evaluation for six different hero characters. 109

5.1 (Top) Schematic of the OpenVDB data structure for sparse volumes and (bottom) a typical cloud model stored as a sparse volume. 121
5.2 Volume rendering of a large dust cloud simulated with a resolution of $N = 1200 \times 195 \times 500$ along with a final frame from the movie *Megamind*. . . . 122
5.3 (Top) Simulated torch fire and (bottom) high-resolution pyroclastic dust and destruction from *The Croods*. 123
5.4 Speedup curve for scalar advection on a grid with $N = 512^3$ grid points using the BFECC advection kernel. 127
5.5 Comparison of solve times for the Poisson equation with N total grid points using MG and FFT solution techniques. 129
5.6 Parallel speedup for the FFT-based Poisson solver (top) and MG Poisson solver (bottom) for various grid resolutions. 130
5.7 (Top) Surface details of a simulated liquid integrated with a surrounding procedural ocean surface, and (bottom) production shot from *The Croods* with character integration and final lighting. 131
5.8 Schematic of the data structure used for liquid simulations. 132
5.9 Schematic of parallel point rasterization into separate grids for threads T_0 and T_1, and then a final reduction to combine the results. 134
5.10 Speedup curve for velocity rasterization from $N = 446$ million points into a $N = 836^3$ (effective resolution) sparse grid using a high-order (MP4) and low-order (BSP2) kernel. 136

6.1 Destruction simulation. 138
6.2 Rigid body pipeline. 139
6.3 Obsolete CPU performance benchmarks. 140
6.4 Host and OpenCL device. 140
6.5 Typical GPU architecture. 142
6.6 Axis aligned bounding box. 146
6.7 Uniform grid. 148
6.8 Projected AABB intervals. 148
6.9 Sequential incremental 3-axis sweep and prune. 149
6.10 Parallel 3-axis sweep and prune. 149
6.11 Binary AABB tree. 150
6.12 Node array with skip indices. 151
6.13 Convex shapes. 151
6.14 Convex decomposition. 152
6.15 Concave triangle mesh geometry. 152
6.16 Dual representation: Surface points and cube map. 153
6.17 Generating contact area by clipping faces. 153
6.18 Single contact point collision impulse. 155
6.19 Multiple contact constraints. 156
6.20 Uniform grid to split batches. 158
6.21 Bullet Physics rigid body benchmark, 112k box stack on a GPU simulated in 70 ms/frame. 160
6.22 Bullet Physics GPU rigid body benchmark, 64k boxes colliding with a concave trimesh, simulated in 100 ms/frame. 160

6.23 AMD CodeXL tool used to debug an OpenCL kernel under Linux. 161
6.24 AMD CodeXL tool used to profile an OpenCL kernel under Windows in Microsoft Visual Studio. 161

7.1   Recursive subdivision of a polyhedron. 164
7.2   Wireframe of Geri's head. 165
7.3   Half-edges data structure. 167
7.4   Non-manifold fan. 167
7.5   Successive subdivision iterations. 168
7.6   Two iterations of uniform subdivision. 169
7.7   One subdivision iteration applied on a pyramid. 170
7.8   The child vertices created from a regular quad face. 171
7.9   Subdivision tables for the pyramid of Figure 7.7: (A) is the vertex buffer, (B) contains topology information, (C) provides the edge and vertex sharpness, and (D) are indices which point into the vertex buffer. 171
7.10 Comparison of CPU and GPU architectures. 173
7.11 Streaming multiprocessors with multiple processing cores. 174
7.12 Several kernels executing in sequence. 176
7.13 Combinations of subdivision rules. 177
7.14 Vertex ranking matrix. 177
7.15 Final execution sequence. 179
7.16 Execution sequence without and with Dynamic Parallelism. 180
7.17 Coalesced global memory access. 181
7.18 Kernel compute times for six uniform subdivision levels of a simple mesh. 182
7.19 Geometric progression of subdivided polygons. 184
7.20 Comparison of off-line and interactive assets. 185
7.21 Discrete and fractional tessellation patterns. 186
7.22 A regular and extraordinary vertex. 187
7.23 Subdivision of regular and extraordinary faces. 187
7.24 Bi-cubic patches around an extraordinary vertex. 188
7.25 Adaptive topological feature isolation. The color coding illustrates how the different types of patches are used to isolate boundaries or extraordinary vertices. 189
7.26 Feature-adaptive display pipeline. 190
7.27 GPU shader stages pipeline. 191
7.28 Wireframe showing the triangles generated by the GPU tessellation unit. . 194
7.29 Boundary patch and corner patch with mirrored vertices. 195
7.30 Matching tessellation across isolation levels. 195
7.31 All five possible transition patterns. 195
7.32 Comparing an example transition pattern drawn with sub-patches against our proposed extension. 197
7.33 Interactive render using GPU hardware tessellation and Ptex displacement textures showing the extremely high density of geometric detail. 199
7.34 Mudbox sculpture showing analytical displacement with GPU hardware tessellation for interactive animation. 200

List of Tables

3.1   Deadlock due to improper use of the GIL.   59

5.1   Hardware used for production computing at DreamWorks Animation from 2008–2013. Note that the processor speed has been flat or decreasing while the processor counts go steadily up.   112

5.2   Asymptotic complexity for several common methods used to solve the discrete Poisson problem.   127

Chapter 1

Introduction and Overview

James Reinders

Intel Corporation

1.1	Introduction	1
1.2	Overview of Case Studies	2
1.3	Motivation	3
	1.3.1 Quickly Increasing Clock Speeds Ended by 2005	3
	1.3.2 The Move to Multicore	4
	1.3.3 SIMD Is Parallelism Too	6
	1.3.4 Highly Threaded Hardware	7
1.4	Program in Tasks, Not Threads	7
1.5	Value of Abstraction	8
1.6	Scaling and Vectorization	9
1.7	Advancing Programming Languages for Parallel Programming	10
	1.7.1 Abstraction	10
	1.7.2 Parallel Programming Needs	10
	1.7.3 Relaxed Sequential Semantics	11
1.8	Parallel Programming in C and C++	11
	1.8.1 Brief Survey of Key Parallelism Options	12
	1.8.1.1 TBB	12
	1.8.1.2 Cilk Plus	12
	1.8.1.3 OpenMP	12
	1.8.1.4 OpenCL	13
	1.8.1.5 GPU Specific Models	13
	1.8.2 More on TBB: Intel Threading Building Blocks	13
	1.8.2.1 Parallel for: parallel_for(...)	14
	1.8.2.2 Parallel Reductions: parallel_reduce	15
	1.8.2.3 Parallel Invocation of Functions: parallel_invoke	16
	1.8.2.4 Learning More about TBB	16
1.9	Data Movement and Layout	16
1.10	Summary	17
1.11	Additional Reading	18

1.1 Introduction

We begin with an overview of the current state of parallel programming; this chapter provides a common basis of information and terminology before the following chapters dive into the various domains and parallel programming experiences. Parallel programming is how we program modern computers anytime we want to reach their full potential. As we will explain, this is because computers themselves have universally become parallel computers.

Parallel programs are comprised of multiple tasks that may be executed in parallel. These programs are designed for concurrency purposefully to utilize parallel computers; we refer to them as parallel programs instead of concurrent programs because we are interested in the benefits of parallelism. Concurrency is the property of having multiple tasks that are active at that same time but not necessarily doing work simultaneously; parallel computers add the ability for concurrent work to be simultaneously making progress.

Parallel programming allows an application to either get more work done in a given amount of time, or allows work to get done more quickly by doing pieces of it (tasks) in parallel. Using parallelism to get more work done in the same time is said to give us increased throughput. Using parallelism to get a given amount of work done more quickly is said to give us reduced latency. Parallel programs often do both, but understanding which is most valuable in a particular situation can be very important. Tools that help animators do their detailed work interactively, in a highly fluid and detailed fashion, is generally a quest to decrease latency. Server farms that seek to render a complete movie in a reasonable amount of time are likely to be most concerned with throughput. While both are parallel programming methods, the approaches are different enough to deserve consideration at the outset of a project.

1.2 Overview of Case Studies

Using parallelism in your application is almost never something you can stick in at the last minute in a program with effective results. We are best off when we think about everything in terms of how to do it in parallel as cleanly as possible and then implement to match our clean thinking about parallelism. The more we are constrained to not modify code or data structures within an application, the less likely we are to take the best advantage of parallel computing. Of course, we almost always find ourselves working to add parallelism to existing applications instead of starting completely from scratch.

Often we do not have the luxury from starting from scratch. We will see in Chapter 2 (Houdini: Multithreading Existing Software) how multithreading can effectively be added to an existing mature application, as was done in Houdini. We will also cover how DreamWorks and Pixar implemented their applications with multithreading in mind from the beginning, when we talk about Presto in Chapter 3 and LibEE in Chapter 4.

The most popular solutions such as Intel Threading Building Blocks (TBB) [57] are designed with this in mind with features like "relaxed sequential consistency" and concurrent replacements for memory allocation routines and STL containers to adapt programs with sequential origins for effective use of parallelism. TBB is the preferred method of parallelism in several chapters of this book.

The case study in Chapter 5 discusses both OpenMP and TBB while offering insights into the relationships between hardware, algorithms, and data structures while simulating fluids.

Of course, if you can rewrite you may consider getting close to the hardware to extract maximum performance from specific hardware using OpenCL. The Bullet Physics case study, in Chapter 6, shows a full rewrite of a rigid body simulator running the entire pipeline on the GPU using OpenCL. All the data structures and algorithms have been chosen to exploit the fine grain massive parallelism of GPUs. Although tuned for GPU, the OpenCL kernels also run surprisingly well on an OpenCL CPU platform.

In Chapter 7 (OpenSubdiv: Interoperating GPU Compute and Drawing), the OpenSubdiv case study is confined to the narrower problem space of manipulating high-level geometry within an interactive application. However, the engineering methods introduced in this chapter break some new ground showing how to interoperate GPU and many-core parallelism with cutting-edge GPU drawing techniques from the latest graphics APIs and hardware. Beyond the optimization of a complex problem, we detail how a complete paradigm shift yielded not only significant performance gains, but also brought to the interactive domain several critical shading features once exclusive to off-line image renderers.

In several of the case study chapters we have chosen to highlight multithreading "gems." These are brief notes that encapsulate what we feel are key points and valuable lessons that we have learned in our own work that we would like to share with our readers. These gems are displayed in the same format as this current paragraph.

By discussing successful work in parallel programming, this book offers multiple learning opportunities. This chapter covers the motivation and foundation for the rest of this book.

1.3 Motivation

All computers are now parallel. All modern computers support parallelism in hardware through at least one parallel feature such as vector instructions, multithreaded cores, multicore processors, multiple processors, graphics engines, and parallel coprocessors. This applies to supercomputers as well as the lowest-power modern processors such as those found in phones.

It is necessary to use explicit parallel programming to get the most out of such processors. Approaches that attempt to automatically parallelize serial code simply cannot deal with the fundamental shifts in algorithms required for effective parallelization.

The goal of a programmer in a modern computing environment is not just to take advantage of processors with two or four cores. Instead, we must strive to write scalable applications that can take advantage of any amount of parallel hardware: all 4 cores on a quad-core processor, all 8 cores on octo-core processors, 32 cores in a multiprocessor machine, more than 60 cores on many-core processors, and beyond. The quest for scaling requires attention to many factors, including the minimization of data movement, and sequential bottlenecks (including locking), and other forms of overhead.

1.3.1 Quickly Increasing Clock Speeds Ended by 2005

Parallel computers have been around for a long time, but several recent trends have led to increased parallelism in all computers.

Around 2005, a dramatic halt to the rise in clocking speeds of new microprocessors occurred, which gave rise to an equally dramatic shift to parallel designs. For decades, computer designs utilized a rise in the switching speed of transistors to drive a dramatic increase in the performance of computers. Figure 1.1 shows this steady growth until 2005 by plotting the actual clock rates of every major Intel processor. Note that in this, and future trends graphs, we plot Intel processors only. The trends are essentially the same across all manufacturers. Plotting Intel architecture alone gives us a consistent multi-decade view of trends while reducing the varying elements of architecture, manufacturer, or process technologies. An increase in clock rate, when the instruction set remains the same as has mostly been the case for the Intel architecture, translates roughly into an increase in the rate at which instructions are completed and therefore an increase in computational performance.

FIGURE 1.1: Growth of processor clock rates over time (plotted on a log scale).

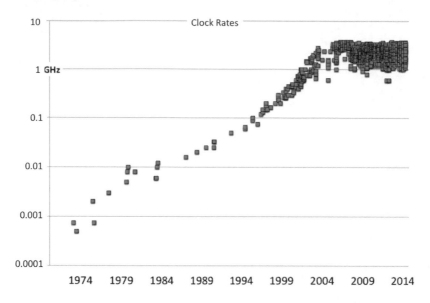

1.3.2   The Move to Multicore

From 1973 to 2003, clock rates increased by three orders of magnitude (1000×), from about 1 MHz in 1973 to 1 GHz in 2003. However, as is clear from Figure 1.1, clock rates have now ceased to grow, and now generally top out around 3 GHz. By 2005, the convergence of three factors served to limit the growth in performance of single cores through rising clock rates, and shift new processor designs to the use of parallel computing instead. Understanding that this was from the convergence of three factors helps us understand that this shift from rising clock rates was inevitable and not the result of a single missing breakthrough. The three factors were unacceptable power utilization, limits in instruction level parallelism (ILP), and the high discrepancy of processor speeds relative to memory speeds. We can refer to these as the Power Wall, the ILP Wall, and the Memory Wall. In order to achieve increasing performance over time for each new processor generation, we cannot depend on rising clock rates, due to the Power Wall. We also cannot depend on automatic mechanisms to find (more) parallelism in naive serial code, due to the ILP Wall. To achieve higher performance, we must write explicit parallel programs. This is especially true if we want to see performance scale over time on new processors. The Memory Wall means that we also have to seriously consider communication and memory access costs, and may have to use additional parallelism to hide latency. Instead of using the growing number of transistors predicted by Moore's Law for ways to maintain the "serial processor illusion," architects of modern processor designs now provide multiple mechanisms for explicit parallelism. As programmers, these are our opportunities to exploit what parallel processor designs offer for parallel programming.

The trend shown in Figure 1.2, known as Moore's Law, demonstrates exponential growth in the total number of transistors in a processor from 1970 to the present. In 1965, Gordon Moore observed that the number of transistors that could be integrated on silicon chips were doubling about every 2 years, an observation that has become known as Moore's Law.

Two rough data points at the extremes of Figure 1.2 are 0.001 million transistors in 1971 and 1000 million transistors in 2011. The gain of 6 orders of magnitude over 40 years represents an average growth rate of 0.15 orders of magnitude every year. This works out

FIGURE 1.2: Moore's Law continues! (plotted on a log scale).

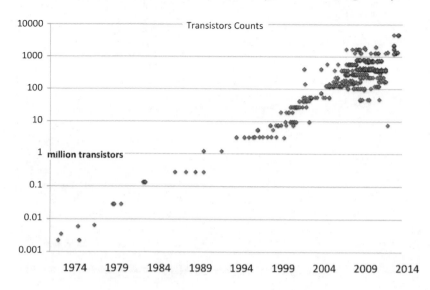

to be 1.41× per year, or 1.995× every 2 years. The data shows that a prediction of 2× per year is amazingly accurate.

This exponential growth has created opportunities for more and more complex designs for microprocessors. The resulting trend in hardware is clear: more and more parallelism at a hardware level will become available for any application that is written to utilize it.

This greatly favors programmers over time, as the increased complexity of design will allow for innovations to increase programmability. The "free lunch" [62] of automatically faster serial applications through faster microprocessors has ended. The "new free lunch" requires scalable parallel programming. The good news is that if you design a program for scalable parallelism, it will continue to scale as processors with more parallelism become available.

Figure 1.3 shows that the number of cores and hardware threads per processor was one until around 2004, when growth in hardware threads emerged as the trend instead of growth in clock rate. The concept of multiple hardware threads per core started earlier, in the case of Intel with hyperthreading this happened a few years prior to multicore taking off. Today, you may find one, two, or four hardware threads per core depending on the processor.

Multicore and many-core devices use independent cores that are essentially duplicates of each other, hooked together, to get work done with separate software threads running on each core.

The distinction between "multicore" versus "many-core" is not strictly defined, but in 2014, multicore is used to refer to products under 32 cores, and many-core devices start at 57 cores per device. The difference will likely blur over time, but for now the design of many-core devices is heavily biased to scaling and not individual core performance while a multicore device is designed with more emphasis on single core performance.

Hyperthreaded cores reuse the same core design to execute multiple software threads at a time efficiently. Unlike adding additional cores for more parallelism, which duplicate the design 100% to add support for an additional software thread, hyperthreading adds single digit (maybe 3%) die area to get support for an additional software thread. The 100% duplication in the case of an additional core can yield 100% performance boost with a second thread, while hyperthreading generally adds only a 5 to 20% performance boost from an additional thread. The added efficiency of hyperthreading is obvious when the small amount of die area that is added is considered.

FIGURE 1.3: Cores and hardware threads per processor (plotted on a log scale).

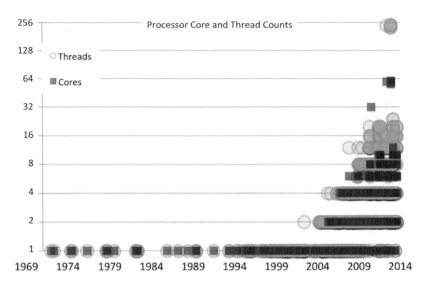

1.3.3   SIMD Is Parallelism Too

In addition to adding more cores to use in parallel, and more hardware threads per core to use in parallel, we can offer each hardware thread the ability to operate on more data in parallel. Figure 1.4 shows the trend of increasing the size of data operations. Until 1995, most mathematical operations in Intel processors utilized single values at a time. In other words, an addition C = A + B would have a single value A added to a single value B giving a single answer C. The introduction of MMX allowed for 64 bit operands that were actually made up of multiple smaller data items that would be operated on in parallel. Byte (8-bit) operations would fit eight per 64-bit word, so that a Single-Instruction could operate on Multiple-Data using what are referred to as SIMD instructions. In MMX, eight bytes at a time could be operands into a SIMD addition that could be expressed as C[0:7] = A[0:7] + B[0:7]. SSE expanded to be 128 bits wide and include floating point (FP) number operations in addition to the integer arithmetic of MMX. Since floating point numbers are either 32-bits wide (single precision FP) or 64-bits wide (double precision FP), an SSE instruction could do four single precision or two double precision computations in parallel. Figure 1.4 shows that data widths have doubled twice more since SSE, with AVX (256-bits wide) followed by 512-bits wide SIMD capabilities. With the 512-bit operations, we have SIMD instructions that can do 16 single precision math operations in parallel per instruction.

Since SIMD instructions are operating on vectors of data, the programming to use SIMD operations is called vector arithmetic. The activity to change an algorithm to use vectors is frequently referred to as vectorization. Just like other forms of parallelism, expressing vector arithmetic was not provided for in programming languages originally. Efforts to have compiler assisted vectorization, even attempts to make "auto-vectorization," are extremely limited when programs are not written to use this type of parallelism. Just like other forms of parallelism, vector parallelism is best used when a program is designed with vector arithmetic in mind.

FIGURE 1.4: Width of largest data (plotted on a log scale).

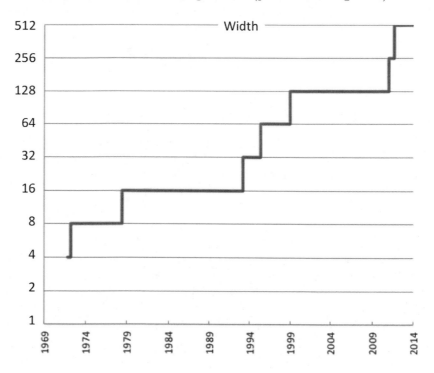

1.3.4 Highly Threaded Hardware

The emergence of "highly parallel" devices, including GPUs and many-core processors, are only interesting to use if a program can harness all these forms of parallelism. Figure 1.5 comes from teaching programming for the highly parallel Intel Xeon Phi Coprocessor [36]. This Intel coprocessor has up to 61 processor cores (x86) each with four hardware threads and 512-bit with SIMD instructions. That means a program that can scale to use 244 hardware threads and use 512-bit vectors effectively will do much better than a program that tries to use few threads or vectors. The key to Figure 1.5 is that scaling is essentially required for such devices because the performance of a single core, or a non-SIMD instruction, is much less for a many-core processor (or GPU) than it is for a multicore processor. For small numbers of threads, or little vector usage, a multicore processor has a much higher performance than a many-core processor or GPU. It is only when a program scales to high levels of parallelism that an advantage can be had. The good news for programmers is that efforts to add parallelism can increase performance regardless of the target if programming models are abstract enough. The highly parallel devices offer an additional upside for the applications that can show the highest levels of parallelism.

1.4 Program in Tasks, Not Threads

A programmer should always think and program in terms of tasks, not threads. This is incredibly important. This means that a programmer's role is to identify a large number of tasks (work) to do. A runtime engine can map tasks onto threads at runtime to match

FIGURE 1.5: Highly scalable coprocessor versus a standard high-end processor.

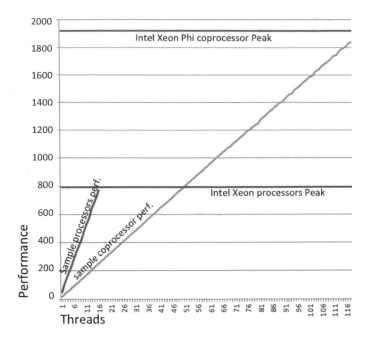

the hardware and the runtime attributes of the application. This works much better than having a programmer's role being to both find and map parallelism.

We are guilty in this book of talking about multithreading while we are actually encouraging programming with multiple tasks. The confusion arises because the program is truly multithreaded to utilize the parallel computing available, but that the programming mindset really should focus on programming in terms of multiple tasks. The Massachusetts Institute of Technology (MIT) Cilk project, which started in the mid-1990s, was key to helping spur this important evolution of programming. The most popular and widely used implementation of these concepts is the open source project Intel Threading Building Blocks (TBB). In retrospect, many on the team responsible for developing TBB would select the name "Tasking Building Blocks" if given the chance again. The TBB library emphasizes having programmers reason and program in terms of tasks while the library maps the programmer's intent onto software threading presented by the operating system and the hardware threading available in the processors. Later in this chapter, there is a brief introduction to TBB since it is so often referred to in the other chapters. On the general topic of not programming to threads, we recommend a paper titled "The Problem with Threads" by Edward A. Lee [41].

1.5   Value of Abstraction

The concept of programming to an abstraction is not new in general but it is relatively new for parallel programming. Fortran was introduced as an abstraction in 1957 to move programmers to a more productive abstraction than using assembly language directly. Programmers were skeptical as they worried about efficiency but were soon won over to the benefits of good abstractions. Little has changed! Many programming abstractions have come along since Fortran. Moving to abstractions for parallel programming creates similar debates about efficiency of the produced code and the benefits that should be expected. Three key motivations to move to an abstraction that we see are: (1) desire to have portability, (2) desire to utilize nested parallelism, and (3) desire to benefit from multiple types of parallelism. The desire to be portable includes wishing for portability across operating systems and platforms, wishing to be "future ready" to run well on future machines, and wanting "performance portability" where code runs reasonably well everywhere without recoding for each platform.

Portability of functionality and performance are both compromised when programming close to the hardware. The more hardware specific an application is coded, the less portable it is. Programs that are coded to use 128-bit vectors using intrinsics designed specifically for 128-bit (SSE) vectors are much less portable than a program that can use general vector arithmetic and allow a library or compiler to use width vector instructions to match the hardware. OpenCL is designed to give high degrees of programmer control over heterogeneous computing. Since that is a key reason to consider OpenCL, code written in OpenCL is generally not as portable as more abstract methods. This may be possible to overcome by programming style with additional effort. It is fair to blame portability challenges of OpenCL on programming which exercises tight control over heterogeneous programming by encouraging specialized versions for different hardware (CPU or GPU or coprocessor, etc.) rather than a single solution aimed at running everywhere. Undoubtably, in such an environment portability is going to rest strongly on the algorithm design and the programming style. As such, OpenCL is not a wise choice for applications in general but may be the perfect solution for a critical algorithm or for tools themselves to target when compiling a higher level abstraction.

Nested parallelism comes in many ways including instances where the caller to a subroutine may not know if the subroutine will have tasks sufficient to offer work in parallel, and the subroutine does not know if it was called from a serial portion of the program or a parallel portion. A good abstract will make it so it does not matter. TBB and Cilk Plus handle this automatically for us. Unfortunately, OpenMP solves the problem by not exploiting nested parallelism by default and in general cannot exploit nested parallelism.

Finally, the use of cores, hardware threads, and vectors are all forms of parallelism an abstraction may help manage. While all three of these forms of parallelism could be utilized through explicit coding in every application, it is better to define a higher-level interface for the programmer, an abstraction, and have every application use that abstraction. Not only is the application simplified, but the implementation of the abstraction can be refined, ported, advanced independently, and potentially benefit all applications with future updates. Such has been the experience with the likes of OpenMP, TBB, and Cilk Plus.

1.6 Scaling and Vectorization

Scaling, the use of cores and hardware threads, is well supported by abstractions today and there is no reason to not be coding in tasks instead of threads to take advantage of these excellent abstractions. Vectorization remains more of a black art, although the #pragma simd capabilities of Cilk Plus and OpenMP 4.0 are instances of advances that are helping create better abstractions for vector programming. Without using an abstraction, a "hard coded" application will advance to new techniques or new hardware support only with effort to modify that application itself.

1.7 Advancing Programming Languages for Parallel Programming

None of the most popular programming languages in use today were designed as parallel programming languages. Despite there being programming languages designed specifically for expressing concurrency or parallelism, widespread adoption of parallel programming will occur using the already popular programming languages.

Programming languages have been extended or modified in some manner to assist in their use for parallel programming. This is an ongoing process; the language standards bodies are examining what additional official changes should be embraced to further support parallel programming.

1.7.1 Abstraction

We can consider language changes from several angles, but regardless of the angle the objective is to support a programming abstraction that divides the effort between the programmer and the language implementation. Ideally, the result is a more productive programmer, portability of functionality, performance portability, and continued high performance. Some flexibility reduction in exchange for ease of understanding can be quite desirable. The battle to stop the use of "GOTO statements" [18] in favor of structured programming is now considered normal; although at the time it was debated as some decried the loss of flexibility of the GOTO statement. Today, a similar quest for structured parallel programming evokes similar debates about loss of flexibility.

It would seem inevitable based on history that additional structure with an appropriate reduction in flexibility will advance the state of the art in programming. Programming to tasks instead of threads is clearly one such trend that has resonated well in the programming community. However, the use of strong typing to eliminate deadlock or race conditions have not found adoption probably because they conflict with the less strict traditions of popular programming languages.

1.7.2 Parallel Programming Needs

A number of features seem desirable in a language to support parallel programming. These would include abstractly expressing task and data parallelism, providing hints for efficiency, avoiding parallel programming errors, and assisting with determinism in the resulting programming. Parallel programming extensions generally tackle a portion of these features leaving us to choose how to solve our particular needs.

An aspect of debate to accompany all these extensions is whether the language should be extended with new keywords, libraries, or directives. New keywords offer the tightest integration with compilers but are generally discouraged because they complicate the core language and potentially change existing programs that were designed prior to a particular word being a reserved keyword. The Cilk Plus project [15], derived from the Cilk work at MIT, defines new keywords for parallel programming. Libraries are generally preferred unless compiler assistance is compelling. Intel Threading Building Blocks is an example of a template library that extends C++ for parallel programming. Directives are a compromise between keywords and libraries because they invoke compiler support but are defined to be hints rather than required elements in a program. In other words, directives should not change the semantics of the program. OpenMP defines a popular set of directives for C, C++, and Fortran that are nearly universally supported extensions for parallel programming.

1.7.3   Relaxed Sequential Semantics

We can imagine writing a parallel program in such a way that it cannot be executed without a parallel processor. In general, this is not what we would advise. The obvious disadvantage is that such a program would not be as portable. The less obvious problem is that such a program is harder for most people to understand. In fact, we have found that parallel programming is considered easier to understand, and easier to debug, if the program semantics stay the same with or without the "parallel" portion of the programming considered. We have also seen the bonus that such programs are more efficient on sequential machines and better at supporting nested parallelism.

Having sequential semantics means that a (parallel) program can be executed using a single thread of control as an ordinary sequential program without changing the semantics of the program. Parallel programming with sequential semantics has many advantages over programming in a manner that precludes serial execution. Sequential semantics casts parallelism as a way to accelerate execution and not as mandatory for correctness. With sequential semantics we do not need to fully understand the way parallelism will proceed in order to understand a program with sequential semantics. To contrast with that, examples of mandatory parallelism include producer-consumer relationships with bounded buffers (hence the producer cannot necessarily be completely executed before the consumer because the producer can become blocked) and message passing (for example, MPI) programs with cyclic message passing. Due to timing, precision, and other sources of inexactness the results of a sequential execution may differ from the concurrent invocation of the same program. Sequential semantics only means that any such variation is not due to the semantics of the program. The term "relaxed sequential semantics" is sometimes used to explicitly acknowledge the variations possible due to non-semantic differences in serial versus concurrent executions. OpenMP, TBB, and Cilk Plus all offer relaxed sequential semantics. For instance, OpenMP directives can be ignored, a TBB parallel_for can be comprehended as a regular for loop, and the Cilk Plus keyword "cilk_for" can be comprehended as a "for."

1.8   Parallel Programming in C and C++

The C++11 standard contains a number of additions for parallel programming, perhaps the most important of them being a defined memory model in the face of concurrency. A memory model explains what order things become visible, for instance if a thread changes the value of variables A, B, and C in code in that order must they be seen as changing in that order by all other threads that may be able to see the same variables? If a program has a=b=c=0; a=1; b=2; c=3; can b=2 while a=0? We know that in the thread doing the assignment the answer is no, but the answer for other threads in the same program is maybe. This seemingly mundane detail turns out to be critical in establishing reliable portability of parallel programs. In practice, portability was often achieved before C++11 because implementations of C++ had already addressed the problem at least partially. The whole topic of a defined memory model seems to largely go unnoticed, in part because many people assume it was already solved.

The more visible issues for programmers are dealing with expressing tasks and helping with vectorization. The C++ community has embraced Intel Threading Building Blocks (TBB) for tasking, while vectorization standards remain more elusive.

In the following sections, we touch on TBB, Cilk Plus, OpenMP, and OpenCL to give a flavor of their purpose in extending C/C++ for parallel programming.

1.8.1   Brief Survey of Key Parallelism Options

1.8.1.1   TBB

TBB matters for C++ because it has been ported to virtually every platform, and is available in open source ensuring its long-term availability while also benefiting from commercial support by Intel as an. TBB is more popular with C++ programmers than any other parallel programming extensions. TBB is designed to work without any compiler changes, and thus be easily ported to new platforms. As a result, TBB has been ported to a multitude of key operating systems and processors, and code written with TBB can likewise be easily ported. As a consequence of avoiding any need for compiler support, TBB does not have direct support for vector parallelism. However, TBB combined with array notation or #pragma simd from OpenMP or Cilk Plus, or auto-vectorization can be an effective tool for exploiting both thread and vector parallelism. More information on TBB can be found at `http://threadingbuildingblocks.org`. TBB is covered in a little more depth in Section 1.8.2, and is used in multiple chapter case studies in this book.

1.8.1.2   Cilk Plus

TBB is fundamentally a C++ template library and therefore has not been popular for use with C programs. Intel, inspired by work at MIT, created another open source effort called Cilk Plus [15] to address C, offer direct compiler support for C and C++, and extend support to vectorization. Intel briefly considered calling Cilk Plus simply "compiled TBB." While this conveyed the desire to extend TBB for the objectives mentioned, it proved complicated to explain the name so the name Cilk Plus was introduced. The full interoperability between TBB and Cilk Plus increases the number of options for software developers without adding complications. Like TBB, Intel has open sourced Cilk Plus to help encourage adoption and contribution to the project. TBB and Cilk Plus are sister projects at Intel.

Cilk Plus matters because it reflects efforts to prove benefits of tighter integration of parallelism into the language and compiler technologies. Cilk Plus is not widely adopted by programmers today. Cilk Plus is an open source project from Intel to define parallelism extensions for C and C++ that involve the compiler. The simple tasking keywords of Cilk Plus offer a simple tasking interface that the compiler understands. While not as rich as TBB, the tasking interfaces are equally approachable in C and C++. Cilk Plus also adds support for vectorization with #pragma simd, which was recently adopted as part of the OpenMP 4.0 specification. Cilk Plus requires compiler changes and therefore is slower to be supported. Intel compilers have supported Cilk Plus for a few years, and gcc support begins with version 4.9. More information on Cilk Plus can be found at `http://cilkplus.org`.

1.8.1.3   OpenMP

OpenMP [54] matters because it has widespread usage in high performance computing (HPC) and support by virtually all compilers. OpenMP is less popular with C++ users, and most popular with C and Fortran programmers. OpenMP is an approach to adding parallelism to C, C++, and Fortran using directives. The OpenMP specification consists of directives and environment variable definitions that are supported by most compilers. OpenMP has traditionally focused on task parallelism since the very first specification in 1997. The latest OpenMP 4.0, finalized in 2013, expands to offer some directives for vectorization and for offloading computation to attached devices. More information on OpenMP can be found at `http://openmp.org`.

1.8.1.4 OpenCL

OpenCL [28] matters because it gives standard interfaces to control heterogeneous systems and is becoming widely supported. The hope of OpenCL is to displace vendor specific efforts to provide proprietary interfaces to their own hardware. OpenCL implementations are still emerging and it is fair to characterize OpenCL as less mature today in many ways versus other longer standing options. OpenCL is not abstract enough to see widespread usage in applications, but is more suited for implementing critical libraries or routines, such as we may find key for visual effects, or being the target of tools where the ability to manage hardware precisely may be useful. OpenCL is purposefully designed to encourage programmers to utilize all the functionality of the hardware by being able to tailor code to specific hardware. This nature of OpenCL programming generally means that it will not offer the portability or performance portability of a higher-level abstraction such as TBB, Cilk Plus, or OpenMP. OpenCL extends C and C++. The Bullet Physics case study, in Chapter 6, rewrites an application using OpenCL specifically to use GPUs but showing results on CPUs as well. The case study helps highlight that some algorithms or programming styles in OpenCL can offer both portability and performance. Like other abstractions, OpenCL encourages programmers to expose parallelism and the results depend most heavily on the programmer's skill at exposing it (in this case by creating Work Items and Work Groups). More information on OpenCL can be found at `http://www.khronos.org/opencl`.

1.8.1.5 GPU Specific Models

There are other programming models which are specific to GPUs which we have not used as heavily in this book. Notably, the very popular NVIDIA® CUDA, which offers vendor specific support for computing on NVIDIA graphics processors. The OpenSubdiv case study utilizes CUDA and notes some efficiencies in CUDA over current OpenCL implementations. The Bullet case study chose a more vendor neutral approach by using OpenCL. We also do not use GPU-only solutions like OpenGL compute, DirectCompute, or the C++ AMP, which feeds into DirectCompute. The Bullet case study chose a route which demonstrated portability to the CPU as well.

1.8.2 More on TBB: Intel Threading Building Blocks

Threading Building Blocks (TBB) is an open source project that has grown to be the most popular extension for parallel programming in C++. Chapter 4 (LibEE: Parallel Evaluation of Character Rigs) discusses the use of TBB to address graph parallelism for an interactive animation system designed to handle production level film character animation. The nested parallelism, natural mapping of graph nodes onto TBB tasks, and variable nature of the workloads makes TBB a good fit for this kind of problem.

Initially released by Intel in 2006, TBB gained widespread usage and community support after Intel created an open source project around it in 2007 and O'Reilly released a book, in their Nutshell series, titled *Intel Threading Building Blocks: Outfitting C++ for Multi-Core Processor Parallelism* [57].

It provided a much-needed comprehensive answer to the question, "What must be fixed or added to C++ for parallel programming?" Key programming abstractions for parallelism, in TBB, focused on the logical specification of parallelism via algorithm templates. This included a rich set of algorithm primitives implemented by a task-stealing scheduler and augmented by a thread-aware memory allocator, concurrent containers, portable mutexes, portable atomics, and global timestamps. TBB interoperates with other solutions for vectorization assistance but does not directly try to address vectorization. The first release was primarily focused on strict fork—join or loop-type data parallelism. TBB has grown through community contributions and additional investments from Intel. New features include affinity hints, graph scheduling, oversubscription threads, and a wide variety of ports.

TBB has been ported to a wide variety of processors and operating systems. TBB is available open source (GPL v2 with class path exception), and also in a GPL-free binary-only release from Intel. Intel actively supports and maintains both. The GPL licensing used by Intel was identical to the licensing of the Gnu C++ runtime library being used in 2007. To the relief of some, TBB has remained with GPL v2 and not moved to GPL v3. Both the GPL and non-GPL versions have remained identical in features over time, with the only difference being the GPL-free binary-only license option for users who choose to avoid using GPL projects. New features have appeared in a community (GPL) version first as "preview" features. This dual licensing echoes the approach that helped fuel the widespread adoption of MySQL.

Through the involvement of customers and community, TBB has grown to be the most feature-rich and comprehensive solution for parallel application development available today. It has also become the most popular.

TBB implements a highly scalable and industrial strength work stealing scheduler to underlay every algorithm that TBB offers. Work stealing is an important concept, invented by the Cilk project at MIT in the 1990s. A work stealing scheduler distributes the queue of work to be done so that there is no global bottleneck involved in the distribution of tasks to the worker threads. The cache behavior of this is also excellent.

Although TBB works fine with older C++ versions, it is simpler to use with C++11. In particular, C++11 introduces lambda expressions and auto declarations that simplify the use of TBB and other template libraries. We strongly recommend using them to teach, learn, and use TBB, because once you get past the novelty, they make TBB code easier to write and easier to read. Additionally, TBB implements a significant subset of the C++11 standard's thread support, including platform-independent mutexes and condition variables, in a manner that allows them to be used with older C++ compilers, thus giving an immediate migration path for taking advantage of these features even before they are implemented by C++ compilers. This path is further simplified by the way that TBB's injection of these features into namespace std is optional.

1.8.2.1   Parallel for: parallel_for(...)

A key element of TBB is the license to ignore unnecessary parallelism that in turn enables the TBB task scheduler to use parallelism efficiently.

The function template parallel_for maps a functor across a range of values.

The template takes several forms. The simplest is:

```
tbb::parallel_for(first,last,func)
```

where func is a functor.

It evaluates the expression func(i) in parallel_for all i in the half-open interval (first,last).

It is a parallel equivalent of:

```
for (auto i=first; i< last; ++i) func(i);
```

A slight variation specifies a stride:

```
tbb::parallel_for(first,last,stride,func)
```

This form is a parallel equivalent of:

```
for (auto i=first; i< last; i+=stride) func(i);
```

Another form of parallel_for takes two arguments:

```
tbb::parallel_for(range,func)
```

It decomposes range into subranges and applies func to each subrange, in parallel.

Hence, the programmer has the opportunity to optimize func to operate on an entire subrange instead of a single index. This form of parallel_for also generalizes the parallel map pattern beyond one-dimensional ranges. The argument range can be any recursively splittable range type.

The most commonly used recursive range is tbb::blocked_range. It is typically used with integral types or random-access iterator types. For example, blocked_range<int>(0,8) represents the index range 0,1,2,3,4,5,6,7. An optional third argument called the grain size specifies the minimum size for splitting. It defaults to 1. For example, the following snippet splits a range of size 30 with grain size 20 into two indivisible subranges of size 15.

```
// Construct half-open interval [0,30) with grain size of 20
blocked_range<int> r(0,30,20);
assert(r.is_divisible());
// Call splitting constructor
blocked_range<int> s(r);
// Now r=[0,15) and s=[15,30) and both have a grain size 20
// inherited from the original value of r.
assert(!r.is_divisible());
assert(!s.is_divisible());
```

The partitioning of some algorithms, including parallel_for, allows the partitioning to be controlled explicitly by a parameter. By default, the auto_partitioner is selected, which uses heuristics to limit subdivision to only the amount needed for effective load balancing. The simple_partitioner subdivides as much as possible even when the heuristic for load balancing does not view this as profitable. In practice, this partitioner is a legacy feature that can be ignored. The newest partitioner, affinity_partitioner, encourages mapping of tasks in multiple algorithms to be biased to be similar in order to reuse caches. Because this partitioner helps with the reuse of data in cache, it is only interesting if instantiating parallel algorithms more than once with the same data. In such cases, the resulting performance benefits can be substantial. The first use of affinity_partitioner uses a parameter to hold state information for replaying the assignment of subranges to threads.

1.8.2.2 Parallel Reductions: parallel_reduce

Function template parallel_reduce performs a reduction over a recursive range. A reduction is a fundamental and important operation for combining results from operations that can be subdivided but ultimately aim for a single result. For instance, summing numbers in a vector can be subdivided into a task of summing sub-vectors. Since each task of summing a sub-vector results in a partial sum, computing the whole sum requires summing the partial sums. The task of summing sub-vectors and then the partial sums in parallel is called a reduction operation (in this case, addition).

A parallel_reduce operation has several forms. The most used form is:

```
result =
   tbb::parallel_reduce(range,
                        identity,
                        subrange_reduction,
                        combine);
```

The scheduled order for a reduction is not necessarily consistent from instance to instance. While that offers the highest performance, it does create challenges in debugging and validating an application. With that in mind, a deterministic reduction operation was a common request among the TBB community.

The template function parallel_deterministic_reduce is a variant of parallel_reduce that is deterministic even when the reduction operation is non-associative. The result is not necessarily the same as left-to-right serial reduction, even when executed with a single worker, because the template uses a fixed tree-like reduction order for a given input.

1.8.2.3   Parallel Invocation of Functions: parallel_invoke

Template function parallel_invoke evaluates a fixed set of functors in parallel.

For example: tbb::parallel_invoke(afunc,bfunc,cfunc); may evaluate the expressions afunc(), bfunc(), and cfunc() in parallel. TBB has templates to support up to 10 functors, beyond that the task_group facility or parallel_for should be used. Because it depends on the parallelism available at the time of evaluation, we say "may" (evaluate in parallel) and not "will." It is important for us not to care about the order that the functors are evaluated. Nevertheless, the goal should be to benefit from them operating in parallel.

1.8.2.4   Learning More about TBB

We have only touched on a few of the many features of TBB here. A good introduction is available in the O'Reilly Nutshell book *Intel Threading Building Blocks: Outfitting C++ for Multi-Core Processor Parallelism* [57], which covers the essentials of TBB. The book was published in 2007 when TBB version 2.0 appeared, so some newer features are not covered, including the affinity_partitioner, oversubscription threads, and graph scheduling. It is nevertheless a solid introduction to TBB. For a more complete guide, see the TBB Reference, Tutorial, and Design Patterns documents, which can be downloaded from `http://threadingbuildingblocks.org/`.

1.9   Data Movement and Layout

We would be remiss if we did not say a few words about data movement and the importance of data layout. As computational capabilities have soared in modern computers the challenge of feeding data in and out of the computations has grown. Computers are generally optimized to stream data from contiguous memory better than access patterns that randomly hop around in the memory. Computations on vectors of data definitely benefit from good data layout; good data layout enables the use of SIMD (vector) instructions such as MMX, SSE, AVX, or AVX-512 through a process called vectorization.

Programs that can minimize data movement win in both higher performance and lower power utilization. In general, programs do best to arrange data linearly in memory to

FIGURE 1.6: AoS versus SoA.

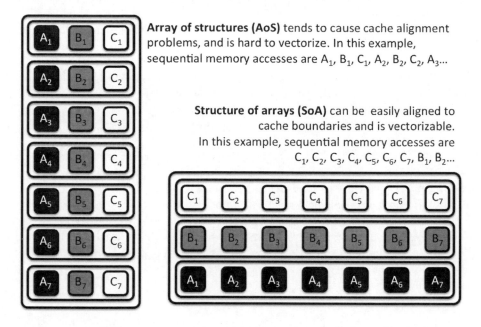

Array of structures (AoS) tends to cause cache alignment problems, and is hard to vectorize. In this example, sequential memory accesses are A_1, B_1, C_1, A_2, B_2, C_2, A_3...

Structure of arrays (SoA) can be easily aligned to cache boundaries and is vectorizable. In this example, sequential memory accesses are C_1, C_2, C_3, C_4, C_5, C_6, C_7, B_1, B_2...

correspond to the order that data would be used in a sequential (not parallel) program. A simple example of data layout is the Array of Structures (AoS) versus Structures of Arrays (SoA) as illustrated in Figure 1.6.

Despite the substantial gains available from good data layout and vectorization, the cases highlighted in the chapters of this book did not generally invest heavily in vectorization work nor precise data layout to enable it. This is not to say that they are terrible at it, just to say it was not the primary focus in optimization done for increasing performance. The performance gains from vectorization range from 2–4× with SSE to 8–16× with AVX-512. While that may seem illogical to not pursue, it is important to note that work done to run an application in parallel by scaling to multiple cores and multiple processors has much more upside available than the 16× maximum for AVX-512 with single precision floating point. For that reason, we encourage that the first focus for speed-up through parallelism is multithreading an application (using lots of tasks). Hence, the title and focus of this book. None of this is to belittle the benefits of vectorization, but rather to encourage threading (through tasks) as the first step for optimizing codes in this modern world. Once a program is scaling through task parallelism, with abstractions such as TBB, then vectorization would be a logical next step to pursue. A good place to start learning more is a three part blog [13].

1.10 Summary

Choice is good. At first the multiple options for parallel programming can seem confusing. The choices are generally easy to pick from when you know what you need. We advocate using an abstraction like TBB or OpenMP as much as possible, and use OpenCL when more control will yield performance benefits for key portions of an application. The loss of portability alone most often encourages other choices. That said, less abstract or less portable interfaces have a place in the world when abstractions fail to offer or allow all the performance or functionality required. For most application developers today, avoiding less abstract programming is likely to be the right answer.

When choosing an abstraction, C++ programmers should start with TBB. C++ programmers will need to explore solutions for vectorization, which will lead them to Cilk Plus or OpenMP to assist with vectorization if libraries do not contain the functionality needed with vector support already. C and Fortran programmers will have to consider OpenMP or Cilk Plus. HPC programmers are most likely to find OpenMP preferable, and others will be more likely to want to examine Cilk Plus.

Regardless of the programming abstraction chosen, the right design in an application is our best weapon in winning with parallelism. While tools and models can help integrate into existing programs, the key to using hardware parallelism is having a good idea of how your application can use parallelism. This almost always means we fall short if we jam parallelism into a program as an afterthought. Nevertheless, with great effort and smart engineering one may be able to show good results, as we will see next in Chapter 2.

The remaining chapters help illustrate successes we have had to help inspire you by sharing ideas and techniques we have found to work.

1.11   Additional Reading

Structured Parallel Programming is designed to teach the key concepts for parallel programming for C/C++ without teaching it via computer architecture. The approach is to teach parallel programming as a programming skill, and show code, and discuss the standard solutions (like map, reduce, stencils, etc.) to solve parallel programming problems. This structured approach to parallel programming techniques supports the objective of architecting parallelism into a program by helping understand known techniques that work.

Chapter 2

Houdini: Multithreading Existing Software

Jeff Lait

Side Effects Software, Inc.

2.1	What Is Houdini?	19
2.2	Rewrite or Refactor	21
	2.2.1 Cleaning Statics	22
	2.2.2 Threading the Simple Cases	27
2.3	Patterns	30
	2.3.1 Always Be Reentrant	30
	2.3.2 Never Lock	31
	2.3.3 Atomics Are Slow	31
	2.3.4 Never Blindly Thread	32
	2.3.5 Command Line Control	33
	2.3.6 Constant Memory versus Number of Cores	33
	2.3.7 Memory Allocation	34
2.4	Copy on Write	34
	2.4.1 Const Correctness	35
	2.4.2 Reader/Writer Locks	35
	2.4.3 Ownership Is Important	36
	2.4.4 Sole Ownership Is a Writer Lock	37
	2.4.5 Failure Modes of This System	38
2.5	Dependencies	40
	2.5.1 Task Locks	41
	2.5.2 Mantra	43
2.6	OpenCL	44

2.1 What Is Houdini?

In this chapter we share the experiences and pitfalls of our ongoing quest to make Houdini fully multithreaded. We will attempt to make the examples as context-agnostic as possible, but we will no doubt still fall into some specialized jargon. In this section we provide the missing context.

Houdini is the flagship package of Side Effects Software, http://www.sidefx.com. Figure 2.1 shows a screenshot of a simulation inside Houdini. It is a complete 3D animation and effects package and is well known for its extremely procedural approach to art creation. Our focus on proceduralism stems from our goal to create tools for artists to express themselves with computers. Computer generated art is distinct from prior mediums in its proceduralism: computers excel at repeating rote tasks. Unfortunately, the act of instructing computers is considered a highly technical task, and often seen as divorced from the act

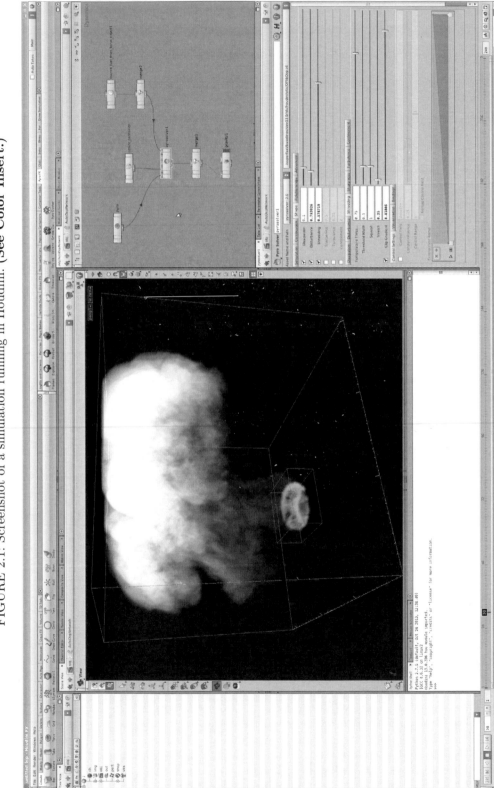

FIGURE 2.1: Screenshot of a simulation running in Houdini. (See Color Insert.)

of creating art. Procedural art tools, such as Houdini, are an attempt to bridge this gap, to ensure that the full potential of computers can be harnessed by artists.

A non-commercial version of Houdini is available for free at the Side Effects Software Web site. This also includes the Houdini Development Kit (HDK), which thanks to the nature of C++, contains header files showing our approach to many threading problems. Of interest to the reader may be `UT/UT_ThreadedAlgorithm.h`, `UT/UT_Lock.h`, and `UT/UT_ParallelUtil.h`.

Central to the Houdini interface is the network editor. The network consists of many nodes (also called operators or OPs) which are wired together. Logically, the data flows down these graphs from the top to the bottom. There are also many different types of networks that reflect the different kinds of data that can be processed.

Terms unique or different to Houdini are covered by this glossary:

OPs, Nodes: The vertices of the network graph. Each one has a type, which determines what computation it represents. Each one also has a page of parameters (based on the type) which act as extra inputs to its computation.

Attributes: Geometry can define extra named data that is attached to all points, vertices, or primitives. Position, color, normal, and texture UVs are all examples of attributes. Note that all points in a geometry have to have the same set of attributes. The meaning of an attribute is decided by naming conventions: N for normal, uv for textures, and so forth.

Mantra: Mantra is a production-proven renderer designed to work with Houdini. It supports micropolygon, raytracing, and physically based rendering (PBR) approaches to solving the rendering equation.

VEX: Our Vector Expression (VEX) language is a shading language similar to the Renderman Shading Language (RSL). It is an interpreted language, so provides the flexibility and extensibility of scripting. However, it also has an implicit Single Instruction, Multiple Data (SIMD) implementation that amortizes most of the overhead of interpretation. We have evolved VEX far beyond its shading roots, however. We now use it for simulation, geometry, and image manipulation. For most computations we can even compile directly to native code. However, the scripting ancestry leads to some problems that we will address in Section 2.5 when we discuss dependencies.

2.2   Rewrite or Refactor

With the release of the Intel Core Duo platform in 2005, we realized that we were no longer going to see a steady increase of single threaded processing power. The multicore, multithreaded world that we had long been warned about was finally upon us. We were faced with a choice. We could start a project to rewrite Houdini in a new, thread-aware manner. Or we could try and change and adapt Houdini to become thread-aware. This type of choice is a common one for programmers to face. Whether it is a new threading paradigm or a new UI programming model, we must choose between rewriting or refactoring. Often we feel the choice is clear—rewriting has so many obvious benefits. We can take what we learned in the first attempt, and bring in the new technology we have learned since, to build something truly next generational. Unfortunately, there are some corresponding costs to rewriting.

First, we do not actually bring what we learned into the new version. We can't. For any nontrivial project, it is too big for anyone to fully understand every detail that went into its construction. There are thousands of subtle choices that were made to address the needs of users that we don't see when we just look at the code as a whole.

More importantly, while building a new version we are not actually moving forward. We are running as fast as we can in the hopes of staying in the same place. While hopefully the new system will let us move faster after it is built, the longer the rewrite, the greater this speed up had better be!

We must realize the shift to multithreading is not the last time we will see a paradigm shift. There will be future shifts that we have not yet predicted. Our new rewrite will find itself in a similar position as our current code within a few years. It behooves us, therefore, to be able to refactor and adapt rather than always having to start from the beginning.

When we analyzed our needs for multithreading, we decided that refactoring would be the best course for us. There are considerable problems we have because of this, most notably addressed in the discussion on dependencies in Section 2.5. Our incremental approach, however, has allowed us to acquire a lot of the low hanging fruit of multithreading without having to stop our forward progress.

Our refactoring consists of two steps which, suitably enough, we can perform in parallel. We convert our legacy code to be threadsafe while we ensure anything that is embarrassingly parallel is actually executed in parallel.

2.2.1 Cleaning Statics

One disadvantage of working with an old codebase is that little of the code was written with multithreading in mind. Even when we did consider multithreading, our approaches tended to be lock-heavy and lacked the modern understanding of what allows code to scale across multiple cores. Before we worry about having too many locks, however, we have to worry about code having too few.

Global variables are a bad idea for many reasons, but never so much so as when we try to multithread libraries. Finding them can be a challenge, however. We do not want to only fix them when we happen upon a memory corruption or a crash, we want to preemptively eliminate them from our libraries.

We could try grepping our source for the static keyword, but this will not find all of them. It will also falsely report constant statics and static functions, both of which are safe. Instead, we can inspect the generated library files to see what was put into the data segment. Under Linux we can use the **nm** command.

```
nm libGEO.so | c++filt | grep -i '^[0-9a-F]* [bcdgs]'
```

This will report all the writeable symbols in the given library, nicely avoiding anything marked const. However, it will leave us with a lot of false positives. We will have our own legitimate statics, including locks and anything stored behind locks. Further, the compiler itself generates a slew of statics. We can use a chain of greps to eliminate our known issues, leaving us with a short list to inspect.

Using the Intel Compiler we could take advantage of the **-ww1711** option to warn about any write to a static variable. This avoids having to prefix read-only statics with const (though we find that diligent application of the const keyword does have benefits for readability).

When we do want to write to a static we can use a macro, such as this:

```
#define THREADSAFE_STATIC_WRITE(code) \
__pragma(warning(disable:1711));      \
CODE;                                  \
__pragma(warning(default:1711))
```

When we have verified that a write to a static variable is properly locked, we can wrap it within this macro, thereby suppressing the warning for that write.

When we sweep our code to remove all global variables, we must exercise care. While some cases of global variable usage are entirely spurious, often there is a good reason the original author decided to use a global. After all, global variables have been recognized as a bad thing for decades now! We found several common patterns for global variable use, and thus also found some common solutions to fix them with minimal impact on the rest of the code. We do not want to spend time debugging algorithms that have already stood the test of time.

Often, when we write a function, we may have potential invalid parameters or undefined values to guard against. The calling code, however, may be intolerant of errors, and expect to always get a valid result. Consider the conversion between a hue-saturation-value (HSV) color and a red-green-blue (RGB) color. If the saturation is zero, the resulting red, green, and blue channels are independent of hue. Conversely, if the red, green, and blue channels are identical, the hue is undefined. Someone with good intentions may write:

```
static float prev_h = 0;

static void
HSVtoRGB(float h, float s, float v, float *r, float *g, float *b)
{
    prev_h = h;
    // code to set r, g, b from h, s, v
}

static void
RGBtoHSV(float r, float g, float b, float *h, float *s, float *v)
{
    if (r == g && g == b)
    {                       /* achromatic case */
        *s = 0.0F;
        *h = prev_h;    /* *h is undefined in the achromatic case */
        *v = r;
    }
    else
    {
        // code to set hsv from rgb
    }
}
```

The intent of this code is noble. Instead of choosing a default hue, it reuses the last hue it saw. A conversion from HSV to RGB and back to HSV will thus preserve the original hue value even when the saturation is zero. In practice, however, this will rarely work, even without taking multithreading into account. When we batch-convert HSV to RGB, we will have the last hue become the default hue value for the entire reverse conversion. We found that the best solution in this example was return a standard default value and accept the potential loss of information in round-trip conversions. For hue we use the standard default of zero.

There were some cases, however, where we could not properly understand the code to confidently pick a new default. With these functions, which were often found in our NURBS (Nobody Understands Rational B-Splines) library, we wanted to preserve the functionality of the old code precisely, and so found it expedient to add an extra reference parameter storing the fallback value.

```
static void
HSVtoRGB(float h, float s, float v, float *r, float *g, float *b, float &prev_h);

static void
RGBtoHSV(float r, float g, float b, float *h, float *s, float *v, float &prev_h);
```

Augmenting the function signatures with a mandatory parameter storing the fallback value forces the tracking of the fallback value to be explicit in the calling code, ensuring both threadsafety and no accidental loss of value when a later programmer rearranges code.

Sometimes it is not just a float that is shared between functions, but an entire set of variables. It is tempting to make these variables thread local storage, but we tried to do this only as a last resort. It is much better if we can make the interrelationship between the functions explicit. At the same time we desire an easy, mechanical fix to the problem. It is imperative we keep our changes simple and error free.

Creating an ad hoc struct forms an easy and mechanical solution to most parameter problems:

```
float knotspace, knotaccuracy, tolerance;

float setup(float a)
{
    knotspace = a;
    tolerance = 0.01;
    knotaccuracy = a / tolerance;
}

float apply(float a)
{
    if (a < tolerance)
        return a * knotspace;
    return knotaccuracy;
}
```

transforms into:

```
struct ApplyParms
{
    float knotspace, knotaccuracy, tolerance;
};

float setup(float a, ApplyParms &parms)
```

```
{
    parms.knotspace = a;
    parms.tolerance = 0.01;
    parms.knotaccuracy = a / parms.tolerance;
}

float apply(float a, ApplyParms &parms)
{
    if (a < parms.tolerance)
        return a * parms.knotspace;
    return parms.knotaccuracy;
}
```

We can build `ApplyParms` on the stack prior to the first invocation of `setup` and add it to the calls to `apply`.

Callback functions are a particularly painful example of functions sharing state. Ideally, these functions take a `void *` or similar, allowing additional state to piggyback into the callback. Unfortunately, it is all too common to find cases where this was omitted. Changing it, however, would often trigger considerable cascading changes. We therefore found ourselves resorting to thread local storage.

Even when we have a `void *` on a callback, we are not out of the woods. A common pattern is to pass `this` into the callback. All the extra parameters are then stored as member data in `this`. Beyond the obvious problems of polluting our object with temporary parameter data, this stops working when our callback is a const method. In those cases where programmers were wise enough to not cast away const, they may still fall into the trap of creating a global variable instead:

```
static float glb_parm;

static void callback(void *vdata)
{
    const MyClass *data = (const MyClass *)vdata;

    data->callback(glb_parm);
}

void program(const MyClass *data, float parm)
{
    glb_parm = parm;

    runalgorithm(callback, data);
}
```

Thankfully the transformation is simple: we realize we do not have to pass the class as `void *`! We instead create an ad hoc struct to hold both our parameters and the `this` pointer, initialize it on the stack, and pass that into our callback.

```
struct CallbackParms
{
    float parm;
    const MyClass *data;
}

static void callback(void *vdata)
{
    CallbackParms *parms = (CallbackParms *)vdata;
    parms->data->callback(parms->parm);
}

void program(const MyClass *data, float parm)
{
    CallbackParms parms;

    parms.parm = parm;
    parms.data = data;

    runalgorithm(callback, &parms);
}
```

Premature optimization leads to the final pattern of global variables we will look at. We all naturally understand that memory allocation is something to avoid in innermost functions. So, sometimes we decide to cache our allocated memory for future use:

```
void
munge_array(float *data, int len)
{
    static float *temp;
    static int templen;

    if (!temp || templen < len)
    {
        if (temp) free(temp);
        temp = (float *) malloc(len * sizeof(float));
        templen = len;
    }

    // Munge data using temp for temporary
}
```

We should first identify if this optimization is even needed. While allocation is expensive, it is not that expensive. We usually found that the cost of allocation was not an issue; the operation that we were applying to the data dominated the cost.

If speed is an issue, we can take advantage of `alloca`. `alloca` allocates variable data on the stack. Unfortunately, our stack is limited, so we must switch between `alloca` and `malloc` depending on size. If the allocation is large, the computation on it will amortize the allocation cost, justifying this switch.

We created the `UT_StackBuffer` class to handle switching between allocation modes. It uses its own member data as the buffer if below a threshold, and allocates otherwise. Our code then becomes much simpler:

```
void
munge_array(float *data, int len)
{
    UT_StackBuffer<float> temp(len);

    // Munge data using temp.array() for temporary
}
```

We found the sweep for globals a very rewarding exercise. Even without considering the improvement to threadsafety, the transformed code is almost universally easier to understand and in some cases shorter.

2.2.2 Threading the Simple Cases

When we describe an algorithm as embarrassingly parallel, we are saying two things. First, that it is embarrassingly easy to parallelize it—the data splits cleanly into many threads with no dependencies. Second, that it is very embarrassing if we leave it single threaded. Despite this, it is not at all uncommon to come across code that operates independently over millions of elements but stubbornly stays on one core. We have some excuse for historical code—with no real benefit to threading, code was left in a single threaded state. Now, however, we want to transform that old code into multithreaded code. To avoid creating new errors, we want to minimize the changes required to turn an old single threaded loop into a multithreaded loop. Interestingly, we found that making such tools had benefits beyond porting old code. It also helps multithread new code. We can write, debug, and optimize our algorithms in a traditional single threaded manner and then, as a final step, port them to a multithreaded version.

We had the misfortune of beginning our modern attempt to multithread Houdini prior to the release of Intel's Threading Building Blocks (TBB). This gave us the joy of developing a lot of our own threading primitives. However, what we built was remarkably similar to what TBB provides. We were able to switch over to TBB by wrapping TBB with our own abstraction layer.

While our model was similar to TBB, it was not equivalent. There are two approaches to threading an algorithm. Consider the following sample function:

```
class UT_Vector
{
    void addScaledVec(float s, const UT_Vector &v);
};

void
UT_Vector::addScaledVec(float s, const UT_Vector &v)
{
    int         i, end;

    end = length();
    for (i = 0; i < end; i++)
        myVector[i] += s * v.myVector[i];
}
```

This is representative of the hundreds of functions that we had to multithread. In particular, we have a (debatably wise) convention of most operations being methods on their respective classes. We should also note that the shown code is not optimized for the single threaded case. Threading should not be a solution to hide slow code! It can be tempting to see the six times increase we get by multithreading and call our job done, leaving another factor of two unrealized!

Our original solution to this problem was thread pools. We would allocate a fixed pool of worker threads. When we wanted to multithread an algorithm, we would use a macro to create the proper boiler plate to marshal its parameters and pass them to the worker threads. Each invocation of the thread-specific functions receive a UT_JobInfo, which tells them how many threads are running and which thread they are. For convenience, we also include an atomic integer in the UT_JobInfo; allowing load balancing to be implemented by requesting next task numbers.

The transformed code then looks like this:

```
class UT_Vector
{
    bool shouldMultiThread() const
    { return length() > 5000; }

    THREADED_METHOD2(UT_Vector, shouldMultiThread(),
            addScaledVec,
            float, s,
            const UT_Vector &, v);
    void addScaledVecPartial(float s, const UT_Vector &v,
            const UT_JobInfo &info);
};
```

```
void
UT_Vector::addScaledVecPartial(float s, const UT_Vector &v,
                const UT_JobInfo &info)
{
    int         i, end;
    info.divideWork(length(), i, end);
    for ( ; i < end; i++)
        myVector[i] += s * v.myVector[i];
}
```

The shouldMultiThread method is often shared across all methods in the class. It acts as a gate on the minimum work size to ensure we do not attempt to thread small tasks. With a generic class like UT_Vector, this is vital, because it may contain 6 items or 6 million. When it contains six items, it is imperative that the overhead is as close to zero as possible. The THREADED_METHOD2 macro handles defining an addScaledVec method to perform these tests and either call addScaledVecPartial directly if threading is not desired, or pass it to the worker threads if it is desired. It also defines an addScaledVecNoThread method at the same time. This version will never multithread. This is very useful for debugging: if we suspect some code is not threadsafe, we can selectively turn off threading to see if the problem still occurs. Similarly, sometimes we only know at runtime if the behavior of a function will be threadsafe. It may, for example, have a callback whose threadsafety depends on its parameters. In these cases, we can switch between the two implementations easily.

While we currently implement our thread pool on top of TBB, it is important to recognize it does form a subtly different paradigm. TBB approaches the `parallel_for` problem by having the caller divide the dataset into many small tasks using a partitioner. Each task must be big enough to avoid excessive task switching overhead, but small enough to allow all the threads to be active. We do not, however, know how many tasks will be created or on which threads they will be run. By contrast, the thread pool approach places the work of dividing the dataset on the callee. Because the thread pool works with a fixed set of threads, it can provide the callee with the number of threads that will be run.

Working with a thread pool paradigm has some nice advantages, especially when it comes to converting old code. Often a function will have considerable setup before the big `for` loop. The thread pool approach provides an upper bound on how many times we have to repeat that setup, allowing us to consider it amortized for large datasets. A task-based method, however, may divide large datasets into a similarly large number of tasks, forcing us to pay more attention to the prequel code. If we want to pull the prequel code out of the task, however, we must perform considerably more code surgery. Newer C++ features, such as lambdas, ease this problem, but we are limited in how quickly we can raise our minimum compiler requirements. Thread pools have a similar advantage with map-reduce functions. Because we know the maximum number of slots ahead of time, we can preallocate an array of outputs, one for each thread. Each invocation can use this array and its job number to write to its own output.

There are, however, very good reasons why TBB does not use this model. The chief problem of thread pools is that they are not composable. Thread pools work well if our program has only a single level of threading. However, it is very easy to find ourselves with multiple levels. The `addScaledVec` may be called from within a blocked matrix algorithm, which itself has been multithreaded across the blocks. We cannot split the `addScaledVec` call across the thread pools because they are all busy. We also do not want to create a new thread pool, both because this would oversubscribe and because thread creation is expensive. We are thus forced to devolve to single threaded behavior for the nested call. However, if the top block-based algorithm did not use all the threadslots, or if some of the worker threads finish much earlier than others, we cannot take advantage of those extra cycles. TBB solves this problem by placing both the block operations, and the `addScaledVec` operations, on the same task list, allowing worker threads to balance between all active processes.

By breaking the data up into a thread-independent number of tasks, TBB also solves the load balancing problem. In a thread pool the simplest approach is to split the task equally, as shown in the earlier example. If the work units take a variable amount of time, however, this can leave idle threads when it comes to synchronization. For example, our volume format breaks a volume into 16 cubed tiles. If one of these tiles has a constant value, it is compressed to a single value. When we process a constant tile, we can often do so very quickly if all we have to do is update the constant value, leading to a factor of a thousand difference in processing time between constant and varying tiles. To balance the thread pool, we make use of the atomic integer stored in the `UT_JobInfo`. Each thread will repeatedly request and increment the shared integer and use it as the linear tile number to process. While this solves the load balancing problem, we have effectively reproduced the TBB paradigm of turning each tile into a task!

Our favorite way of writing multithreaded code is to eschew either TBB or the thread pool approach. Instead, we write the algorithm directly in VEX, our vector expression language. VEX code is written as an inner body of a for-loop, much like kernels in OpenCL, so it is multithreaded by default. Unlike OpenCL kernels, however, we have the full flexibility of a general purpose computer and can invoke all the domain specific functions we have implemented for visual effects programming. We are often surprised that rewriting an algorithm in VEX results in a 10 times speed increase over the same algorithm in C++.

Of course, when we investigate, we find the C++ algorithm was not optimized. However, neither was the VEX code! Naturally fully optimized C++ code will beat VEX once more in speed, but this requires attention to multithreading, vectorization, and caching; all of which were ignored in the VEX version. For a lot of code, however, it is more important for it to be flexible and readable so we can improve it and debug it. For these tasks, VEX shines, as being an interpreted language, we can change it directly in the application with no need to restart. Increasingly, we now turn to VEX first to solve any problem that smacks of an embarrassingly parallel nature, and we often find it produces sufficiently scalable results that, much as we rarely go below C++ to assembly, we rarely must go below VEX to C++.

2.3   Patterns

Over the many years of multithreading Houdini we have made many mistakes. We hope that by describing them we can help others avoid the same mistakes. Some of these mistakes predate the modern push for multithreading, for this is not our first foray into the world of threads.

2.3.1   Always Be Reentrant

When we create a lock on a resource, we are often given a choice of whether that lock should be reentrant or not. Reentrant locks, also known as recursive locks, allow the same thread to reacquire the lock. A non-reentrant lock will block, creating a deadlock. There are advantages to non-reentrant locks—we do not need to track the owner, so may be able to process them faster or use less memory. However, it requires more care on our part.

```
class foo
{
public:
    void interface1()
    {
        UT_Lock::Scope scope(ourlock);
        // Do computation.
    }
    void interface2()
    {
        UT_Lock::Scope scope(ourlock);
        // Reuse interface1
        interface1()
    }
};
```

Adding the call to `interface1` inside of the lock in `interface2` creates a deadlock. We could argue the programmer is at fault: they have broken the rule that interface functions should be separated from internal functions. However, why did we create such a dangerous rule? The real crime of the hapless author was trying to reuse code. Reusing code should be one of the greatest virtues, but we have managed to turn it into a sin!

It certainly does not help that, during the dark early days of our lock code, we had different policies on different platforms. Irix locks were reentrant, while Windows locks were non-reentrant. Thus some developers would execute that code without hassle, and others would face a deadlock. The message we learned from this experience was to make all locks reentrant by default. There must be a good and clear reason to do otherwise! Efficiency is not one of them: if you are locking, you have already given up on speed.

2.3.2 Never Lock

The hardest lesson we learned? If you lock, you are not multithreading.

This does not match what we had learned in our studies. We would build clever diagrams to prove our system would work well, and see nice effects on single threaded machines. Any attempt to scale, however, would see our CPU monitors hit 100% in kernel times, not in process times. Lock-based algorithms are predicated on an assumption that we know something about the machine we are running on. Perhaps if we actually had separate CPUs for each of our threads that would sync in step our locks would work efficiently. But our threads do not remain on one CPU. They live in a complex ecosystem of mp3 players, YouTube windows, background renders, and other cycle-suckers. In our system monitor, we configure the CPU graph to color kernel times a bright red versus a soft blue for normal tasks. Algorithms that lock then bleed across the graph, giving a quick visual indicator that we had better investigate closer. Once, when running a simple VEX expression on a 100 million voxels, we noticed the CPU graph turn red. Intrigued, we brought out our profiler (Intel VTune Amplifier XE in this case) and swiftly found that calls to `UT_Interrupt::opStart` were triggering a lock. These calls are used with our cooperative interrupt system. Algorithms are expected to periodically check to see if the user has requested an interrupt and stop execution if so. Normally, the VEX workload for a block of voxels would be high enough to mask the cost of this check, but for this lightweight operation the lock became contentious and slowed the entire operation by a factor of two! We learned from these sorts of encounters that non-contentious locks do not necessarily remain that way. Just because our current use case, or our current number of cores, does not make the lock contentious, does not mean some future use or future machine might not invert our assumptions.

Of course, we still use a lot of locks in our code. The admonition "Never Lock" applies anywhere where we expect multithreading to gain a speed advantage. There remain many non-speed related thread synchronization problems for which locks are a natural solution.

2.3.3 Atomics Are Slow

When we realized locks could not be relied upon, we naturally turned to the next best thing: atomics. A lot of traditional locking algorithms can be replaced by the judicious use of a few atomic variables. While nothing like a lock in cost, we must still exercise caution when using these. Any atomic must, by definition, be synchronized across CPUs. In particular, this means that it often cannot remain cached locally. The cost of an atomic should be treated like that of a guaranteed uncached memory fetch. Which is to say: very expensive.

```
class FOO_Array
{
public:
    shared_ptr<float> getData() const
    { return myData; }
private:
```

```
    shared_ptr<float> myData;
};

float
sum_array(const FOO_Array &foo)
{
    float total = 0;
    for (int i = 0; i < foo.length(); i++)
        total += foo.getData()[i];
}
```

As longtime users of C++, we are very excited by `shared_ptr`. It provides a way to abdicate responsibility for tracking ownership of data. The `FOO_Array` does not have to worry if the caller destroys it after fetching its data—the fetched data will still be valid. We will have more to say about the danger of this abdication in Section 2.4 when we discuss copy on write.

There is a hidden cost to `shared_ptr`, however. Because `shared_ptr` is threadsafe, it must do some form of atomic operation to track its uniqueness. Every time we invoke `getData` it must increment and decrement this shared resource. When we invoke `sum_array` on a single thread the overhead is there, but perhaps hidden by the cost of accessing the actual data of the array. When we decide to multithread `sum_array`, however, things change drastically. The shared resource can no longer be cached and performance will plummet, rather than seeing our summation run faster; we will see it slow down!

2.3.4   Never Blindly Thread

In any discussion of TBB's `parallel_for` there will be a discussion of the importance of grain size. This cannot be stressed enough. We go even farther and insist that it must be considered if any multithreading should be attempted at all. While the per-task overhead is made as small as possible, it is still there. We can often have data structures, like vectors, that may store anything from 1 to 1 billion elements. Overheads that we can ignore when processing even 100 elements can be crippling when processing a single element!

When using our thread pool interface we do not have to worry about grain size. We implicitly set a maximum number of tasks to be the size of our worker pool. We still, however, have to worry about whether to thread or not. We make it a mandatory part of our interface for that reason. We do not want, in a fit of laziness, to cripple simple code.

For   TBB   we   wrapped   the   `tbb::parallel_for`   in   two   versions: `UTparallelForLightItems` and `UTparallelForHeavyItems`. These implicitly set a grain size of 1024 and 1, respectively. Both version chain down to `UTparallelFor` which further tests if only a single task will be created. In this case, it does not actually enter the TBB scheduler at all, instead just directly invoking the body.

Despite the best efforts, it is still possible to forget to consider grain size. We noticed when duplicating geometry we were able to duplicate different attributes independently, so thus tried to multithread it if there were sufficient number of attributes. However, some cases may have hundreds of attributes but only a few points in the geometry, causing the overhead of threading to dominate. We had to choose to thread based not just on the number of attributes, but also on the number of elements in each attribute. In this case, a final version of our wrapper became very useful: UTserialFor. This variant merely executes the body directly. The chief advantage is that it has the same signature as the parallel variants, making it trivial to write code that switches between the parallel and serial versions.

2.3.5   Command Line Control

We believe that all stand-alone applications should have command-line options to set their maximum thread count. We use -j, where the j stands for jobs. Our choice was inspired by make and provides a consistent way for people to create scripts that limit their thread usage.

A good selfish reason for this is debugging. When we get a troublesome file, we can easily run both with and without threading and determine the locus of the fault. If the problem still shows up with -j 1 we breathe a sigh of relief—it is not a threading bug, just a garden variety normal bug.

A practical reason is speed. Multithreading is less efficient than single threading. If we have the memory and bandwidth, it is more efficient (in terms of throughput) to single thread multiple copies of our program than run a single copy multithreaded. After all, we do not have just one job to do. On a render farm we will have thousands of frames to process, so it will be faster to run six frames at once, each single threaded, than try to balance one frame across six cores. Naturally, there are exceptions and trade-offs. We must balance memory use, network bandwidth, and the importance of fast artist turnaround time. The choice of this balance, however, lies with the render wranglers that know their machines, their common scenes, and their deadlines. By providing a command line thread control we make it very straightforward for anyone to adjust our program's behavior to what they have found works best for their farm and their shots.

2.3.6   Constant Memory versus Number of Cores

We often want to write to the same object from multiple tasks. A common example in visual effects is stamping points into a volume. With single threaded code this is easy: loop over all particles and for each one write to the voxels it overlaps. But if we multithread this across particles, many particles will try to write to the same voxel at the same time.

One solution we can immediately discard is the idea of acquiring a write lock on the volume, or even on a subset of the volume. Locks are simply too expensive and do not scale.

If we cannot lock, perhaps we can just ensure no conflicts occur. In our volume format, we break the volume into 16 cubed tiles. While two threads cannot safely write to the same tile at once, it is threadsafe for two threads to write to different tiles at once. Thus, we could assign each thread a subset of tiles. Then each thread could process all of the particles, but only perform writes to the tiles they owned. We have, however, incurred the cost of recomputing the bounds of every particle for every thread.

Another approach, which motivates the title of this section, is to create a separate destination object for each thread. We could create an empty volume for each thread and composite them together into a single version at the end. We can optimize this by either using a thread pool approach or using thread-local storage to ensure we only create one temporary volume per thread, not per task. However, even then we may be in for a surprise. What works well on a 12 thread machine may not be so pleasant when run on a four-socket, 10 core machine with hyperthreading. We will see 80 copies of the volume, for an 80 times increase in peak memory! We may ameliorate this somewhat by using sparse volumes. Either with constant tiles or with a hierarchical structure such as VDB, we can ensure that the memory cost of empty space is kept small. Unfortunately, if we apply the particles in a first-come manner, probabilistically we are still looking at an 80 times memory peak. The particles we get from artists do not tend to be ordered spatially, instead they are intermixed and scattered throughout the volume. We therefore still must perform a prepass on the particles, bucketing them into separate regions to ensure that the per-thread volumes have minimum overlap. At this point, we may note, we could use the same bucketed particles to speed up the threadsafe write pattern.

2.3.7   Memory Allocation

Traditional memory allocators lock. As such, `malloc` and `new` are not things we want to see in the innermost loops of our threaded algorithms. Thankfully, this is a rather general principle that applies to non-threaded code as well, so usually is not a problem.

But what if we really need to allocate memory? What do we do when `alloca` does not suffice? Traditionally, the answer was to write our own small object allocator. And we have written a few. More recently, `tbb::scalable_malloc` provides a ready-made solution for highly contentious allocations. Unfortunately, with memory allocation we face not just the threat of slow performance; memory fragmentation is a very serious problem that can easily halve our effective working set.

Thankfully, we have found an easy solution for Linux. We continue to use `malloc` *and* `new` *as normal, but we link against* `jemalloc`. `jemalloc` *replaces our standard allocator with one that does all the proper tricks of small object lists and thread local caches, but it does it in a way which aggressively avoids fragmentation. On platforms where linking to* `jemalloc` *is not practical, we resort to* `tbb::malloc_proxy`. *The cost of fragmentation is balanced by the significant performance improvements.*

2.4   Copy on Write

As we analyzed most of our embarrassingly parallel algorithms, we commonly found we had random overlapping reads from shared data structures and sequential independent writes to another data structure. From this, we identified two usage scenarios that we must deal with to make data structures threadsafe. First, we must ensure that the structures are threadsafe for reading—it should be clear when and how it is safe for multiple threads to read from the data structure, and, as importantly, what operations constitute reads in the first place. Second, we must have the ability to define a safe write operation. Usually, there are constraints on what sort of writing can be performed in parallel. With our volume data structure, for example, it is possible to write to different tiles of the structure simultaneously, but not to the same tile from two different threads. We expose these guarantees and requirements so we do not have to lock on the write—locking, after all, will defeat our performance goals. These rules can suffice when a single algorithm wishes to spawn multiple threads to write to an object, but they are untenable if separate algorithms wish to update the same data structure. Thus, we need to separate these cases so we can provide raw access for writing with known threads without having to worry about foreign threads playing havoc with our data in the meantime.

2.4.1 Const Correctness

We are very fortunate with Houdini that two historical accidents work in our favor: our code is written in C++ and we have maintained const correctness. When it comes to determining read-safety of code, it is the second accident that aids us. const is one of our favorite keywords in C++. It exemplifies what the language does right: allowing us to build contracts that the compiler will enforce. Our original motivation for const correctness was a mistaken belief that future compilers would be able to use this information to better optimize the code. While this may have never come to pass, the rewards we have reaped in code maintenance have easily justified our continued use of the practice.

In the single threaded context, the const keyword is a contract to the caller that the invoked code is side-effect free. This knowledge leaves one less thing for us to worry about when we encounter the function in someone else's code. It is essential that the compiler enforces this relationship. Unlike comments or names of functions, this particular contract cannot easily drift. While there are still `const_cast`, `mutable`, and C-casts to worry about, in practice, we have found these to be remarkably rare exceptions. We can understand why when we remember what causes function names and comments to drift from the truth. It is usually a harried programmer eager to get something done that adds a small change to a function and fails to update all of the boilerplate. We have found that when we (for we are all at some point that harried programmer) are in that state, our solution is to merely not use the const keyword at all. The const keyword is instead usually introduced in a bottom-up fashion when we are carefully performing code-hygiene. We have found it to be a remarkably trustworthy indicator of the nature of the function.

As the use of multithreading spreads through our codebase, the const keyword has now become an essential tool. Not only can it be used to imply the code is side-effect free, it can also be used to imply the code supports many readers. Again, care must be taken due to the risk of mutable caches or global variables, but still it allows the easy validation of large swathes of code. Further, by ensuring we send const structures to the multiple threads, we can have the compiler enforce that we do not accidentally call an unsafe function.

2.4.2 Reader/Writer Locks

When a single algorithm invokes multiple threaded tasks to write to a data structure, we can assume the author of the algorithm is able to reason about the write pattern and generate a lock-free method of changing the data. However, often data will not belong to a single data structure, but be shared across the session to provide both speed and memory optimizations. For example, a large piece of geometry with 10 million points may have a three-float color attribute for each point. This 192 megabyte array does not need to be copied every time the geometry is copied. If a deformation operation is performed the color is unchanged, so the deformed geometry can share its color attribute with the original. When we do choose to update the color values, however, we wish to ensure any simultaneous readers do not see an inconsistent state. A traditional solution to this problem is to create a reader/writer lock. This special type of lock can allow many readers into the data structure at once, but only allow a single writer, and only if no readers are present. Such a lock would have quite an unacceptable performance cost—we would lose even the lock-free ability to read the geometry from multiple threads. In the following sections we will present our solution to this problem, which avoids the need for locking.

2.4.3 Ownership Is Important

A misunderstood feature of C++ is its lack of garbage collection. Critics deride this decision as a foolish choice based on antiquated notions of efficiency. They claim memory leaks and dead pointers abound in C++ code, leading to crashing programs and inefficient software. While we acknowledge some truth to these objections, we believe there is a silver lining to this cloud. Lacking the safety net of a garbage collector, C++ programmers have developed practices to track ownership of objects. We use techniques like Resource Acquisition Is Initialization (RAII) to solve many of the pitfalls of manual memory management and maintain a strong sense of object ownership.

Our clear understanding of both object ownership and object lifetimes solves a lot of problems. A common example is disk files—who should write to them and when they should be closed is straightforward in an ownership based model. We also contend that this sort of thinking can help solve multithreading problems in a way that minimizes locks.

Unlike Java, where every reference to an object is considered an owner of that object, C++ encourages us to keep ownership simple. In particular, the `shared_ptr` device, while incredibly useful, should be kept to a minimum. Consider again our simple array class:

```
class FOO_Array
{
public:
    shared_ptr<float> getData() const
    { return myData; }
private:
    shared_ptr<float> myData;
};
```

We saw earlier how this can result in problems with multithreading; but this implementation also has an important conceptual problem. Who owns `myData`? Why does someone who merely wants to inspect `myData` have to acquire ownership? Usually, `shared_ptr` aficionados argue that the caller of `getData` does not know the lifetime of the `FOO_Array`. Acquiring a `shared_ptr` will insulate us from the `FOO_Array` suddenly vanishing. However, the caller does know the lifetime! We must already hold a reference to the enclosing `FOO_Array`, or it would not have been possible to invoke the getData function in the first place. It is only if we are planning on keeping the returned pointer after we have released ownership of the containing `FOO_Array` that we would require a `shared_ptr`. But, in this case, we are conceptually caching the result of the call, so we should not be surprised that we have to explicitly signal this by taking ownership.

```
class FOO_Array
{
public:
    float *getData() const
    { return myData.get(); }
```

```
    shared_ptr<float> copyData() const
    { return myData; }
private:
    shared_ptr<float> myData;
};
```

We have made this transformation explicit in this version: we invoke `copyData` if we want to maintain the data beyond `FOO_Array`'s lifetime, and `getData` if we merely want to inspect it locally. As an added bonus, we will avoid any performance surprises when we do multithread our accesses.

2.4.4 Sole Ownership Is a Writer Lock

We make lock-free the case of many readers and no writers by ensuring all functions used by the readers are threadsafe. We use the const keyword so the compiler validates this requirement. But what happens when we want to write to data?

A reader/writer model needs a way to keep track of the active readers. It is not safe to start writing if there are any active readers. We want to avoid that overhead, however, since we want reads to be lock-free. Our solution is to cheat and redefine our problem. We solve a slightly less general problem, and gain an efficient solution that avoids any locking on the part of the readers.

When we design multithreaded algorithms that write to shared data structures, there are two types of readers we must worry about. The first are the reads our own algorithm will generate. We can reason about these and create solutions for our planned read pattern. We do not need special reader/writer locks, we instead just need safe access patterns. The second, and more troubling, are the reads generated by other concurrent algorithms. We find these reads a scary proposition since we cannot reason about them or predict them.

How then do we detect if there are any external readers? If we are not tracking individual read requests, we can only detect if there is the possibility of an external reader. For an external algorithm to be able to read from a data structure, it must have a reference to that data structure. Our concept of data ownership can now provide a solution: for an external thread to be able to unexpectedly read from our structure, that thread must also have ownership of it. After all, if they have not acquired ownership, they have no guarantee on the lifetime of the object, so should not be reading from it at all!

Our write-lock problem is hence simplified. Before we can write to a potentially shared data structure, we must first ensure that we have sole ownership. Provided we are the only owner, we know that no other system can gain ownership—after all, we have the only reference! Provided we have ensured all caches properly own the object, we have no fear of surprisingly increasing our ownership count because, again, there must be no references to our object outside of our algorithm.

So, what do we do if we want to write to an object and discover its ownership is shared? We simply copy it. In almost all of our use cases, the share is due to a cache, in which case a copy is the right thing to do; it is unexpected for a cached version to be updated. Even if we do want to update the shared object, however, it is still semantically correct to work on a copy. This means that other threads will see the old version until the new version is posted, which is almost always advantageous since we then eliminate the risk of inconsistent states being exposed mid-algorithm. Further, we can always imagine that all the would-be readers just happened to block until the algorithm was complete, making this instant posting of the result something the overall system should be able to handle.

This approach is equivalent to copy on write, a technique often used to share memory. We have found, however, it is also an effective way to manage multithreaded access to shared structures. Again, let us look at the FOO_Array built in this fashion.

```
class FOO_Array
{
public:
    const float *readData() const
    { return myData.get(); }

    float *writeData()
    { makeUnique(); return myData.get(); }

    shared_ptr<const float> copyData() const
    { return myData; }

private:
    void makeUnique()
    {
        if (myData.unique()) return;

        shared_ptr<float> copy(new float*[size];);
        memcpy(copy.get(), myData.get(), sizeof(float)*size);
        myData = copy;
    }

    shared_ptr<float> myData;
};
```

We have made the readData function const correct. It returns a const float *, which makes it more difficult for us to accidentally write to shared data when we have a const FOO_Array. If we do want to write to the data inside the FOO_Array, we have to instead use the non-const writeData. It guards all access with a makeUnique invocation to ensure that the caller is the only owner of the underlying data. Our claim is that after the makeUnique call we will be the only owner of the underlying data.

We must stress that this uniqueness is not guaranteed by the code! A malicious caller can easily stash a pointer to the FOO_Array else-thread and call copyData, violating this assumption. However, provided the ownership model is respected, the guarantee will hold. We already use this sort of contract to avoid memory leaks, and we have found the same sort of coding practices can be used to ensure there are no surprising behaviors.

While our ownership contract ensures there can be no surprising increases to the unique count of myData, it says nothing about surprising decreases. As such, after the unique call and until the assignment to myData, it is possible another thread will decide it is done with its own copy of the data and leave this as the only copy. In that case, however, the only penalty we face is making an extra copy. Further, the extra copy is something that, but for the timing of threads, may have been otherwise required.

2.4.5   Failure Modes of This System

While we have successfully used copy on write to solve our reader/writer problem, we have found that it does have its own set of pitfalls. As expected from a system that requires a contract with the programmer, a violation of the contract can cause things to fail.

The main problem we encounter is being too liberal in acquiring ownership. It is tempting when using `shared_ptr` to fall into a Java-style model of programming in which everything is owned by everyone. Not only does this result in a lot of unnecessary atomic operations, with copy on write it can cause writes to disappear into the ether.

For example, consider this multithreaded code:

```
void applyPartial(FOO_Array foo, RANGE partialrange)
{
    float *dst = foo.writeData();

    for (i in partialrange)
    {
        dst[i] *= 2;
    }
}


FOO_Array bar;

invoke_parallel(applyPartial, bar);
```

We have treated `FOO_Array` as a lightweight container, so we have passed it by value to our threaded tasks. In the original definition, where `FOO_Array` was a wrapper of a `shared_ptr` to `myData`, this would work, but now with copy on write the result is different. Each of the tasks will build their own copy of the array, write to that, and then delete the copy. When we return at last to the caller, it will find its copy in `bar` unchanged. The solution is to ensure none of the threads gain ownership of the `FOO_Array`, but we leave that ownership in the caller:

```
void applyPartial(float *dst, RANGE partialrange)
{
    for (i in partialrange)
    {
        dst[i] *= 2;
    }
}

FOO_Array bar;

invoke_parallel(applyPartial, bar.writeData());
```

Because the lifetimes of the subtasks are contained by the invoker, it is correct to use raw pointers and not give them ownership.

Another nasty situation we found if proper care is not taken is:

```
void apply(float *dst, const float *src)
{
    for (i = 0; i < size; i++)
    {
        dst[i] = src[i] * 2;
```

```
    }
}

void process(FOO_Array &foo)
{
    const float *src = foo.readData();
    float *dst = foo.writeData();

    apply(dst, src);
};
```

This contrived example of pointer aliasing creates a few problems. First, whether `src` == `dst` depends on the share count of the incoming `foo` reference. If `foo` is already unique, the `readData` and `writeData` will report the same pointer and we will get the expected aliasing. However, if it were shared, `writeData` will cause `dst` to have a duplicate copy, leaving us with two independent blocks of memory. This is not the most serious problem, however. Consider if `foo` was shared during the invocation, but the other copy was released after the `readData` and before the `writeData`. After the `writeData` completes its copy it will free the original data as it now is unshared, leaving `src` pointing to freed memory.

Using copy on write to solve the reader/writer problem is not a silver bullet. We have found it requires some additional care and code hygiene. However, we do not believe these requirements are much more onerous than what is already posed by C++'s lack of garbage collection, making the technique familiar and accessible.

2.5   Dependencies

Each parameter or input to an algorithm is a dependency for that algorithm. When we wish to scatter points into a volume, for example, we have a dependency on computing the point positions. We also have a dependency on knowing the parameters for the scatter—things such as filter kernels or density prescales. Evaluating these dependencies can become arbitrarily complicated. The filter kernel, for example, could be an expression, and this expression's value could require the computing of still other geometry in the scene. Traditionally, dependencies are always evaluated in a just-in-time manner. This allows natural efficiencies if some parameters imply that other parameters do not need to be evaluated. A switch-geometry operation, for example, selects one of several geometries to be its output. It would not just be inefficient to evaluate all of the possible inputs when only one is needed, quite often the unselected inputs are actually invalid and would trigger an error if evaluated.

TBB provides support for dependencies. When we create tasks we can create a task-graph making the dependency explicit. We may then evaluate our tasks blindly, relying on the scheduler to ensure our explicit dependencies will be computed prior to our own evaluation. We are, however, required to explicitly prebuild this dependency graph, a difficult job when faced with code written with ad hoc dependency invocation.

Our problems go beyond explicit dependencies, however. We have a rich set of expressions to query live, upstream geometry. The actual shape of the dependency graph can be a function of what is being processed. Further, these expressions are not rare exceptions, but form a core of a lot of procedural workflows. It is quite common, for example, to inspect upstream geometry for certain attributes and invoke a separate chain of initialization operations if they are missing. We cannot, therefore, simply break into a two-pass system that first builds a full dependency tree, and then evaluates it. Instead, we would have to build a recursive system where we alternate between building dependencies and evaluating operations.

Even with such a system, however, we would still encounter the problem of some dependencies being only discoverable partway through performing an operation. Our VEX programming language allows the inspection of live geometry elsewhere in Houdini. This inspection can then require the computation of that geometry. The geometry to be requested is not known to the higher level operation. It merely is aware of a block of VEX code that it must execute, it cannot predict the implications of that text without executing it. This Turing trap means we must always be able to handle the case of dependencies that are being discovered during execution.

2.5.1 Task Locks

How, then, do we handle the case where we have this delayed realization of dependencies? A simple solution is to treat the dependency as a lock. We can acquire a lock on the object we need to evaluate, thereby ensuring only one of the tasks dependent on the value will evaluate it. With the case of VEX, we perform this by acquiring a lock on the geometry engine.

Our geometry lock, however, serves multiple purposes. It is not just to keep separate VEX threads from computing geometry at the same time, but is also used to keep the Python thread and the main thread from both computing geometry at the same time. Thus, when a VEX task wishes to acquire this lock, it will already be acquired by the VEX task's parent thread—which if it is a worker thread, will be a separate thread id. Any attempt to get the geometry lock from a VEX task scheduled on a different thread than the parent thread will hence deadlock.

To solve this we created a task lock, a more general form of the reentrant lock. When we create tasks we store their parent task group. Then, when we try to acquire a task lock, we will successfully acquire it not if the thread-id matches, but if the task's parent matches the owner of the lock. The acquiring task is then pushed as the new holder of the lock, ensuring sibling tasks will properly block.

There are two major problems we have found with this approach. The first is efficiency. We effectively devolve to single threaded performance during the task lock. In the common case, if one of the VEX tasks requests this lock, all the tasks will. Thus, each TBB worker-thread will become blocked on the task lock, excepting the single thread that acquired the lock. The second problem is more insidious: as described, it can lead to deadlocks.

Not only are locks a bad idea for obvious performance reasons, the task-stealing nature of TBB can lead to unexpected deadlocks when they are used. The fundamental principle that must be obeyed is that the TBB scheduler must never be entered while a lock is held. Let us take a closer look at why this is a problem.

Consider a system with two worker threads, W1 and W2. We decide to execute a VEX operation that creates three tasks, T1, T2, and T3. Each of these tasks will require external data D. The best approach is to first compute D, and then compute the VEX operation in a lock-free manner. However, we may be unable to discover that we need D without first executing the tasks. In this case, we can create a lock, L, to guard our computation of D.

An example execution order is this: Threads W1 and W2 execute T1 and T2. T1 discovers it needs D, so acquires lock L. T2 likewise needs D and so blocks on the lock L. We complete D with a single thread active, and when done, T1 and T2 can complete. T3 will be executed by the first of W1 and W2 to finish, and our job is finished.

However, what happens if we decide to speed up the computation of D by multithreading it? The first problem is that it will not actually multithread. No matter how many tasks we create, only W1 is free to execute as W2 is blocked on L. If this were the only problem, we could leave it as an optimization exercise for the artist to make the dependency on D explicit. However, when we return to the TBB scheduler, it does not know about the dependency on D either. Thus, it is free to select from any available task, not just the ones enqueued by D. In particular, it could decide to assign T3 to W1. T3 will then try to acquire the lock on D but be blocked because it is a sibling to the current owner, T1.

One solution is to embrace the single threaded option. Because we have wrapped our TBB invocations, we are able to set a thread-local flag to disable all further calls into the scheduler. `UTparallelFor` will devolve to `UTserialFor` and we will avoid the deadlocks. This does not, however, help us with third-party code. Third-party code will often directly invoke TBB rather than use our wrappers because it is often designed to be platform agnostic.

Newer versions of TBB provide a better solution: the task arena feature. Task arenas provide a way to create a logically disjointed subset of worker threads. They will share the main thread pool, but will not steal work from it. Whenever we create a task lock, we are already committing ourselves to an expensive operation. Thus, we can justify creating a new task arena for it. By putting our computation of D into its own arena, any attempts it makes at threading will stay in its own scheduler, preventing T3 from being enqueued. While this often will still result in single threaded performance, there is some hope that if the other tasks did not actually depend on D, those worker threads can still migrate to D's arena.

We show a concrete example of the potential deadlock with this simple function to update a global cache. Normally, a lock suffices to protect a cache. If the `compute` method calls into `buildCache` we need a reentrant lock. But if the `compute` method multithreads, and those child threads wish to invoke `buildCache`, we both need a task lock and need to guard against the described deadlock.

```
static UT_TaskLock glb_lock;
static CACHE *glb_cache;

void *
buildCache(...)
{
    // To access glb_cache we need to lock.  Because we
    // can be re-entrant, it must be a re-entrant lock.
    // However, we could be re-entering from a child
    // thread of the original processor, thus a Task Lock.
    UT_TaskLock::Scope       scope(glb_lock);

    if (glb_cache->hasItem(...))
        return glb_cache->getItem(...);

    // This call to compute may:
```

```
// a) thread
// b) call buildCache from a sub-thread
void *item = compute(...);
glb_cache->addItem(item);
return item;
}
```

We can fix this by ensuring that the compute method is invoked as a new task inside a task arena:

```
#define TBB_PREVIEW_TASK_ARENA 1

static UT_TaskLock glb_lock;
static CACHE *glb_cache;

struct compute_Delegate
{
    compute_Delegate(...)
    { /* Localize Parameters */ }

    void operator()()
    {
        myResult = compute(...);
    }

    void *myResult;
};

void *
buildCache(...)
{
    UT_TaskLock::Scope        scope(glb_lock);

    if (glb_cache->hasItem(...))
        return glb_cache->getItem(...);

    // Build a task arena for our computation
    tbb::task_arena arena();
    compute_Delegate        computer(...);
    arena->execute(computer);

    void *item = computer.myResult;
    glb_cache->addItem(item);
    return item;
}
```

2.5.2   Mantra

Threading a renderer is supposed to be easy. Especially in raytracing mode, the problem seems embarrassingly parallel. Divide the image into small tiles, make each tile a task, and send it to a `parallel_for`. However, much like the case of executing VEX, it is very hard to know when you start a tile just what things that tile will depend on.

When we wish to trace a complicated model we will first build an acceleration structure for that model. We do not want to prebuild these, however, since not all models will show up in the scene. They may be totally obscured, or totally obscured for the set of tiles assigned to this particular render pass. We thus delay building acceleration structures until a ray risks hitting a model. If one task's tile triggers a hit, the other tasks will likely do otherwise, leading to many worker threads wanting to build the acceleration structure simultaneously. Somewhat reluctantly, we throw a lock around the construction. And everything seems fine.

As models become larger, however, constructing this data structure becomes more expensive. We find ourselves waiting minutes for the first tile to complete as Mantra laboriously builds the acceleration structure. We look at our CPU graph, see but a single process working, and grumble that we should multithread the building process. After much sweat and tears, we build a nice multithreaded construction algorithm. But our CPU graph? It stays locked at a single process. After all, all the other potential threads are locked waiting for this structure, so are unable to contribute to the job.

Our ideal situation would be to have a `yield(LOCK)` method which returned a worker thread to the task scheduler until the given lock becomes free. However, this is not possible in TBB. Task arenas come close to a solution. If the `wait_until_empty` method can be supported, we could use a task lock to guard the building operation. We would first do a try-lock and, if the lock fails, find the arena created for the task lock and invoke its `wait_until_empty`, thereby donating our thread to the cause.

Another solution we considered was cancelling the tile when we found we had a block on a dependency. We could abandon our computation of the current tile, re-enqueue it on the scheduler with a dependency, and return to the scheduler. Unfortunately, this may waste considerable work prior to hitting the dependency. Further, we may spend our time attempting a series of partial tiles until we happen to be assigned a task that actually contributes to finishing the building task.

Our current solution relies on the simplicity of the top level of multithreading. Splitting tiles among a thread pool is a simple form of scheduling that requires none of the subtleties of TBB. Thus, we create a pool of threads separate from TBB's worker pool. This primary pool of threads performs all of the normal tile rendering, but when we need to invoke TBB we can rely on it having its own full contingent of worker threads, even if all of our tile threads are blocked. Unfortunately, this can result in oversubscription—in theory we could use twice the active threads as was requested on the command line. However, in practice, if one tile blocks the successive tiles will also block, so we remain close to the requested active thread count.

2.6 OpenCL

The CPU is only half of the power of the modern desktop machine. The other half lies in the GPU. When we are not drawing to the viewport, we would like to bring it into the mix to speed up our computations. This is especially tempting with large simulations. We may have a considerable delay between frames in any case, so the graphics card would otherwise be unused while we are computing the next frame of the simulation. We have watched with interest many of the excellent results that have been achieved using GPUs. They can, however, be hard to properly compare with an equivalent CPU algorithm. All too often we see an algorithm described as ten times faster, but 10 times faster than a single threaded CPU implementation!

Nonetheless, there are cases where GPUs are able to significantly outperform CPUs, and we would like to be able to take advantage of these cases. We have added support for OpenCL to our simulation environment. We chose OpenCL for its device agnostic nature. In particular, the existence of Intel's CPU drivers mean that a simulation created for the GPU can still be sent to a farm of headless machines. With the maximum memory on video cards often still in the single-digit gigabytes, very large simulations simply must be processed on the CPU regardless of their comparative speed. We are very happy we can use the same kernels for both the low-resolution GPU-driven desktop version and the high-resolution CPU-driven farm version. We were also concerned that using any GPU mechanism leaves us at the mercy of the quality of the drivers. To ameliorate this risk, we restricted our use to the basic OpenCL 1.0 specification. Further, we maintained pure CPU versions of all our code, providing both a baseline comparison and a fallback when drivers are not available.

We do, however, run into some of the limitations of working with a GPU. A core problem we face is the lack of unified memory. Since the GPU and the CPU have separate memory spaces, any time data has to transfer between the two there is a huge cost. This often completely eradicates the gains of using the GPU, leading to cases where even if the GPU took zero time, the algorithm would still be faster if it ran solely on the CPU. The usual solution to this problem is to put the entire system on the GPU. Ideally, we could use the actual screen images as our final output, leaving all operations to live on the GPU. The output of our simulations, however, tends to be the dense data. If we have a smoke simulation, we intend to render it in Mantra, so will require the full 3D volume data. We also run into the problem of VEX. Because we have provided this language for manipulating simulations, it has been commonly used for just that purpose. It, however, cannot be simply ported to the GPU. Its scripting roots, particularly its ability to inspect arbitrary geometry elsewhere in Houdini, mean that only a fraction of its features would be sensible on the GPU side of the bus. Further complicating things, our simulation itself is not fixed in order. We can, within Houdini, rewire the simulation, reordering operations and injecting new operations in between old ones. The operation order itself may be determined by the results of the simulation, preventing any static analysis of the data flow between the CPU and the GPU.

Our solution to the bandwidth problem is to keep both CPU and GPU backed versions of each volume. We lazily update each one on demand, so if the CPU does not require the output of a GPU computation, it will never retrieve the resulting volume from the GPU. We take advantage of the const keyword to differentiate writes to a volume from reads. If a CPU operation only reads from a volume, we know that any GPU backed version must still be valid so we do not have to update it.

We handle this logic in SIM_RawField, key methods of which are listed below:

```
/// Fetches a read-only CPU field.
const UT_VoxelArrayF       *field() const
{
    if (myFieldOutOfDate) { updateFieldFromGrid(); }
    return myField;
}

/// Fetches a writeable CPU field.
UT_VoxelArrayF             *fieldNC() const
{
    if (myGrid) { clearGrid(); }
```

```
    return myField;
}


/// Fetches the GPU grid, returns 0 if not present.
CE_Grid                    *grid() const;

/// Fetches the GPU grid, creating if not present.
CE_Grid                    *requireGrid() const;

/// Mark the GPU grid as out of date, but only if we have a valid grid.
void                       markGridAsChanged()
{
    if (myGrid) myFieldOutOfDate = true;
}


/// Copies GPU grid to CPU if CPU out of date and frees
/// the GPU grid
void                       clearGrid() const;
```

We distinguish the terms field and grid for the volume stored in the CPU and the one stored in the GPU, respectively. Note in particular that we do not name the non-const accessor for the CPU field the same as the const accessor. Because the non-const accessor has such significantly different behavior, we felt it important to make it clear which version was being used. Because GPU memory is very precious, we are very quick to evict the grid version of the field. Whenever the CPU version is about to go out of sync, as determined by a `fieldNC` call, we will immediately clear any corresponding GPU version. In the converse case, we believe it is reasonable to leave the old CPU grid in memory. This also allows us to store some of our metadata, such as resolution, in the CPU version of the volume. We use a flag, `myFieldOutOfDate`, to track if the grid has changed. This is a manual process because we do not know what the OpenCL kernel plans to do with the volume, so we require the kernel implementer to call `markGridAsChanged` if they have a result to post back.

Our simulations are cached in memory by default. As described, the cached versions of the volumes will retain their GPU-backed grids, swiftly exhausting GPU memory. We had to resort to a small bit of hackery: when we copy a volume out of a cache, we give ownership of the GPU-backed grid to the new copy, not the cached copy. Even with this being accounted for, caching causes every volume that is modified on the GPU to be retrieved, so we often disable it for OpenCL simulations.

We are very happy with the flexibility we have gained by our hybrid approach. We have been able to slowly grow the amount of GPU-based code in our simulations without having to fully convert our pipeline.

Chapter 3

The Presto Execution System: Designing for Multithreading

George ElKoura

Pixar Animation Studios

3.1	Introduction		48
	3.1.1	A Note about Interactivity	48
3.2	Presto		49
	3.2.1	Presto Objects	50
	3.2.2	Rigging in Presto	51
	3.2.3	Animation in Presto	52
3.3	Presto's Execution System		52
	3.3.1	Phases of Execution	53
		3.3.1.1 Compilation	53
		3.3.1.2 Scheduling	54
		3.3.1.3 Evaluation	54
	3.3.2	Engine Architecture	54
		3.3.2.1 Network	55
		3.3.2.2 Schedulers	55
		3.3.2.3 Data Managers	56
		3.3.2.4 Executors	56
		3.3.2.5 Engine Architecture and Multithreading	56
3.4	User Extensions		57
	3.4.1	Dependencies Declared *a Priori*	57
	3.4.2	Client Callbacks Are Static Functions	57
	3.4.3	Presto Singletons Are Protected	58
	3.4.4	Iterators	58
	3.4.5	And Then There's Python	58
		3.4.5.1 Global Interpreter Lock	58
		3.4.5.2 Performance	59
3.5	Memory Access Patterns		59
3.6	Flexibility to Experiment		60
	3.6.1	Modular Design	60
	3.6.2	Targeting Other Platforms	60
3.7	Multithreading Strategies		61
	3.7.1	Per-Node Multithreading	61
	3.7.2	Per-Branch Multithreading	62
	3.7.3	Per-Model Multithreading	62
	3.7.4	Per-Frame Multithreading	64
3.8	Background Execution		64
	3.8.1	User Interaction	65
	3.8.2	Frame Scheduling	65

	3.8.3	Interruption	66
	3.8.4	Constant Data	67
	3.8.5	Problematic Data Structures	67
3.9		Other Multithreading Strategies	69
	3.9.1	Strip Mining	69
	3.9.2	Predictive Computations	70
3.10		Debugging and Profiling Tools	70
3.11		Summary	71

3.1   Introduction

In this chapter, we present an asynchronous computation engine suitable for use in an animation package. In particular, we describe how this engine is used in Pixar's proprietary animation system, Presto.

We will start by describing what Presto is and concentrate on how it is used in two different disciplines, rigging and animation. We will then dive into Presto's execution system, its phases and the structures that make up its architecture. We then describe how several different multithreading strategies can be implemented using the architecture. We focus on Background Execution, a feature that allows users to keep working while soon-to-be-needed computations are performed in the background. We discuss the requirements and considerations from a user interaction perspective. We then end by briefly discussing debugging and profiling tools necessary for such a system.

3.1.1   A Note about Interactivity

Multithreading can be used effectively to speed up many different kinds of computations often used in the visual effects industry. Before we choose multithreading as the answer to our performance problems, we must at least consider our target performance characteristics. Some computations take hours or days, others can take milliseconds. The most appropriate approach varies with the scale of the computation we are trying to optimize. For example, if you are targeting a day-long task, you probably would not be too concerned with the cost of starting up the threads. Whereas for interactive rates, this overhead would be of great importance to you.

In this chapter we concentrate on interactive-rate computations. In Presto, our targets are generally computations that are performed in under 0.1 second. One tenth of a second is an important threshold. Even regular human conversation over the telephone starts to breakdown when the latency exceeds this limit [14]. The three important limits for response times that have been established in the usability community are 0.1 second, 1 second, and 10 seconds [50]. At or below 0.1 second, the user feels that the application is responsive and no lag is perceptible. Between 0.1 and 1 second, users typically will not lose their concentration or lose their focus on the task at hand. Go too far above 1 second and the user's focus will shift elsewhere. If the delay is over 10 seconds, the user will likely switch tasks.

We found that 0.1 second (100 ms), is a bare minimum for interactive rates, and users actually start to feel comfortable around 65 ms. We have set 42 ms as our target rate for frequent animation-related interactions. This allows us to hit an important playback rate of 24 fps, for example. Higher frame rates are often requested, however, and being asked to hit rates of 60 fps is becoming more common.

Other factors that force us to hit high frame rates include the use of input devices such as camera trackers. When Presto is used with these kinds of input devices, ensuring that we can keep up with the input stream that these devices generate often requires higher than 24 fps frame rates.

3.2 Presto

Presto is Pixar's proprietary, fully featured, animation package. In addition to the main interactive application, many other interactive and batch-mode tools are built on top of the same set of reusable libraries that are used by Presto.

The application supports integrated workflows for a variety of feature film departments including rigging, layout, animation, and simulation. It also provides built-in media playback and asset management tools. Figure 3.1 shows a screenshot of a sample session in Presto.

For the purposes of this chapter, we will mainly discuss Presto's execution system. We will use two common disciplines, rigging and animation, to illustrate how the system works. Much of what will be discussed applies to other disciplines as well. Though we will mainly talk about computations used for posing points, the execution engine itself is generic and is used for other kinds of computations as well.

Figure 3.2 roughly shows how the execution system libraries fit in with the libraries around them. In this case, the figure is showing just one client, the viewport, but of course

FIGURE 3.1: Screenshot of a session in Presto, Pixar's proprietary animation system. Presto provides an integrated environment that supports rigging and animation workflows, among others. The editors shown here (the spline editor and the spreadsheet editor) are commonly used for animation. This chapter describes Presto's execution system, which is responsible for posing the characters and other such computations at interactive rates. **(See Color Insert.)**

FIGURE 3.2: High-level view of where the execution system libraries fit in the overall system.

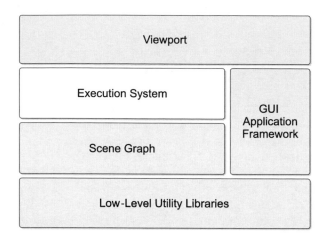

many other clients exist in the actual system. Also note that the execution system itself is a client of the libraries providing the scene graph, which we will discuss a little later, as well as some lower-level libraries.

One of the challenges in Presto is its integrated architecture. In a single session, the user may wish to animate, do some rigging, run a simulation or all three without an explicit context switch. Some of these tasks do not lend themselves well to multithreading, and yet must coexist seamlessly with all features of the application.

Before we begin let's go through a quick overview of the types of objects in Presto that play an important role in execution. We will then dive into a description of the disciplines of interest and some of the workflows they use. Then we will be ready to get into the details.

3.2.1 Presto Objects

We do not want to get too bogged down in the details of Presto's object model, so we will define only a few terms and concepts. These concepts should map roughly to concepts that exist in other visual effects packages with which the reader may be familiar.

The objects that can hold values are called "attributes." Attributes are used to represent both inputs and outputs. Attributes can be assigned values by the user, and can also be used to extract computed values. The radius of a sphere, for example, would be represented by an attribute. The radius of the sphere can be explicitly set by the user, and it can also be affected by computations that are specified by the user. The two are not mutually exclusive in Presto, meaning that the value entered by the user may be used by the computations to produce the computed value for the same attribute.

Attributes may send and receive traditional data flow values through "connections." These are objects in the scene that describe data flowing from one attribute to another. Nearly all 3D applications provide a mechanism that allows you to do the same thing.

Attributes are owned by "prims." These are high-level objects that contain, among other things, collections of attributes. One would represent a Subdivision Surface, for example, using a prim. Prims are typically classified by their behavior. For example, geometric prims are called gprims. Prims that provide behavior to modify point positions are called deformers, and so on. Lights, cameras, bones, and widgets are all examples of prims.

FIGURE 3.3: Objects used to build a scene graph in Presto.

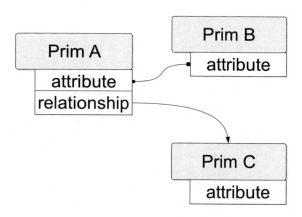

In addition to attributes, prims can also own "relationships." Like connections, relationships allow users to express associations between objects. While connections can only associate one attribute to one or more other attributes, relationships can associate prims to attributes, to other prims, or to other relationships. Also, while a majority of relationships serve to express powerful computation behavior, they do not necessarily imply any—they simply express associativity. How a particular prim's behavior interprets that association is up to the prim.

These are some of the "scene objects" that are used to express a scene graph in Presto.

Figure 3.3 shows three prims: Prim A, Prim B, and Prim C. They each have an attribute and Prim A has a relationship. The relationship on Prim A targets Prim C in this case. Prim A's attribute has a connection to Prim B's attribute, meaning that Prim B's attribute value is retrieved from Prim A's attribute.

A typical rig is made up of at least two different kinds of prims: gprims and deformers. Gprims describe the geometry of the model; and deformers describe how the geometry changes under a given set of parameter values. There is a third type of prim that is frequently used called a weight object. Weight objects, in their simplest form, merely assign weights (scalars) to the points. These weights can be used in a variety of ways by deformers, for example, to attenuate the deformations. There are many other kinds of prims used by the system, and users invent new ones every day, however, we have enough background now to delve in and learn how these concepts are applied.

3.2.2 Rigging in Presto

Rigging is the process of modeling the posing behavior of the characters and props for a show. Riggers describe how, given a set of inputs, a character poses. They use what is effectively a visual programming language to describe the structure and behavior of their models. From a rigger's point of view, the structure consists of the human-readable objects we described earlier: the prims, attributes, connections, and relationships. These objects are transformed into a different representation before we execute them.

Later in the chapter, we will discuss in more detail the different phases of execution and what purpose this transformation serves. For now, it is sufficient to know that before a final result can be delivered, the system produces a data flow network from the objects that users create. The execution structures are designed specifically for efficient computation. Ideally, riggers never have to know that a transformation is taking place between the objects they directly author and the objects used by the execution system. In practice, it helps to be aware of this process and how it works, especially when optimizing rigs.

Typical rigging workflows often involve making topological changes to the execution network. For example, changing a connection between two attributes, or changing the order of deformers, all result in a topological change to the network that must be applied before additional values are computed by the system. Making this fast is an important part of making sure that the abstraction does not get in the way of a rigger's work. If we blew away and regenerated the execution structures every time a rigger changed topology, for example, the system would be far too slow for riggers to work comfortably. We therefore have to update the execution structures incrementally as the rigger is working.

Geometry topology also changes during character rigging, but is fixed once the rig is finalized. In other words, the character rig itself does not modify the topology of the geometry. Some kinds of rigs do modify geometric topology, though we generally try to avoid such behaviors in character rigs because our system is able to take advantage of fixed topology for faster computation.

3.2.3 Animation in Presto

Animation is responsible for bringing characters to life. Animators supply input values to the rig in order to hit desired character poses.

The topology of the character's geometry does not change during the course of typical animation workflows. Network topology may change, but does so infrequently. We said earlier that Presto is a fully integrated application. This means that animators are free to change the rigging of the character in their shot, in whichever way they please. However, this is generally discouraged since it could lead to hard-to-debug problems as well as continuity issues. Riggers set aside an area in the rig that can be used for animation rigging. Restricting this extra shot rigging to a well known location allows riggers to better understand and control how it may interact with the rest of the character's rigging.

Common examples of per-shot animation rigging include adding lattice deformations and post-deformation sculpts. Animators add these lattices and sculpts using the same underlying architecture that riggers use. So the speed up we mentioned earlier for faster incremental updating of the execution network applies equally well to some animation workflows.

Another, much more common, way in which the network topology is changed by animators is through the addition of constraints. Adding constraints imposes new structure on the data flow network. New dependencies need to be established, for example. This, too, invokes the incremental network update process, and must be performed at interactive rates in order to avoid interrupting the animator's concentration.

3.3 Presto's Execution System

Presto's execution system is a general-purpose computation engine. Given a set of inputs (e.g., animation splines) and an execution network (e.g., derived from a rig), the job of the execution system is to provide the computed result (e.g., point positions) as quickly as possible. Common computations include posing points, calculating scalar fields, determining object visibility, and so on.

Like many other similar systems, at its core, the execution engine in Presto evaluates a data flow network. Presto's data flow network is vectorized, meaning that many uniquely identifiable elements may flow along a single connection. We do not need to get into the details of this aspect of the system to talk about multithreading, but it is worth noting as it will come up now and again. Note that we use the term "vectorization" much in the same way as it is used when talking about CPU SIMD instructions. However, the two are not the same thing and can, in fact, be combined. More on that later in the chapter.

In the following sections we will explore the architecture of the execution system, how the parts fit together, and how they lead to a framework that is amenable to multithreaded computation.

3.3.1 Phases of Execution

The purpose of the execution system is to produce computation results to clients as efficiently as possible. It accomplishes this work in three phases:

- Compilation

- Scheduling

- Evaluation

We will see why that is beneficial as we describe the phases in more detail, but the biggest benefit is that each phase amortizes costs for the next phase. The phases are listed in the order that they run, also in the order of least-frequently run to most frequently run and from most to least expensive, in terms of runtime costs.

3.3.1.1 Compilation

As we said earlier, riggers author scene objects using a rich, high-level, visual language. This allows riggers to work efficiently. By abstracting away details of the execution system, we allow riggers to concentrate on building the rigs. However, the paradigms that enable a fast rigging process may not always lend themselves to fast rig evaluation. Compilation is the phase of execution that converts the human-readable scene objects into optimized data structures that can be used for fast, repeated evaluations of the rig (e.g., during animation).

The result of compilation is a network of nodes and connections between them. While riggers deal in various concepts like connections, deformers, weight objects, and so on, once compilation is done, the execution system sees only a network consisting of homogeneous execution nodes.

Full network compilation typically happens only when a character is first loaded in a session. Rigging workflows invoke an incremental recompilation code path that builds or rebuilds the network in pieces as the rig is developed. This is important to keep the system responsive for rigging activities.

As we mentioned, our main motivation for the compilation phase is to produce data structures that are fast to evaluate repeatedly. In addition, compilation provides a layer of abstraction that allows us to keep the representation of the assets separate from the data structures required by our system. Assets are time-consuming and expensive to author, and we would like them to be independent from the implementation of the execution system. That is to say, if we decide to change how the execution system's data structures are organized, we could do so without having to also modify the assets.

Compilation also provides a convenient place to perform optimizations at the network level. Constant folding, node fusion, and no-op elision are examples of the kinds of optimizations that are most conveniently done at compilation time. Constant folding is the analysis performed on the network to determine sets of nodes that will always produce the same answer and to replace them with a single node that produces the constant value. Node fusion can be an arbitrarily complex analysis that determines which set of nodes can be combined into fewer nodes that produce the same answer. No-op elision is a simple optimization where the system removes nodes that are known to have no effect on the output. These are, of course, a few examples; the main point is that the system provides a phase for implementing and experimenting with these kinds of algorithms.

Since the network-level optimizations we just described are destructive to the network, and thus difficult to incrementally recompile, we perform them only for animation workflows, that is, when we know that the intent is to no longer modify the internals of the rig. Edits made by animators that modify the network topology outside the rig must still be incrementally recompiled, of course.

For animators, we can also avoid the cost of full network compilation by serializing the results of compilation during a preprocessing step for each model.

3.3.1.2   Scheduling

Given a set of desired outputs (e.g., the posed point positions of a character), which we call a "request," scheduling serves to amortize dependency analysis costs that would otherwise have to be incurred during each network evaluation. The specifics of the analysis performed during scheduling is up to the implementation. For example, this typically includes the set of nodes that need to run in order to satisfy the request. It may be beneficial for certain schemes that scheduling determine the partial ordering in which the nodes run, and for others, it might be more efficient if scheduling only determines what nodes need to run, and the ordering is left to the evaluation phase. Scheduling occurs every time a client (e.g., the viewport, a simulation, etc.) requests a new set of outputs to evaluate.

Scheduling is performed more often than compilation, but not as often as evaluation. For requests that have already been scheduled, scheduling must be performed again after network topology changes caused by incremental recompilation, and therefore occurs more often during rigging workflows, and relatively rarely during animation workflows. Animation workflows may cause scheduling, for example, when adding a new constraint or creating new deformers.

3.3.1.3   Evaluation

Evaluation is the most frequently run phase of execution. Its job is to run the nodes in the network as determined by the schedule in order to produce computed values for the requested outputs. Evaluation is run every time an input value changes, or a new output is requested, and the results are pulled on (e.g., to satisfy a viewport update).

3.3.2   Engine Architecture

The execution engine is made up of several components: Networks, Schedulers, Data Managers, and Executors, which we will now describe in more detail. The relationship between these components is shown in Figure 3.4.

As we describe these components, keep in mind that the driving principle behind this architecture is to facilitate efficient multithreaded execution. For example, we will see how splitting up the network from the data storage in data managers can help us avoid synchronizing between threads.

FIGURE 3.4: The components of the execution system's architecture.

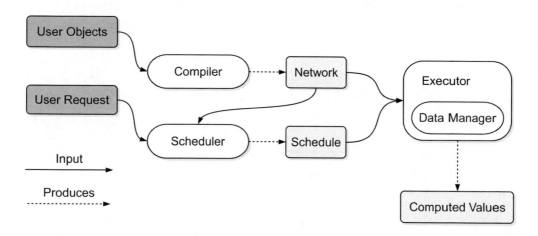

3.3.2.1 Network

The network is generated from user-authored scene objects and is a static representation of computations and the dependencies among them. A network is made up of nodes and connections. A node is made up of zero or more inputs and zero or more outputs (a leaf node with zero outputs is only used for tracking and broadcasting dependencies to external systems and is never run). Client code requests computed values by specifying desired node outputs.

As we mentioned earlier, this network is similar to the data flow networks that are commonly found in systems such as ours. The main difference is that connections in our networks may represent multiple data elements. Masks on the connections are used to track fine-grained dependencies and to index each element individually. Much like SIMD instructions on modern CPUs, this kind of vectorization in our network allows us to process elements more efficiently in big batches. Point posing, for example, is a great candidate for this kind of optimization because one operation is usually performed on multiple points at once.

Also, the vectorization we set up in our networks make it easy to use the CPU SIMD instructions to operate on the data. Nodes in our network can take advantage of the data's layout in memory to make SIMD calls to speed up their work.

Finally, it is important to note that no state is stored in the network, it embodies only the computation's static structure.

3.3.2.2 Schedulers

Schedulers are responsible for the scheduling phase of execution and produce schedules that are used by the executors for repeated evaluations. Clients (e.g., the viewport) hold on to schedules through an opaque object that is returned to them when they make a request. They then pass that object back to the system when they request a value evaluation.

Beyond providing a list of nodes to run, schedulers can also perform extra analysis that can be taken advantage of by executors. Schedulers give us a convenient place to perform this kind of expensive analysis and cache the result. When we find the executors performing an expensive operation, we often ask ourselves, "can this work be done, instead, by the scheduler?" When the answer is "yes," we get a boost to the runtime efficiency of the system, for a relatively small cost to scheduling. The kind of analysis that cannot be moved to scheduling is that which depends on the dynamic content of the executors. For example, knowing what nodes ran and what nodes did not is only available to the executor that ran (or did not run) the nodes—this information is not available at scheduling time. Schedulers can also be specialized for different kinds of multithreading schemes.

3.3.2.3   Data Managers

Data managers are simply data containers for nodes in the network. They are used by the executors to store the computed data. Each executor uses one data manager to store the data for the whole network. The simplest data manager stores a map from output to computed value. You would specialize a data manager if you wanted to provide a faster implementation or if you wanted to change where the data was stored (e.g., a VRAM data manager). The abstraction data managers provide, that is: not storing data in the nodes themselves, is an important architectural feature of our network.

Data managers store computed data as well as validity masks, which keep track of the dirty state of the outputs, and other per-node or per-output data that is required by the executor.

3.3.2.4   Executors

Executors are the workhorses of the execution system. Executors orchestrate evaluation using the compiled network, a schedule, and a data manager. They run the inner loop and need to do so as efficiently as possible.

Executors can be arranged in a hierarchy, where the child is allowed to read from (and sometimes even write to) the parent in order to avoid redundant computations. This feature is put to use in a few different ways in the system, but for the purposes of multithreading we will discuss specifically how it is used for Background Execution a little later in this chapter.

Executors can be specialized to use different algorithms to run the network. You might want to specialize an executor to implement different multithreading techniques, for example, or to target a different hardware platform. Later, when we discuss different multithreading strategies, we will see that they are primarily implemented by writing different kinds of executors.

3.3.2.5   Engine Architecture and Multithreading

Now that we have seen all the components, let's see how they can be put together to enable efficient multithreading algorithms.

The network is a static representation of the overall computation to be evaluated. It contains no state and does not get modified during evaluation. This means that the network can be used from multiple threads without locking.

The same applies to schedules. They contain the results of static analysis and can be reused during evaluation without modification. Again, multiple threads can use the same schedule without locking.

Finally, an executor directly embodies a multithreading scheme. Background Execution, for example, uses one executor per thread. Since the executors each use their own data manager to store the stateful data for the network, they are all free to run independently of one another without locking. More multithreading schemes are discussed later in this chapter.

3.4   User Extensions

One of the problems that often complicates multithreading is having to call out to plugin code. Not knowing what the clients are going to do, and what resources they might acquire, makes it difficult to create a resilient and robust system, let alone one with predictable performance characteristics. Our system is no different, but we do take a few extra precautions in order to minimize the chance that a user will accidentally shoot themselves in the foot. Dogged determination to shoot oneself in the foot, on the other hand, is impossible to guard against.

Since we have always intended for our system to be run in a multithreaded environment, we needed to carefully consider the responsibilities we impose on clients of the system. One of our goals was to make it as safe as possible for users to write plugin code without requiring them to worry about multithreading in most cases. The structure of the system described here helps avoid common multithreading pitfalls for users in the following ways:

- Dependencies are declared *a priori*

- Client callbacks are static functions

- Key singletons are protected

- Data access is through provided iterators

3.4.1   Dependencies Declared *a Priori*

The system is set up in such a way that users declare, ahead of time, the inputs that their node computations will consume. They can make certain dependencies optional (meaning that if they are not available, the node can still produce a reasonable answer), but they cannot add more dependencies at runtime. The static structure of the network is fixed and is built based on the dependencies that the user declares.

3.4.2   Client Callbacks Are Static Functions

All client callbacks of the execution system are expected to be static functions (i.e., not class methods) that are passed a single argument. They take the following form:

```
static void MyCallback(const Context &context) {
   ...
}
```

The callbacks are disallowed from being methods on objects by structuring the code in such a way as to force the binding of the callback before the user can have access to any of the specific instances of the objects in question. This is accomplished by providing a type-based registry where users declare the callback based on the type of their object. This is the same registry that clients use to declare their dependencies. When declaring these callbacks and dependencies, users only have access to the type of their object.

Clients must read inputs and write to outputs using only the API provided by the passed-in context. This structure discourages users from storing any state for a node that is not known to the execution system. Users are not intended to derive new node types.

3.4.3　Presto Singletons Are Protected

Some of Presto's libraries provide APIs that allow client code to access system functionality through singleton objects. Some of these libraries are not threadsafe and are not allowed to be called from user-code running inside of execution. As a safety measure for client-code, we detect and prevent the use of such singletons while running execution plugin callbacks. Users are, of course, still free to create their own singletons and access static data, but doing so adds the burden on them to make sure that their code remains threadsafe.

3.4.4　Iterators

Access to large, vectorized, data (e.g., points) is provided through iterators that are easy to use and hide from the user the details of where in memory the data is stored, or what subset of the data their callback is dealing with. This allows us to modify memory allocation and access patterns, as well as our multithreading strategies, without changing client code. As we will see later in this chapter, this also allows for more efficient single-threaded execution.

3.4.5　And Then There's Python

Python is Presto's main scripting language—it is used extensively by users to automate repetitive tasks. However, it is famously known for not playing well within a multithreaded system. For this reason, we initially disallowed the use of Python for writing execution system callbacks. However, there are some clear advantages to supporting Python:

1. Python allows for quicker prototyping and iteration.

2. Python is accessible to a wider range of users than C++.

3. Python has a rich set of packages (e.g., numpy) that users would like to leverage.

These benefits make it difficult to adopt alternatives (e.g., a different existing language or a custom-written language).

3.4.5.1　Global Interpreter Lock

The Python interpreter is not threadsafe—it cannot be run from multiple threads simultaneously. Python provides a global lock, the Global Interpreter Lock (GIL), that clients can use to make sure that they do not enter the interpreter from multiple threads simultaneously [3]. A thread that needs to use Python must wait for its turn to use the interpreter.

Getting the locking right is tricky; it is easy to find yourself in classic deadlock situations. Consider the following user callback (though this code should be discouraged due to its use of locking to begin with, it nevertheless happens):

```
static void MyCallback(const Context &context) {
    Auto<Lock> lock(GetMyMutexFromContext(context));
    ...
    EvalMyPythonString(str); // A function that takes the GIL
    ...
}
```

Now consider the sequence of events in the threads which result in a deadlock, shown in Table 3.1.

TABLE 3.1: Deadlock due to improper use of the GIL.

MAIN THREAD	OTHER THREAD
Python command acquires GIL	Work started
Computation requested	`MyCallback` runs and acquires `MyMutex`
	`MyCallback` now waits for GIL
`MyCallback` runs and waits for `MyMutex`	(waiting for GIL)

One thing to note about this situation is that if, in the main thread, the call was made from C++, then there would be no need to hold the GIL in the main thread, and everything would be fine. If, however, it is called from Python, we get the hang. Moreover, neither subsystem knows about the other: the locks are taken in client code. The client code could be smarter about the order in which the locks are acquired, but that is not always a viable solution. In this case, the client is calling out to a function in a library, and may be unaware about it taking the GIL to begin with.

One solution in this case is that, in the main thread, we no longer need to be holding the GIL once we make a computation request in C++. Ideally, you would structure your bindings to always release the GIL upon reentry. However, there is a small cost to acquiring and releasing the GIL, so we need to be careful to not introduce undue overhead in following this policy.

> *This is a good example of why global, system-wide locks are a bad idea. Use lock hierarchies [63] to avoid the common deadlock patterns if you must have wide-reaching locks. Better still, prefer locks that have local, easy to reason about scope if you must lock at all.*

3.4.5.2 Performance

Anything running in Python is the only thing running in Python. This means that if your execution callbacks are all implemented in Python, you lose much of the efficiency gains of a multithreaded system. However, Python can still be effective for writing the control logic and have the heavy lifting be performed in C++ (with the GIL released).

3.5 Memory Access Patterns

Although we tried to construct the system in as flexible a way as we could, we did not want to sacrifice performance. Therefore, a major guiding principle was to make sure that we paid attention to memory access patterns. How memory is accessed is extremely important for performance, and we wanted to make sure that our desire for a flexible system did not impose any detrimental patterns for memory access.

> *Optimizing memory access patterns is one of the most important ways to improve performance. An algorithm with poor memory access characteristics will tend to scale poorly when multithreaded. In general, it is best to make sure that your algorithm is optimized for the single-threaded case to get the biggest gains from multithreading—and paying attention to memory access is one of the most important optimizations.*

It is important that bulk data is processed in a way that is compatible with the processor's prefetcher [1]. Luckily, modern processors are clever and do a good job at prefetching memory—but you still need to be careful to remain within the patterns that the processor can detect and prefetch. Hardware prefetchers typically work best with ascending access order. Though more complicated patterns, such as descending and uniform strides, may be detected, it is always best to check your hardware specifications for your target platforms. Arranging your data in a structure-of-arrays rather than an array-of-structures often helps the prefetchers improve your application's performance.

Locality is important for performance. Most common multicore platforms available today use non-uniform memory access, meaning that the location of the data in memory relative to the processor affects the time it takes to access it [55]. Therefore, keeping memory and code access local to each core will improve the scalability of a multithreaded system. Using the right memory allocator can help achieve this goal. Using an allocator written with this sort of scalability in mind, like jemalloc [24], is preferable to a multithreading-unaware allocator.

It is important to always measure the performance of your system and monitor how changes to the code affect it. Modern hardware architectures are sufficiently complicated that intuition and educated guesses often fail to predict performance. Always measure performance.

3.6   Flexibility to Experiment

3.6.1   Modular Design

We designed the system with two main unknowns:

1. We did not know exactly what architecture it was going to run on.

2. We did not know how the user requirements were going to evolve.

We did not want to base our architecture on the current state of hardware and user desires. We attempted to build in as much flexibility as we could.

For example, we have written a variety of different executors to satisfy different multithreading strategies. As our hardware's capabilities and requirements change, we expect to only update our executor code, which is relatively small. Schedulers are not often specialized, though they may be in order to add acceleration data for use with specialized executors.

Another example is if user requirements change such that the objects they deal with need to be rethought or redesigned, only compilation would need to be rewritten—the rest of the execution system can remain untouched. This would actually involve rewriting a lot of code. In practice, a total rewrite is unlikely, but this separation has allowed the user model to evolve over time while the execution system's internals remained isolated.

3.6.2   Targeting Other Platforms

As we mentioned, the structure of the system allows us to experiment with other platforms. The factoring into phases of execution described earlier gives us an opportunity to write different kinds of executors and compilers.

For example, to run all or part of our rigs on the GPU, we would need to at least write a new GPU executor and a VRAM data manager. We would also likely want to change certain parts of compilation to produce different kinds of networks that are more suitable for running on the GPU.

Similarly, our architecture can be adapted to take advantage of hardware platforms that provide large numbers of cores, such as the Intel Xeon Phi coprocessor. Getting the best utilization from any platform is challenging, it is therefore important that we can adapt quickly.

3.7 Multithreading Strategies

Finding the right granularity for the tasks to run in parallel is critical for getting the most performance from the hardware. Too many small tasks cause too much time to be spent in context switching and other thread management overhead. On the flip side, tasks that are too large can lead to poor utilization.

One of the factors we have to keep in mind while choosing a granularity for our specific domain is that we have a fairly small time budget for evaluating the network. We would like to aim for running the rig and drawing the character at 24 fps or better. Even if we ignore the costs of drawing the character, that gives us less than 42 ms to run approximately 30,000 nodes (e.g., for a light character). We therefore have to choose a granularity for the units of work that is compatible with this target time budget.

We have found the architecture described above allows for easy experimentation with various multithreading strategies in order to find the right granularity for the greatest performance. In this section we will explore only a few of the possibilities. Note that these strategies are not mutually exclusive—they can be combined.

3.7.1 Per-Node Multithreading

By per-node multithreading, we mean that each node runs its own computation in a multithreaded fashion. So long as the algorithm in the node is efficiently parallelizable, this might be a viable way to get a performance boost from multithreading.

A node does not typically need to synchronize or inform the system in any way that it intends to run its algorithm in multiple threads. It is also free to use any multithreading infrastructure that is deemed appropriate, for example Intel TBB or OpenMP, or through an abstraction API that is provided by the system. The advantage of using the system's API is that it can coordinate the total number of threads in flight and can help avoid oversubscription.

This approach works very well for slow nodes. We saw improved performance from multithreading the slow nodes in our system in this way. Unfortunately, this scheme does not work very well for nodes that execute quickly. For fast nodes, the threading overhead overcomes the cost of running the node's computation and we end up with the same, or worse, performance than the single-threaded version. The granularity of the work for these kinds of nodes is too small. Since most of the nodes in our system execute very quickly, we need to find a larger granularity of work to achieve bigger performance improvements from multithreading.

FIGURE 3.5: Per-node multithreading.

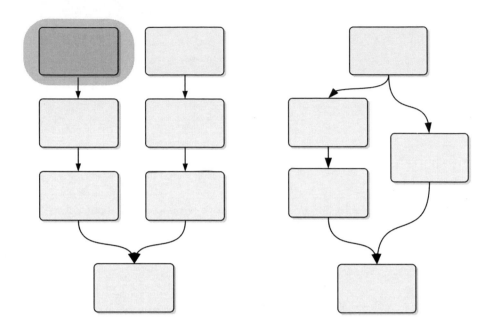

3.7.2   Per-Branch Multithreading

Another strategy is to launch a thread per branch in the network. Once the executor reaches a node that needs multiple inputs to be satisfied, each input branch can be launched in its own thread and can execute in parallel.

In order to implement this scheme, the executor must be specialized as well as the scheduler.

The amount of work that can be done in each thread here is much greater than the per-node scheme, and we can therefore get a bigger speed up from multithreading, provided that your network has enough branches relative to the number of available cores and that they each have a significant amount of work to do. This assumption does not typically hold in our networks, and we find that often the largest amount of work is along a linear spine, and the branches are relatively cheap in comparison.

3.7.3   Per-Model Multithreading

An even larger level of granularity is to run each model in its own thread. This is fairly straightforward to implement. The scheduler first finds all the disconnected subgraphs in the network, and the executor launches a thread per subgraph.

This is a special case of the per-branch scheme, providing a larger amount of work to do per-thread. It generally works well but does run into a couple of hurdles.

The first is that animators, when they can, often choose to work with a small number of characters loaded at any one time, often smaller than the typical number of cores found in modern hardware. This means that some cores can sit idle, which is not desirable.

FIGURE 3.6: Per-branch multithreading.

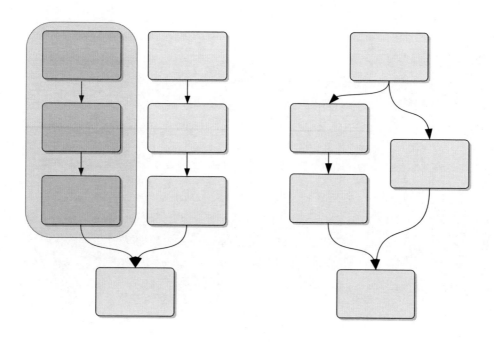

FIGURE 3.7: Per-model multithreading.

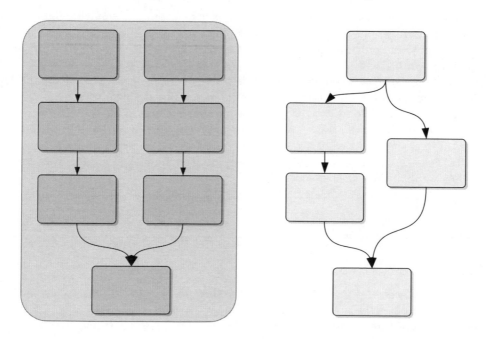

FIGURE 3.8: Per-frame multithreading.

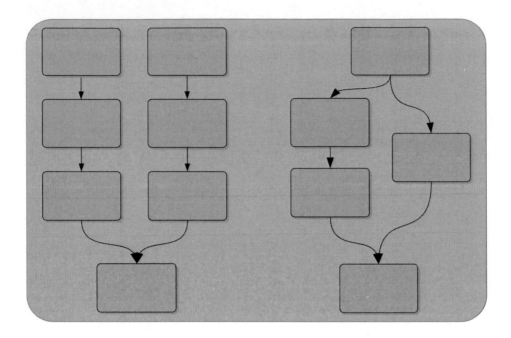

Second, characters are often dependent on one another—outputs from one model feed into inputs on another. These constraints limit the available parallelism, decreasing the system's potential performance.

3.7.4   Per-Frame Multithreading

Until now, the strategies we have discussed do not take advantage of any domain-specific knowledge. We could employ these techniques for the evaluation of any data flow network. If we consider that our software's primary goal is animation, we find a whole new dimension along which to parallelize: time.

By allowing the system to compute multiple frames concurrently, we can significantly boost the performance of very common workflows. This approach lets us design a system where thread synchronization is not necessary while the concurrent tasks are running, and only needed when storing the final results. This approach also introduces its own set of challenges that are due to its asynchronous nature.

We call this feature of our system Background Execution, and that is the multithreading strategy that we found to be most successful.

3.8   Background Execution

Background Execution is the ability of our system to schedule frames, one per time sample, to be computed in asynchronous background threads, allowing users to continue working while frames are computed. When the user changes to a frame that has been computed in the background (e.g., during playback) the system can use the results of the computation right away without having to wait for the potentially expensive computation to complete in the main thread.

The system architecture allows for easy implementation of the feature in its most naive incarnation: collect the frames that you need to compute in parallel, create an executor for each thread that you have available, and start doling out frames as tasks for the executors. This approach leads to several practical issues that need to be considered when embedding in an interactive application.

3.8.1 User Interaction

A typical use case is that a user will change an attribute value and then scrub or play back on the timeline to see the effect the change has had on the animation. We would like to use the Background Execution feature to make sure that the computations of neighboring frames have completed by the time the user scrubs to them. So as soon as the user stops modifying the value, background threads are kicked off to compute the frames that have become invalid due to the modification. How these frames are scheduled is discussed below. By the time the user scrubs over to the new frames, the idea is that the system would get cache hits for the frames and be able to return much quicker than it would have if it had to perform the full evaluation.

We kick off as many background threads as we have cores available, except for one that we save for the main thread. Ideally, the main thread would spend most of its time drawing frames and handling the user's interactions, and not executing the computations that can be run in the background. Occasionally, the main thread requires results that have not finished executing in the background. In that case, we go ahead and compute those results in the main thread rather than wait. When that happens, the system briefly appears slower until the background threads catch up and overcome the main thread.

While the background threads are actively computing, the user is free to modify attribute values again, possibly invalidating the in-flight computations. The user's work should not be delayed by what the system is doing in the background. We also do not want to wait for the background threads to finish before allowing the user to interact with the system. Therefore, being able to quickly interrupt the background threads is critical. We will discuss interruption policies a little later.

> *It is unacceptable for the system to pause or hitch at random times due to work that was not explicitly initiated by the user and that the user is not expecting: Avoid performance surprises.*

Along the same lines, providing users with feedback that work is happening in the background can inform them of what to expect in terms of performance. For example, providing visual feedback when a frame has been computed in the background helps the user predict that moving to a filled-in frame will be faster than moving to a frame that has not yet been computed. This feedback is also valuable for those trying to debug the system.

3.8.2 Frame Scheduling

In order to perfectly schedule the next frames to be computed, you would need to be able to accurately predict what the user will do next. For example, if the user wants to play the frames in order after making a modification, then you would want to schedule them in ascending order. If, on the other hand, the user will scrub back and forth around the dirtied frame, then you will want to schedule the frames to bloom out from the dirtied frame. But we do not know ahead of time which the user will do. We would prefer not to make this an option to the user because the user is only in a marginally better position to make this decision. The choice is not necessarily known to the user *a priori* either.

Some of the possible approaches are:

1. Pick a scheme and stick to it (e.g., always ascending, or always bloom out).

2. Base the decision on how the frames were dirtied. For example, if the user is dropping in key poses in a spreadsheet editor, then use the ascending order scheme; if refining a tangent in a spline editor, then bloom out. The task that causes the frames to be dirtied can be a clue as to what the user will likely do next.

3. Keep a record of the user frame changes and match the dirty frame schedule to the pattern observed in past frame changes.

4. Combine #2 and #3: record the user's actions and the frame change patterns and use that information to predict which frames to schedule.

In our system, we currently always schedule in ascending order. That captures the most common use cases and is the simplest to implement.

3.8.3   Interruption

The user is free to modify the state of the application while background tasks are in flight. In particular, the user is free to modify the state in such a way as to make the currently scheduled tasks invalid, meaning their results are no longer useful. One of the major problems we therefore need to deal with is interruption of these invalid tasks. It is critical during common animator workflows (e.g., changing spline values or playing back) that background tasks do not interfere with foreground work. Any hitch or delay can immediately be detected by the users and may annoy them or, worse, can contribute to repetitive strain injury. These kinds of hitches are particularly irritating because users cannot predict when they will occur or how long they will last. Therefore, we cannot block the user while waiting for invalid in-flight threads to finish.

The first thing we do is find any opportunity we can to avoid interruption altogether. We structured the system such that common animator tasks (e.g., changing spline values) can take place without having to interrupt at all. We will discuss how we take advantage of that a little later in this section. There is a second class of user actions (e.g., setting constraints) that alter the topology of the network for which we have to interrupt, since the network is shared among threads.

When we must interrupt, we have to do so as quickly as possible. We do not explicitly kill threads (e.g., through `pthread_cancel` or `pthread_kill`) because that is a problematic approach [64]. For starters, most of our code is not exception-safe. We also felt that tracking down resource cleanup problems that resulted from abrupt interruption of threads would be time-consuming and a constant source of bugs. So we decided to avoid it altogether.

We also did not want to burden clients by requiring them to check for an interruption flag. That approach is problematic as well, as some clients may either perform the checks too often or not enough.

The system therefore completely controls interruption and checks for interruption after each node has completed. Since our nodes are typically fast, that granularity seems appropriate. Unfortunately, we occasionally have nodes that do take longer to run and waiting for those nodes to complete before interruption is unacceptable for some workflows. Although we may want to support a cooperative scheme in the future, our experience so far has been that it is always better to avoid the long running computation altogether, for example, by splitting it up into smaller sub-computations. No one node can be allowed a very long runtime if we expect to stay within our 42 ms budget.

While animators are adjusting spline values, adjusting tangents, inserting and deleting knots, and so on, we cannot afford to wait for interruption at all. Animators can change values several dozens of times per second, and cannot be interrupted. These common, high frequency, edits do not change the topology of the network, and, as mentioned earlier, we do not have to wait for background tasks to complete before responding to the edits. We take advantage of this fact by not interrupting at all during these workflows. Instead, we remove any pending tasks and set a flag telling in-flight threads to throw away their results once the next node is done computing. This means that the main thread does not block at all. It only pays for setting a flag, which is significantly faster than waiting for the nodes to finish. This approach lessens the negative effects of having many background threads running for animators.

3.8.4   Constant Data

Since we would like to avoid synchronization among threads while the computations are in flight, each thread manages its own network data. We quickly noticed that there can potentially be a lot of redundant computations performed by different threads. In particular, time-independent computations will yield the same results in all threads. These computations also tend to be slow and memory intensive—for example, the kinds of computations that set up large projection caches or acceleration structures that do not change with time. Launching many threads to compute the same data at the same time saturates the bus and decreases the system's throughput. We would like to avoid running computations redundantly, and yet avoid introducing locks to the execution engine.

Our solution is to first launch a single thread, which we call the starter thread. The starter thread's job is to compute all the constant data in the network and make it available to the other threads that compute the time-varying data. The starter thread uses a starter executor to compute the constant data, then schedules the background frames and kicks off the concurrent threads. For each concurrent thread, we create a new executor that is allowed to read from the starter executor. This multiple-reader scenario is supported without needing to lock since the starter executor's data is read-only while the other frames are being computed. Since it lets us share the expensive-to-compute, and often memory-intensive, data, this scheme reduces our memory consumption and lets us scale much better with the number of available cores.

The starter thread allows the main thread to remain free to respond to user interaction while the expensive data is being computed in the background. It also runs infrequently: once at load time and again only when time-independent data is invalidated. We further decrease the amount of time this thread needs to execute by allowing it to also locklessly read constant data (i.e., data that cannot be invalidated through the model's animation interface) that is computed only once per model.

3.8.5   Problematic Data Structures

Sometimes we encounter data structures that cause trouble in our multithreading scheme. Consider the following pseudocode:

```
class MeshAlgorithm {
public:
        // Constructs a MeshAlgorithm object with a fixed topology
        // for the lifetime of this object.
        MeshAlgorithm(Topology *meshTopology);

        // Sets the point positions to be used for subsequent calls to
        // Compute().
        SetPoints(Sec3 *points);

        // Uses the topology passed in at construction, and the
        // point positions passed into SetPoints(), and performs
        // algorithm and returns the result.  It is an error to call
        // this method without first having called SetPoints().
        Result Compute();
};
```

Typically, with these kinds of classes, users create a `MeshAlgorithm` object that does something expensive with the mesh topology and is then passed on to the computation that performs the points-dependent, usually cheaper, operation. That goes something like this:

```
void ProcessMeshForAllTime(mesh, timeRange) {
        MeshAlgorithm ma(mesh.GetTopology());
        foreach(t, timeRange) {
                ma.SetPoints(mesh.ComputePoints(t));
                Result r = ma.Compute();
                // do something with r;
        }
}
```

The assumption is that the construction of the `MeshAlgorithm` object is very expensive and that computation is reused later to make the `Compute()` call with the different sets of point positions much faster than they would otherwise be.

Now consider a simple multithreading approach to `ProcessMeshForAllTime` that you might like to implement. The for loop seems like a reasonable loop to multithread, except that, unfortunately, the pattern used for `MeshAlgorithm` forces the `Compute()` calls to all run serially. Since the calls to `Compute()` must be preceded by a call to `SetPoints()`, the data structure relies on stateful behavior which is problematic for multithreading.

Using this data structure, unmodified, in our system is equally problematic. We detect that the construction of `MeshAlgorithm` is not time dependent and we compute it once, we then launch multiple threads to perform the inner body of the loop. Used in this way, and without locking, the system would crash or exhibit other unspecified behavior and hard to track bugs.

To make this pattern more multithreading friendly, we can reorganize the code to look like this:

```
class MeshTopologyResult {
public:
    // Constructs a MeshTopologyResult object that performs any
    // necessary pre-computations on the topology that will speed up
    // subsequent calls to ComputeMeshAlgorithm.
    MeshTopologyResult(Topology *meshTopology);
```

```
};

// Performs the MeshAlogrithm computation using the passed-in point
// positions and the pre-computed topological information in a
// previously constructed MeshTopologyResult object.  This function is
// re-entrant and threadsafe.
Result
ComputeMeshAlgorithm(Vec3 *points, const MeshTopologyResult &mtr);
```

And our processing function would be modified like this:

```
void ProcessMeshForAllTime(mesh, timeRange) {
    MeshTopologyResult mtr(mesh.GetTopology());
    foreach(t, timeRange) {
        Result r = ComputeMeshAlgorithm(mesh.ComputePoints(t), mtr);
        // do something with r
    }
}
```

In this case, we have broken up the expensive computation that used to be performed inside the construction of `MeshAlgorithm` into its own class, `MeshTopologyResult`. And we have made it so that the `ComputeMeshAlgorithm` call does not depend on any state in `MeshAlgorithm` itself, it instead gets the acceleration structures from `MeshTopologyResult` that is also passed-in. With this setup, the multithreading can be done without needing to lock.

3.9   Other Multithreading Strategies

There are many other multithreading strategies for executing computations. Though our system was designed to support these strategies, as of this writing, these features have not yet been exploited.

3.9.1   Strip Mining

As we alluded to earlier, our data flow graph is different than a traditional one in that each edge can flow multiple elements, each tracked independently for dependency analysis. We provide a simple, public iteration API for users to access these elements, which abstracts the underlying representation. The users, therefore, do not need to be concerned with where the data is coming from.

One of the benefits of the iteration API that we have mentioned before is how it allows us to provide fast memory access patterns to users. Another benefit of this structure is that it allows us another form of multithreading strategy called strip mining. With strip mining, all the requested elements are processed in parallel, in equal chunks among the available number of cores.

This strategy complements Background Execution and we believe it would be useful in improving the speed of single frame evaluations where Background Execution does not help. We think this approach has the potential to scale well with the increasing number of cores available on user desktops.

3.9.2   Predictive Computations

In an interactive animation package, knowing the previous few input values to a computation can give us the ability to guess at the next few input values. For example, if a user entered rotation values 30, followed by 30.5 and then 31, it is reasonable to assume that they will next ask for 31.5, 32, and so on.

In other words, while a user is continuously changing a value on an input, we can schedule computations for input values that the system predicts the user will ask for next, and run those computations in parallel. The results would then be available much sooner when the user eventually gets to them. This would require only a small modification to our Background Execution infrastructure.

One of the challenges of this approach is that it may introduce inconsistencies in the user's interaction rates. The application will be more responsive when the user enters values that have been predicted, and less responsive if the inputs have never been computed before. If there are enough mispredicted values, this inconsistency can lead to a frustrating user experience.

3.10   Debugging and Profiling Tools

As programmers, we appreciate good debuggers and profilers for the software we write. Similarly, it is also important to provide these kinds of tools to the users of our software. As we said earlier, riggers use our software like a visual programming language, so we need to make sure that we provide them with tools to help debug and profile their rigs.

Since our system does not strictly enforce a one-to-one mapping between user-facing objects and objects used by the execution system, one important step in making sure that these tools are useful is to be able to provide a mapping from the execution objects back to the objects in the scene that the users are familiar with. We do this by maintaining a mapping during the compilation step. The profiling and debugging happens at the node level and then we map that back to the user objects in generated reports and interactive tools.

At a bare-minimum, we needed a profiler that can tell users how much time is being spent in each computation in their rig. They need to be able to see and sort the objects (e.g., deformers) they created and reason about their costs. We additionally show the number of elements processed by each computation and the amount of memory allocated. The former is useful in finding computations that were unintentionally processing many more elements than expected, and the latter can help identify and eliminate memory hogs.

In addition to the tools provided to riggers, other users also need help debugging their work. For animators, layout artists, and other users not interested in the rigging details, we provide a tool that identifies areas of slowness in their session. For example, the tool may identify expensive hardware shaders in a shot, or meshes with a high number of points, or that the user has turned off caching. The tool is plugin-based and is designed such that our QA department can add more scenarios and criteria as they are discovered (during a production) by writing small Python scripts. This tool also gives users the opportunity to fix the identified problem immediately, if the particular plugin provides such a capability (e.g., by turning on the cache settings).

We have also developed in-house tools to help us measure and optimize our code. The heart of our optimization toolset is an extensive performance test suite. The test suite tracks the speed of the software, provides us with reports, and allows us to quickly identify regressions and improvements. This is the single most important tool we have for improving the speed of our software and making sure that we do not cause it to regress.

The profiling tool we rely on most was also developed in-house and consists of a small library of functions and macros used to instrument our code. We find the fine control we have over this profiler, and its integration into our application, to be of benefit to us. In particular, being able to precisely define which functions are profiled and reported, and which are not, lets us generate succinct reports that are simple to reason about. We complement this tool with a sampling profiler (also built in-house).

3.11 Summary

In this chapter we outlined the architecture of our animation system's computation engine. The purpose of this engine is to enable users to work at interactive rates. A modern high-performance engine must take advantage of the increasing number of cores available on users' desktops. We described how this architecture is flexible enough to accommodate several kinds of multithreading strategies. We discussed the advantages and pitfalls of supporting background computation and how they can be used to significantly speed up common animation workflows.

Writing multithreading code is challenging and available hardware is evolving quickly. By appreciating that there will be better algorithms and better hardware in the future, and by designing for multithreading from the start, along with a little modularity, we will be better able to overcome the challenges of multithreading, and maybe even have fun doing it.

Chapter 4

LibEE: Parallel Evaluation of Character Rigs

Martin Watt

DreamWorks Animation

4.1	Introduction	74
4.2	Motivation	76
4.3	Specific Requirements for Character Animation	76
	4.3.1 Animation Graph Goals	77
	4.3.2 Animation Graph Features	77
	4.3.2.1 Few Unique Traversed Paths through Graph	77
	4.3.2.2 Animation Rigs Have Implicit Parallelism	78
	4.3.2.3 Expensive Nodes Which Can Be Internally Parallel	78
	4.3.3 Animation Graph Constraints	78
	4.3.3.1 No Graph Editing	78
	4.3.3.2 No Scripting Languages in Operators	78
4.4	Graph	79
	4.4.1 Threading Engine	79
	4.4.2 Graph Evaluation Mechanism	80
4.5	Threadsafety	80
	4.5.1 Node Threadsafety	81
	4.5.1.1 API Layer	81
	4.5.1.2 Parallel Unit Tests	81
	4.5.1.3 Threading Checker Tools	82
	4.5.1.4 Compiler Flags	82
	4.5.1.5 LD_ PRELOAD	83
	4.5.1.6 The Kill Switch	84
	4.5.2 Graph Threadsafety	84
4.6	Scalability: Software Considerations	85
	4.6.1 Authoring Parallel Loops	86
	4.6.2 Overthreading	87
	4.6.3 Threading Fatigue	87
	4.6.4 Thread-Friendly Memory Allocators	88
	4.6.5 Oversubscription Due to Multiple Threading Models	88
	4.6.6 Cache Reuse—Chains of Nodes	89
	4.6.7 Cache Reuse—Scheduling Nodes to Maximize Sharing	89
	4.6.8 Task Priorities	89
	4.6.9 Graph Partitioning	89
	4.6.10 Other Processes Running on System	91
	4.6.11 The Memory Wall	91
	4.6.12 Failed Approaches Discussion	91
4.7	Scalability: Hardware Considerations	92
	4.7.1 CPU Power Modes	92
	4.7.2 Turbo Clock	92

	4.7.3	NUMA	92
	4.7.4	Hyperthreading	93
	4.7.5	CPU Affinity	94
	4.7.6	Many-Core Architectures	94
4.8		Production Considerations	95
	4.8.1	Character Systems Restructure	96
	4.8.2	No More Scripted Nodes	96
	4.8.3	Optimizing for Maximum Parallelism	96
4.9		Threading Visualization Tool	97
4.10		Rig Optimization Case Studies	100
	4.10.1	Case Study 1: Quadruped Critical Path Optimization	100
	4.10.2	Case Study 2: Hair Solver	100
	4.10.3	Case Study 3: Free Clothes!	100
4.11		Overall Performance Results	104
4.12		Limits of Scalability	104
4.13		Summary	106

4.1 Introduction

Computer-generated characters are central to an animated feature film and need to deliver appealing, believable on-screen performances. As such, character rigs continue to expand in complexity (for example, higher fidelity skin, clothing, and hair). This leads to growing computational demands as animators wish to interact with complex rigs at interactive frame rates. Since single threaded CPU performance is no longer increasing at previous rates, it is necessary to find alternative means to improve rig performance.

This chapter focuses on the multithreaded graph evaluation engine called LibEE, which is at the heart of the new DreamWorks Animation tool called Premo (Figure 4.1), which

FIGURE 4.1: Animator working interactively on a character in Premo. **(See Color Insert.)**

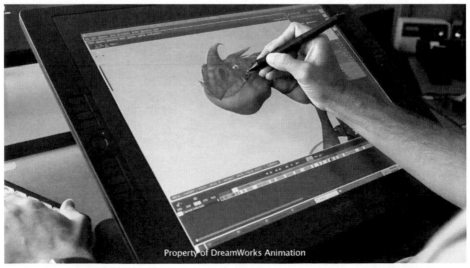

FIGURE 4.2: Detail from a still frame from the DreamWorks movie *How to Train Your Dragon 2*, showing character animation generated by using the parallel dependency graph engine LibEE running in Premo. This is the first movie to be released that was animated using this engine. (**See Color Insert.**)

was first used in the movie *How to Train Your Dragon 2* (Figure 4.2). The chapter also describes changes to the character rig setups that were made to take maximum advantage of this parallel evaluation system.

A heavily multithreaded graph requires not just that individual expensive nodes in the graph are internally threaded, but that nodes in the graph can evaluate concurrently. This raises numerous concerns, for example, how do we ensure that the cores are used most effectively, how do we handle non-threadsafe code, and how do we provide profiling tools for riggers to ensure character graphs are optimized for parallel evaluation?

This chapter discusses the motivation, design choices, and implementation of the graph engine itself, developer considerations for writing high performance threaded code, including ways to optimize scalability and find and avoid common threading problems, and finally covers important production adoption considerations.

4.2   Motivation

The previous generation in-house animation tool at DreamWorks Animation has been in use for many years. With each animated film, the filmmakers raise the bar in terms of the characters' on-screen performances and therefore in terms of the computational complexity of the character rigs. More expensive evaluation has partially been addressed over the years by taking advantage of the "free lunch" associated with the increased performance delivered by each generation of processors. However, for the past few years, processor architectures have been constrained by basic physics and can no longer provide significant increases in core clock speed nor from increasing instructions per clock. CPU performance improvements are now being delivered by offering CPUs with multiple cores.

Given the relentlessly single threaded nature of the existing animation tool, it was not possible to take advantage of multicore architectures. We had reached the point where the execution performance of the animation tool was no longer accelerating due to hardware gains, while show demands, of course, continued to increase with each film. In short, our appetite was pushing us beyond the limit of what could be delivered in the existing animation environment, and we had to change.

To retrofit multithreading into the core architecture of the existing animation tool would have been extremely difficult. Instead we embarked on a studio initiative to write a new animation tool from the ground up. A key component of this new tool is a highly scalable multithreaded graph evaluation engine called LibEE.

The primary benefits of the new system are:

- A framework to deliver significant graph level parallelism for complex character rigs which can run concurrently with internal node threading. The graph engine is optimized for the specific requirements of character animation. In contrast, typical animation applications today achieve character rig threading scalability primarily through internal node concurrency.

- The system scales to meet the demands of feature film production. We provide details of many of the challenges encountered and solutions delivered.

- We built a parallelism visualization tool to enable riggers to optimize character setups for maximum performance. We found this tool to be an essential aid for the creation of scalable character rigs.

This chapter first presents the graph engine architecture and design choices for character animation. We then explore the implementation details including the threading engine, graph evaluation, threadsafety, and implementation challenges. We finish with a discussion of production considerations and results.

4.3   Specific Requirements for Character Animation

The core engine for the animation tool is a dependency graph (DG), a commonly used approach for animation systems, also implemented in commercial packages such as Maya. The basic building block of the graph is a node, which is a stand-alone Compute Unit that takes in data via one or more input attributes, and produces data via one or more output

FIGURE 4.3: A typical hero character graph. The leftmost panel is the full graph. Each panel to the right is a zoomed-in region showing a small part of the graph view to the left of it. This graph has over 100k nodes. **(See Color Insert.)**

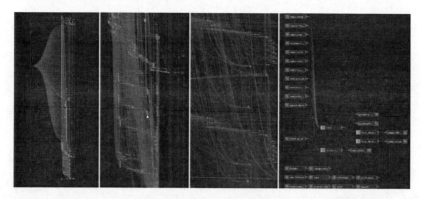

attributes. A dependency graph is constructed by binding output attributes on individual nodes to input attributes on other nodes. The dependency graph is evaluated to obtain the required outputs for display, usually geometry, when driven by changing inputs, typically animation curves. Although the principle is well known, we have made a number of design choices given the target workload of animation posing and playback.

The following sections describe the goals of the system, the specific features of animation systems that were used to guide the design, and some deliberate restrictions that were placed on the implementation to constrain the problems.

4.3.1 Animation Graph Goals

The graph for a hero character can have 50k–150k nodes (see Figure 4.3). Although not all nodes will evaluate every frame, there are still typically thousands of nodes that need to be evaluated in a frame. The goal is to provide consistent interactivity within the animation environment. We have set a benchmark of at least 15 fps for executing a single full-fidelity character. Since the graphs can contain thousands of nodes, all of which need to be scheduled and run in this time interval, we need a very low overhead scheduling system.

Note that there was no expectation to hit these performance levels when running a character-based simulation that must evaluate the graph multiple times through a range of frames.

4.3.2 Animation Graph Features

Our goal was to deliver a high performance evaluation engine specifically for character animation, not a general multithreading evaluation system. As a result, the design is driven by the unique requirements of a feature animation pipeline. Listed below are some of the distinctive characteristics of character animation evaluation that were used to inform design choices for the specific implementation adopted.

4.3.2.1 Few Unique Traversed Paths through Graph

Although the graph may contain a very large number of nodes, the number of unique evaluation paths traversed through the graph during a session is relatively limited. Typically, there may be a hundred or so controls that an animator interacts with, and the output is typically a handful of geometric objects. Posing workflows involve manipulating the same sets of controls repeatedly for a series of graph recomputes. As a result it becomes feasible to cache a task list of nodes that require evaluation for a given user-edit to the graph. Walking dependency graphs to propagate dirty state and track dependencies can be expensive, and is not highly parallelizable, so avoiding this step offers significant performance and scalability benefits. Of course, if there are a large number of controls available to the user the application will still perform well, though cache sizes for these task lists might need to be increased, or we take the extra hit of walking the graph for some evaluations.

4.3.2.2   Animation Rigs Have Implicit Parallelism

Characters usually have components that can be computed in parallel at multiple levels. As an example the limbs of a character can often be computed in parallel, and within each limb the fingers can similarly usually be evaluated concurrently. Such concurrency will vary from character to character. We have suggested that our filmmakers explore storylines involving herds of millipedes to demonstrate the full potential of the tool, but even with conventional biped characters we are able to extract significant levels of parallelism. A very important aspect of this, however, is that the rig must be created in a way that expresses this parallelism in the graph itself. No matter how well the engine can run tasks concurrently, if the rig expresses serial dependencies in its construction, those dependencies must be respected. We cannot outguess the riggers. This was a very challenging area, and is discussed in more detail later.

4.3.2.3   Expensive Nodes Which Can Be Internally Parallel

Nodes such as deformers, tessellators and solvers are expensive, but can in many cases be threaded internally to operate on data components in parallel. We want to take advantage of this internal concurrency potential while also allowing such nodes to evaluate in parallel with other nodes in the graph. As a result we require a system that offers composability, that is, nested threading is supported by making full use of the cores without oversubscribing the system.

4.3.3   Animation Graph Constraints

The following are constraints applied to the system to limit the implementation challenges.

4.3.3.1   No Graph Editing

We developed an evaluation-only dependency graph for the animation environment, which does not need to account for editing the characters. This enables us to take advantage of a graph topology that is relatively fixed. We do not need to build an extensive editing infrastructure, and can strip out from the graph any functionality that would be required to easily modify the topology. This reduces the size of nodes and connections, leading to better cache locality behavior.

4.3.3.2   No Scripting Languages in Operators

One controversial restriction placed on node authors was that they could not use any authoring language that is known to be low performance or inherently non-threadsafe or non-scalable. This means we do not allow authors to write nodes in our in-house scripting language, which is not threadsafe, nor do we allow Python which, while threadsafe, is not able to run truly concurrently due to the Global Interpreter Lock. Python is also significantly slower than C++. This limitation caused concern among riggers, who author nodes for specific show requirements, since scripted nodes are typically easier to write than their C++ equivalents. We discuss this in more depth later.

Try to constrain application functionality if it makes the threading challenges more manageable. Threading is hard enough already without trying to handle every case that a user may wish to have available to them. Future work may allow relaxation of some restrictions once a solid reliable framework has been built.

4.4 Graph

4.4.1 Threading Engine

There was a requirement to build or adopt a threading engine to manage the scheduling of the graph. There are several upfront requirements for this engine:

- The graphs can have up to 150k nodes for a single hero character, which we wish to evaluate at close to 24 fps, so the engine needs to have very low per-node runtime overhead.

- The threading engine needs to deliver good scalability since our animator workstations have between 16 and 20 cores already, a number which will only increase in future, and we wanted to make effective use of these current and future hardware resources.

- We require a system that supports composability, i.e., nested threading, since we intend for some nodes to be internally threaded as well as the entire graph running in parallel, and want the two levels of threading to interoperate seamlessly.

We considered writing our own engine from the ground up, but that would be a very major effort in which we did not have specific domain expertise, so we decided to focus resources on the higher level architecture rather than devote effort to building the low-level components. We chose to adopt Intel's Threading Building Blocks (TBB) as the core threading library. This library offers composability, high performance, and ease of use, as well as being industry proven, being used in commercial tools such as Maya and Houdini.

Explore existing threading libraries before deciding to roll your own, or there is a danger you may spend a lot of time in maintenance of this library rather than the code that runs on top of it.

TBB has a component called a task scheduler. This assigns user-defined tasks to available cores, ensuring that all cores are kept busy while avoiding oversubscription. By mapping the nodes in the graph onto TBB tasks, we can use the TBB dependency mechanism to allow the graph to evaluate by having the TBB scheduler assign each node to a core once all its upstream inputs have been computed.

Since we have threading at the graph and node level, and node authors can potentially call any code in the studio, we needed to ensure that all this threaded code worked well together. As a result we made a studio-wide decision to adopt TBB as the threading model globally for all new code we write. We also retrofitted existing code to use TBB where possible. This ensures node authors can safely invoke other studio code from their nodes and have the threading interact well with the graph level parallelism.

4.4.2   Graph Evaluation Mechanism

DGs are typically implemented as two-pass systems. In the first pass, input attributes to the graph are modified and marked dirty. This dirty state propagates through the graph based on static dirty rules which define the dependency relationship between attributes within a node. Then a second pass occurs for evaluation, where the application requests certain outputs from the graph, such as geometry. If the node that outputs the geometry has the relevant attribute marked dirty, it will recompute itself. If the node has inputs that are dirty it will recursively reevaluate those input nodes, potentially triggering large sections of the graph to recompute.

The second evaluation step is a challenge for threading since recursive node evaluation limits potential scalability. We have chosen to modify this evaluation model. In the evaluation pass we traverse the graph upstream to decide what to compute but, rather than computing the nodes right away, we instead add them to a "task list" along with the dependencies between the tasks. Then we add a third pass where those tasks are evaluated by the core engine, extracting all potential parallelism given the dependencies in the list.

Although this approach provides good concurrency, it does mean that we can potentially overcompute, since some nodes may only know the required inputs once they are inside their compute routine. In our case we will compute all inputs that could potentially affect the given dirty output given the static dirty rules, even if the inputs are not actually required based on a dynamic analysis of the node state during evaluation. This can be a problem for "switch" nodes that can select between, for example, low and high resolution geometry based on an index control. To address this problem, we do an additional one or more passes over the graph to evaluate the inputs to such nodes. If the switch index changes, we prune out the unwanted code path before doing the main evaluation pass. Since switch indices rarely change during an animation session, the pruning pass has minimal overhead in graph evaluation.

4.5   Threadsafety

Threadsafety is one of the biggest challenges of building this system. Unlike regular data level parallelism, a parallel graph involves running potentially dozens of different algorithms concurrently with each other in ways that can change every frame depending on which parts of the rig are being computed. Thus, we need to worry not only about regular threadsafety within a node, but safety at the much broader graph level, to ensure all nodes can run concurrently with each other.

When this project was started, threadsafety was one of the largest areas of concern. There was a risk that the project might fail because of the level of threadsafety required and potential for a continuous stream of hard-to-find threading bugs and regressions. As a result we preemptively worked on approaches to make and keep the code threadsafe. There is no single solution to ensuring threadsafe code, so we adopt a variety of different approaches to try to minimize potential problems, while allowing exceptions for cases where we know we cannot guarantee threadsafety, as discussed in the items below.

4.5.1 Node Threadsafety

The studio has a large existing codebase dating back 20 years, and significant parts of the codebase are not threadsafe. Since node authors can potentially call anything in the studio codebase, pulling in non-threadsafe code is a concern. In addition, any new code can introduce threadsafety issues.

This section discusses the approaches taken to ensuring threadsafety within individual nodes.

4.5.1.1 API Layer

We wrote an API for the studio code that provided one layer of insulation from direct access to the studio code. This is partly to ensure that users do not get hold of raw memory since the design of the graph requires the graph itself to do memory management. However, this API layer can also be used to block access to classes and methods that are known to be non-threadsafe. We endeavor to keep this API complete enough that developers would not need to bypass it and obtain raw access to external data structures, although in some cases that is still required.

4.5.1.2 Parallel Unit Tests

There is a mandate for developers to write unit tests for each node. Since threading problems can manifest intermittently, one brute-force technique to catch a class of threading bugs is to create parallel unit tests by wrapping these unit tests in a framework that will run them concurrently using code similar to that below, so invoking multiple instances of the original unit test that will run in parallel. The optional runId parameter supplied to the main test can be used to avoid conflicts between the parallel instances, for example, if the test writes a file to disk it can use the runId to generate a unique filename for each instance of the test.

```
// regular unit test
void TestXformNode::test(int runId) {
    [...]
}


// parallel unit test
void TestXformNode::testParallel()
{
    // OpenMP parallel loop
    #pragma omp parallel for
    for(int i=0; i<numParallelIterations(); ++i) {
        test(i);
    }
}
```

A test plan was set up to run these parallel tests continuously to look for such intermittent failures. The thread count was specified via the OpenMP environment variable OMP_NUM_THREADS to be a non-integral multiplier of the core count to try to force more unpredictability, and the number of iterations was set to be as large as possible while keeping the entire test suite runtime to within an hour or so.

Over time the number of failures in these tests has dropped, although it has not reached zero. Instead it has reached a low level where background noise, that is, hardware problems and resource issues such as full disks, cause as many crashes as threading bugs. Because threading bugs are almost by definition hard to reproduce, remaining bugs are the ones that happen very rarely and so are the most difficult ones to track down.

It is highly likely that threading bugs still persist in the code, and new node authoring means there is likely to be introduction of new threading problems, but they are now at a level that crashes from threading are fewer than crashes from other parts of the application, and are not a major productivity drain. This is usually the best that can be hoped for—guaranteeing that an application is fully threadsafe is generally impossible.

In addition to the parallel stress test, crash logs were also tracked using Google's Breakpad to look for repeating patterns of failure that might indicate a threadsafety issue.

4.5.1.3 Threading Checker Tools

Intel's Parallel Inspector tool was used to check for race conditions. This tool can be useful in catching threading problems, but runs on large complex codebases can result in many false positives, which makes tracking down the genuine race conditions challenging.

It is possible to generate suppression files to suppress false positives from Inspector. We looked into using this with our parallel unit tests to have a test plan that would run Inspector on the parallel test regularly looking for any new race conditions that might have been introduced. However, this proved unsuccessful since the code evolved rapidly enough that it required constant maintenance and updates of the suppression files. As a result, the approach was abandoned. The concept is still appealing though, and it is hoped that Inspector or similar tools will evolve over time to become more usable in this regard.

4.5.1.4 Compiler Flags

There are some very useful compiler settings with the Intel compiler that can warn for access to static variables, which is a common source of race conditions. The warnings, with example code, are as follows:

```
static int x=0;
if(x>1)    //warning #1710: reference to statically allocated variable
x = 1;     //warning #1711: assignment to statically allocated variable
int* p=&x; //warning #1712: address taken of statically allocated variable
```

Warning 1712 currently triggers in a lot of system-level code that cannot easily be avoided. Warning 1710 triggers for stream access like std::cout calls, which are also relatively common in the code. As a result, we choose to use only the 1711 warning, which is also the most useful of these warnings. Example:

```
int x = 0;
int main()
{
    x++;
}


>icc -c -ww1711 test.cc
test.cc(8): warning #1711: assignment to statically allocated variable "x"
    x++;
    ^
```

We enable this warning in the build environment, and add macros that allow a user to disable the warning if it is considered harmless. So:

```
#define DWA_START_THREADSAFE_STATIC_WRITE __pragma(warning(disable:1711))
#define DWA_FINISH_THREADSAFE_STATIC_WRITE __pragma(warning(default:1711))
#define DWA_THREADSAFE_STATIC_WRITE(CODE) __pragma(warning(disable:1711));\
       CODE; __pragma(warning(default:1711))
```

and example usage:

```
static int x = 0;
DWA_THREADSAFE_STATIC_WRITE(x = 1; ) // safe as code called only once
```

or:

```
static int x = 0;
DWA_START_THREADSAFE_STATIC_WRITE
x = 1; // safe since code is called only once
DWA_FINISH_THREADSAFE_STATIC_WRITE
```

Ultimately, we hope to turn this warning into a global error setting so any new usage will cause builds to fail. However, we are not yet at the point where existing warnings have been fixed, so this warning-as-error is enabled on a per-library basis as libraries are cleaned up, rather than globally.

Note that this flag is only available with the Intel compiler, which is used for production releases. We also build with gcc as a validation build, and for that compiler the above macros are redefined to be no-ops. We found this flag useful enough to recommend using the Intel compiler as a validation tool just for this purpose, even if the final executables are not built with this compiler.

There is no single technique to assure threadsafety in code, so use as many methods as possible to reduce threading problems in code, with the knowledge that you will not catch them all.

4.5.1.5 LD_PRELOAD

LD_PRELOAD is a way on Linux to override functions with user-defined alternatives. We can use it to track calls to known non-threadsafe functions. If we are not sure whether code is making calls to such functions, we can redefine those functions, build them into a library, and preload that library. The redefined function can (for example) print a message to indicate an unsafe function has been called, and dump the stack trace to show where the call originated from. We used this to track calls to a specific function in LAPACK that was known to be non-threadsafe, so we could run our test workloads and verify whether this function was being called or not. It would even be possible to have the preloaded method create a lock before calling down into the original function, thereby rendering it threadsafe.

4.5.1.6   The Kill Switch

The one saving grace for threading bugs is that they can be "fixed" by disabling threading in the application. If the problem can be narrowed down to a specific node that is not threadsafe when run concurrently with other nodes of the same type, for example, it works with static data, we can tag that node to be non-threadsafe. This option, described later, forces the graph to run the node while no other nodes are evaluating concurrently, thus ensuring that the threading problem is not encountered. Of course, we would expect the developer to fix their node so it is threadsafe, this is intended as a temporary solution to get the user up and running quickly.

In the extreme case where the problem is hard to diagnose, or affects multiple nodes, the user has a runtime option to simply disable all graph threading. This will of course severely affect performance, but the animator will at least be able to continue working. Such a control is also useful for developers to determine if problems in the application are threading-related. If a bug persists after threading is disabled, it is clearly not just a threading bug.

It is highly recommended that all parallel applications feature a global "kill" switch, which allows all threading to be disabled, since you will never catch all threading bugs, and this allows a user to keep working even in the presence of such a bug, and a developer to test code in serial mode.

Such a switch is not just a way to enable an application to run in an emergency, but it can also be used as a self-defense mechanism for multithreading authors. As any intrepid multithreading developer will know, as soon as threading is introduced into an application, all bugs instantly become threading bugs. Having the global kill switch allows a developer to fend off such attacks, as in the following (slightly) fictional account:

Developer 1 (assertively): *My code is crashing. I believe it is your multithreaded code that is to blame, since my code appears to be flawless.*

Developer 2: *Did you test by turning off all threading in the app using the kill switch we told everyone about?*

Developer 1 (more quietly): *No. Let me try that.*

[pause] Developer 1 (meekly): *The problem is still there. I guess it is a bug in my code after all.*

4.5.2   Graph Threadsafety

This section discusses the approaches taken to ensuring threadsafety at a higher level than within individual nodes, by addressing graph level threadsafety concerns.

Given graph level parallelism, a new challenge is that every developer needs awareness of threading even if they are not explicitly writing threaded code themselves, since the code they author can be running concurrently with any of the other code in other nodes in the graph. For example, accessing a third-party library that is not threadsafe can work within one node, but if a different node is accessing the same library at the same time, it will be a problem. This is a real challenge given the varying level of expertise among node authors and given that node development spans both R&D and production departments.

Ideally, all nodes in the graph would be fully threadsafe and we could simply allow the scheduling engine to assign tasks to cores as it sees fit. In practice, there is always the need to allow for the possibility of non-threadsafe nodes, as in the following examples:

- An author wishes to prototype an operator for testing and does not want to worry about making the code threadsafe right away.

- The author is not sure if the code they are calling is threadsafe, and wishes to err on the side of caution until it can be fully validated.

- The code calls a library or methods known for sure to be non-threadsafe.

For these cases, a mechanism is provided to allow the author to declare that specific nodes are not fully threadsafe. The evaluation mechanism can then take appropriate precautions in the way it evaluates such nodes. The following potential levels of threadsafety are possible:

Reentrant: The node can be evaluated concurrently with any other node in the graph and also the same instance of the node can be evaluated by more than one thread concurrently.

Threadsafe: The node can be evaluated concurrently with any other node in the graph but the same instance of the node cannot be evaluated by more than one thread concurrently.

Type Unsafe: The node cannot be evaluated concurrently with other instances of the same node type (e.g., a node that works with internal static data) but can be evaluated concurrently with instances of different node types.

Group Unsafe: The node cannot be evaluated concurrently with any of a group of node types (e.g., nodes that deal with the same global static data or the same third-party closed source library).

Globally Unsafe: The node cannot be evaluated concurrently with any other node in the graph (i.e., calls unknown code, or user is just being very cautious).

In practice, the only categories needed in production are Threadsafe, Type Unsafe, and Globally Unsafe. The graph evaluation implementation does not allow the same instance to be evaluated concurrently, so the Reentrant category is not required, and the Group Unsafe category was considered too difficult to maintain. For the latter case we simply default to Globally Unsafe.

If the scheduler sees a node is in a category other than Threadsafe it will ensure that the node is run in such a way that it will not encounter potential problems by using an appropriate lock. A Type Unsafe node will not run concurrently with another node of the same type by using a lock specific to that node type, and a Globally Unsafe node will not run concurrently with any other node by using a global lock. Of course, these latter states can severely limit graph scaling. The goal is to have as few nodes as possible that are not threadsafe.

In production rigs it has been possible so far to run characters where almost every node is marked as Threadsafe with just one or two exceptions over which we have no control. One example of such a node is an FBX™ reader node, since the FBX library itself is written by a third party and is not yet (as of 2014) threadsafe. Thus, it is marked as Type Unsafe since it cannot run concurrently with other FBX reader nodes, but can run concurrently with other types of nodes in the graph.

Provide an option that allows authors to write non-threadsafe code by protecting it so it will still run safely in a multithreaded environment.

4.6 Scalability: Software Considerations

In this section, we discuss approaches that were taken to attempt to extract maximum performance from the system. We discuss both successes and failures, on the assumption that the latter is often at least as interesting as the former when deciding what approaches to adopt for other application areas.

4.6.1   Authoring Parallel Loops

The standard TBB parallel_for loop is somewhat complex to author. Newer versions of TBB support a simpler interface using lambda functions, however, the syntax of a lambda can still be intimidating, particularly to less experienced developers who we want to encourage to write parallel code. We adopted some simple macros to allow easier threading of parallel loops. An example macro is shown below:

```
#include <tbb/parallel_for.h>
#define DWA_PARALLEL_FOR_BEGIN(VARTYPE, VARIABLE, MINVAR, MAXVAR) \
    tbb::parallel_for(MINVAR, MAXVAR, [&] (VARTYPE VARIABLE)

#define DWA_PARALLEL_FOR_END                                      \
    );
```

Then the developer can express their parallel loop as follows:

```
// transform all positions in array by xform
DWA_PARALLEL_FOR_BEGIN(int, vertexId, 0, numVertices) {
    outPositions[vertexId] = inPositions[vertexId] * xform;
}
DWA_PARALLEL_FOR_END
```

One benefit of using a macro like this is that it is possible to disable threading by simply redefining the macro to implement a regular for loop. Another benefit is that alternative behavior can be implemented, for example, timing information can be recorded as shown below by adding code to the macro to have each parallel loop print out a report showing the execution time and line number:

```
#define DWA_PARALLEL_FOR_BEGIN_TIMING(VARTYPE, VAR, MINVAR, MAXVAR) \
{                                                                    \
    int tbb_loop_trip_count = (MAXVAR - MINVAR);                     \
    START_TBB_TIMER                                                  \
    tbb::parallel_for(MINVAR, MAXVAR, [&] (VARTYPE VARIABLE)

#define DWA_PARALLEL_FOR_END_TIMING                                  \
    );                                                               \
    STOP_TBB_TIMER(__FILE__, __LINE__, tbb_loop_trip_count)          \
}
```

We can use code like this to decide on a threshold above which parallelism is worthwhile by running the loops with and without threading enabled and comparing runtimes of each loop.

We have other versions of this macro that support the TBB grain size concept, which is the smallest piece into which the problem range will be decomposed. Allowing the problem to be subdivided too finely can cause excessive work for the scheduler, so it is important to choose a grain size that still allows significant concurrency while maintaining a reasonable amount of work. The timer code can be used to decide on a good grain size to choose for each loop by tweaking the grain size and rerunning the tests.

Unfortunately, TBB (as of version 4.1) does not have a version of the parallel_for lambda function that works with grain size, so currently it is somewhat cumbersome to code this case.

4.6.2 Overthreading

Any new discovery initially leads to overuse before a happy medium is found. We encountered the same with multithreading. Once developers learned about it, some were keen to use it wherever possible, and even code like the following was in some cases being expressed as a parallel loop:

```
for (int i=0; i<4; i++)  x[i] = 0;
```

Clearly, in this case the overhead of threading the loop vastly outweighs the benefits achieved. The rule of thumb is that invoking a parallel region costs 10k clock cycles, so unless the work in the loop is significantly greater than this, the benefits of threading are not there. It can be hard to apply that threshold to real code—we recommend timing the loop with and without threading at different trip counts to decide if it is worthwhile to parallelize it.

Another aspect that might be considered overthreading is to attempt to extract parallelism from short-running algorithms, since it may impede larger performance gains available from longer-running tasks. Imagine a small parallel computation that spawns parallel tasks, which consume all the machine cores. An instant later, a large expensive parallel algorithm begins evaluation. The work is broken into multiple chunks, but no cores are available, so that the tasks wait, and then perhaps just run one at a time. This is where a good grain size selection for TBB is important, so that the tasks are small enough to be able to expand to use additional machine resources as they become available. We have found that even though there are benefits from threading small nodes when tested in isolation, those benefits often turn to disadvantages once a large graph is running, and we have in some cases removed threading from such nodes.

4.6.3 Threading Fatigue

The initial excitement of a large speedup from parallelizing a loop can quickly pall when the inevitable threading bugs are encountered and production deadlines loom, as the following e-mail from the rigging trenches attests to:

This whole foray into DWA_PARALLEL_FOR has been a pretty miserable experience. There's just nowhere near enough people or docs in support of it, and it's just a bit too bloody complex a task when I can't stay concentrated on it due to production demands.

—Anonymous Rigger

Clearly, if we are to ask developers to author parallel code, we need to provide and maintain a support system for them.

Expect developers to struggle with threading, not just in implementation but also in optimization and future proofing, and be prepared to provide guidance.

4.6.4   Thread-Friendly Memory Allocators

There are a number of thread-friendly allocators which hold per-thread memory so that malloc calls do not go to the global heap and therefore contend with each other. We have chosen to use TBB's allocator as it has delivered very good performance for our needs, giving us a 20% performance boost over regular malloc. Note that there is no requirement to use the TBB allocator in conjunction with TBB, nor do the versions need to be in sync. We are using TBB 4 with the TBB allocator from TBB 3, since it delivers better performance for our specific use case with the older allocator. We also evaluated jemalloc and found the TBB allocator to deliver better performance for our workloads, but other authors in this book have found the opposite for their workloads, so testing the various candidates is highly recommended to find what works best for any specific application.

Note that a thread-aware allocator will in general consume more memory than regular malloc as it holds onto large blocks of memory per thread to avoid going to the global heap where possible. We find the TBB allocator increases memory footprint by around 20% over usage of regular malloc, a trade-off that we consider acceptable.

Ideally, all required memory would be allocated upfront during initialization, and there would be no allocation at all during regular graph evaluation. In such a situation there would be no benefit to a threaded memory allocator, and we could just use regular malloc. This would be preferable since the extra allocator introduces complexity, build dependencies, and memory usage. However, we are not at the point where this is feasible yet, although ongoing efforts to avoid allocation at runtime are leading to reduced benefits from the TBB allocator over time. We do hope at some point to get to the point where no heap allocation happens during regular graph evaluation. Tracking down such cases should be as simple as running a profiler on the running application after startup initialization and looking for calls to malloc.

Use a thread-aware memory allocator if you are allocating memory during parallel evaluation.

4.6.5   Oversubscription Due to Multiple Threading Models

If all parallel code is written using a library like TBB there are no concerns about oversubscription. However, in some cases other libraries may be used, which can lead to oversubscription. An example is the Intel Math Kernel Library (MKL) which internally uses OpenMP to parallelize loops in some methods. This library is optimized for heavy compute so prefers OpenMP to TBB due to the slight performance benefits. However, calling into a parallel MKL routine from a TBB task now runs the risk of oversubscription. We have been able to generate synthetic test scenes where multiple nodes running in parallel each call into an MKL parallel solver and exhibit such performance degradation. However, in practice, this has not been a significant problem in our production rigs. It is, however, something to be aware of, particularly if heavy simulations are running in the rig, which may spend a lot of time in MKL or similar routines. As a rule of thumb, we find oversubscription by a factor of 2 is not significantly detrimental to performance. Any more than this though does start to show significant problems.

Try to use a single consistent threading implementation across a shared memory application for best performance.

4.6.6 Cache Reuse—Chains of Nodes

In general, the scheduling system treats each node as a separate task to be scheduled by the TBB task scheduler. This ensures we get maximum possible scaling by extracting all the potential parallelism from the graph. One exception to this is that the scheduling system treats chains of nodes (nodes with a single input and output, all connected together) as a single task for scheduling purposes, since there is no potential scalability benefit to treating each node as a separate task for the scheduler (see Figure 4.4). This reduces the number of tasks, reducing scheduling overhead. For our graphs the reduction in task count was typically 4× since there were a lot of chains in the graphs. Since TBB tasks are assigned to cores, this also has the benefit of ensuring chains of nodes all run on the same core, improving cache reuse.

Note that it is possible for the OS to migrate a task between cores during evaluation. In practice, we found that tasks are short running enough that this very rarely happens. In a graph with 10k nodes, we found at most one or two tasks that were moved to a different processor core to the one they started on.

We investigated treating "hammocks"—where there is a fan-out from one node to several chains and then a fan-in again to a single node—as a special case, but found the relative benefit to be far smaller than for chains, and the management complexity significantly larger, so we did not pursue this further.

4.6.7 Cache Reuse—Scheduling Nodes to Maximize Sharing

Related to the previous section, it might be asked whether it is worth scheduling more general node patterns than just chains in a way that maximizes cache reuse by having downstream nodes run on the same core as upstream nodes which use the same memory. We built a test system where we tracked every memory access of every node, then attempted to statically schedule the nodes such that those with the most common memory accesses were placed on the same core. This was a large amount of work, and data collection needed to be run offline. On analysis it was found that there was very little benefit to scheduling tasks this way rather than just letting TBB schedule the nodes itself. This was actually a huge relief, as the extra processing and bookkeeping would have been a considerable amount of work. However, it is worth pointing out that with 75% of the nodes in chains and already scheduled on the same core to maximize cache reuse, most of the benefits of this approach to cache reuse have already been obtained with the simple chained scheduler approach.

4.6.8 Task Priorities

We explored various schemes for assigning priorities, for example, giving graph-level tasks priority over node-level tasks, or giving specific nodes higher priority. None of these approaches proved significantly better than the default of giving all tasks equal weight. In some cases there were minor gains, but most actually hurt performance. Again this could be considered good news, since the simple approach of letting TBB schedule the tasks proved almost as good or even better than any such more complex mechanism.

4.6.9 Graph Partitioning

We investigated statically partitioning the graph in various ways, for example, grouping all the nodes related to the right arm together and scheduling them as one task. This did not work well for several reasons. First, it requires very consistent naming conventions, which is not always something we can guarantee. Second, the levels of hierarchy available

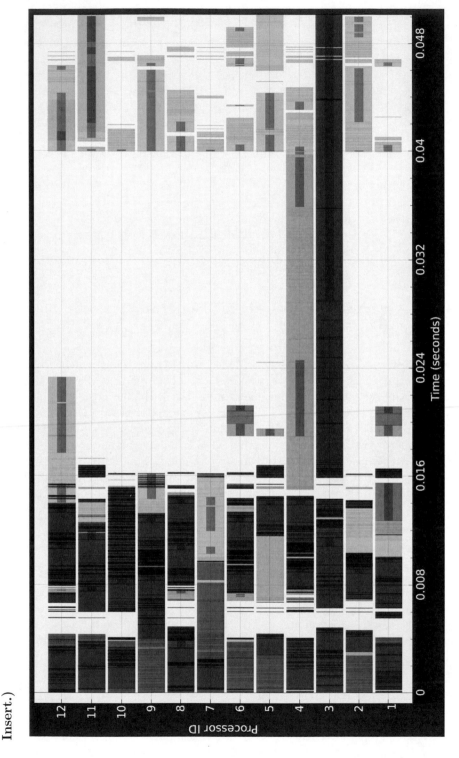

FIGURE 4.4: Tasks plotted against processor ID for a 12 core system. Note the two chains of nodes on cores 3 and 4, respectively, between 0.016s and 0.04s. These nodes have a consistent color along each chain, indicating they are from the same part of the character, and closer inspection shows that they are serially dependent. Because of this dependency they are explicitly treated as a single TBB task and so scheduled on the same processor core, thereby maximizing cache reuse along the chain. (**See Color Insert.**)

are somewhat crude (finger, hand, arm) and do not necessarily map well onto the available number of cores. Attempting a more refined dynamic partitioning based on the topology of the graph each frame proved too time consuming. As a result this approach was not pursued, and again TBB was allowed to do its own scheduling.

4.6.10 Other Processes Running on System

Since the application is an animation tool which is primarily running live rather than in batch mode, and which has the artist's primary attention, we have found that users do not often run multiple concurrent animation sessions. However, it is common for artists to be running other applications on their systems, for example, a Web browser playing videos. This can make heavy use of one or two cores. Since TBB assumes it has the full machine at its disposal, this could potentially lead to choppy behavior as the machine cores are oversubscribed.

In testing so far we have not found this to be a serious problem. However, we may not be so lucky in the future, so we have added a control over the total thread count being used in the application by TBB, so we can in principle dial back the number of threads used by the graph if the machine is being overloaded. As core counts increase, the relative loss of one or two cores becomes less and less significant.

4.6.11 The Memory Wall

One of the key nodes in the graph is a tessellator that smoothes the final output character mesh. This algorithm appeared to scale very well, giving 8× speedup with 8 cores. However, an optimization pass resulted in greater performance, but scaling dropped to 5×, to the initial disappointment of some who had focused on the impressive scaling number. This was a useful lesson that the highest scalability number is not the ultimate goal.

What was more interesting was to understand why scalability dropped. It turns out that the algorithm for tessellation is very memory bound since vertex values queried to compute the finer resolution position are widely scattered in memory, leading to cache misses. When the algorithm was optimized, compute time dropped and this main memory access bandwidth became the new bottleneck which limited performance, so beyond 5 cores we found we saturated the memory bus and additional cores just ended up waiting on memory. The TBB scheduler still creates many tasks to run the algorithm, and the task manager will schedule them all as long as there are idle cores, but in this case the extra tasks just spend their time waiting on memory.

Ideally, we might want a way to limit the number of tasks running the tessellator at this stage to free up resources for other parts of the graph, but it is not possible to explicitly ask a particular loop to use a smaller number of cores with TBB. This is one of the downsides of using a system like TBB, although in this case it is a relatively small one since tessellation happens at the end of the graph when little else is happening that might be blocked by the tessellator. However, it is an interesting example of a pattern to be aware of.

4.6.12 Failed Approaches Discussion

The fact that many attempts to outsmart the default scheduling proved unsuccessful was in some ways welcome news. It meant that we could use the default TBB scheduling and know we were getting good performance. This is not to say that everything we attempted failed. Some approaches did indeed offer speed improvements, but they were generally small enough (<10%) that the extra cost of the additional code and bookkeeping was not worth the benefit. We continue to investigate possible optimizations like these, and may revisit some in future if we can find more compelling approaches.

4.7   Scalability: Hardware Considerations

4.7.1   CPU Power Modes

The workloads on any particular core during parallel graph execution are very spiky (see Figure 4.4). This causes individual cores to switch between busy and idle states very frequently at sub-millisecond intervals. We found the power saving modes in Sandy Bridge processors to switch too slowly into high performance mode for our needs, which meant that the processor was often in a low clock speed mode for a significant portion of the time it was doing heavy compute. Because of this we chose to enable the BIOS settings for performance rather than power-saving modes on our systems to keep the processors running at their full clock speeds all the time. This provided a very significant 20% performance boost over power saving mode, with the obvious downside of greater power consumption when the machine is idle. It is to be hoped that future revisions of processor hardware can enable faster transitions between power savings and full speed modes. (Note that enabling full performance mode is not necessarily trivial as there are OS as well as BIOS settings that need to be coordinated for maximum performance to be achieved.)

4.7.2   Turbo Clock

While power saving modes can downclock cores, turbo clock settings allow cores to temporarily overclock above their nominal frequency if they have thermal headroom. This means looking at the default clock speed of a CPU is not always a good indicator of actual performance. In addition, headroom is greater when fewer cores are running, since the overall power consumption of the processor is lower. This means that a single task running on a single core can potentially run faster as the number of tasks running on the other cores is reduced. This becomes interesting in the case where threading gains are marginal. For example, if an algorithm scales poorly, it may be better to run it on fewer cores, which thereby run at higher clock speeds rather than spread the work across more cores that will then run at lower speeds. Clock speed is controlled at the hardware level, so taking advantage of and measuring this behavior is challenging.

4.7.3   NUMA

The workstations provided to animators are dual socket systems, therefore, NUMA is an area of concern. Currently, we do not actively allocate memory on the banks nearest to the cores doing the work, as TBB can assign work to arbitrary cores. We have not yet found this to be a significant performance issue, although it is something we are monitoring closely. However, experiments with four socket systems have shown that this becomes a real issue on such topologies, since memory can be multiple hops away from the cores where the compute is being done (see Figure 4.5). At this time, deployed systems for animators are two socket systems, so this has not yet been a problem. As core counts per sockets continue to rise, it seems likely that two socket systems will remain the sweet spot for price/performance for some time.

FIGURE 4.5: Scalability dropoff with four socket systems compared with two socket systems for a single hero character workload. The first set of bars track performance on a system with four 8 core processors. The second set of bars indicate performance on a system with two 8 core processors. Per-core performance of the four socket systems is slightly lower so the lower performance at low thread counts is expected. However, as the thread count increases, the power of the additional cores on the four socket system is not effectively harnessed due to NUMA effects, and indeed performance degrades significantly.

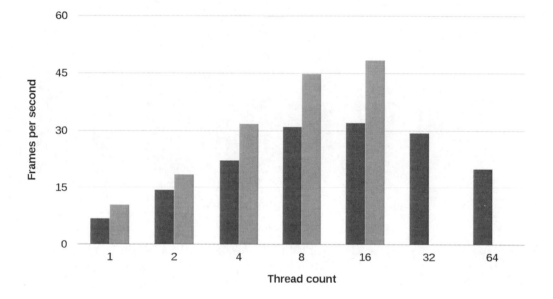

4.7.4 Hyperthreading

Hyperthreading (HT) enables a single physical core to be exposed to the operating system as more than one logical core, so work can be scheduled to take advantage of otherwise idle execution resources on that core. It is usually enabled via a BIOS setting since it does not always benefit performance. The user should test their application to determine if they get a benefit or not.

In our case we found an interesting pattern. If we ran a regular workload across all the cores, we found that enabling HT typically reduced performance by ~15%. As a result, we chose to disable HT on all artist workstations. However, when we later ran some scalability tests that limited the workload to run on a smaller number of cores, we found the situation reversed, with HT providing up to a 20% performance boost (see Figure 4.6). This can be explained by the fact that a typical workload does not heavily stress all the cores, so hyperthreads can cause unbalanced system loads with lighter workloads, while with a heavier compute load all the core resources can be used effectively.

Since hyperthreading is a BIOS setting, it is nontrivial and time consuming to toggle its state. Animators switch between lighter and heavier scenes frequently enough that rebooting constantly to change it is not a realistic option. We currently choose to leave it disabled, but this is an area of ongoing monitoring.

One last point—enabling hyperthreading will cause a threaded application to use more memory. This is because additional threads will be running on the extra logical cores,

FIGURE 4.6: Hyperthreading performance impact. The first set of bars show performance for the walk cycle of a character with hyperthreading disabled, the second set of bars show the same workload with hyperthreading enabled.

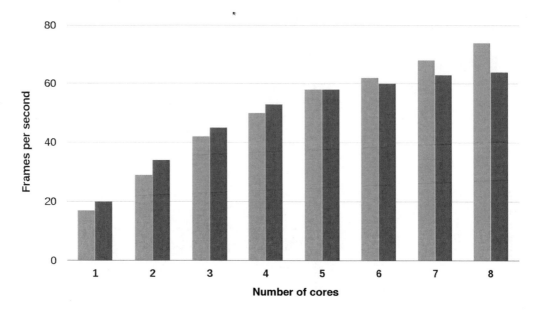

and so per-thread memory such as thread-local storage and stacks will increase the overall footprint. In addition, using the TBB allocator will increase memory overhead due to its use of per-thread memory pools to avoid accessing the global heap.

4.7.5   CPU Affinity

Although we found affinity was not useful in binding individual nodes to cores within the graph, at the application level it is a different story. If we wish to limit the number of cores being used by the graph, we have found it beneficial to set CPU affinity to bind the process to particular cores. TBB itself is affinity-unaware, so on Linux we need to use the taskset command to bind the task to a subset of cores. Figure 4.7 shows a graph running with four threads with and without CPU affinity set. The reason this is beneficial is that it ensures that the threads can be assigned to the same socket thus maximizing both per-core cache and per-socket cache reuse and leading to both higher and more consistent frame rates, both good things for the animator experience.

4.7.6   Many-Core Architectures

The question arises whether an application like this will run well on a processor with more cores, such as Xeon Phi. Xeon Phi in particular is appealing because the porting effort is relatively low. However, optimization for the architecture requires not just high scalability, but also extensive vectorization, which is a separate massive effort that has so far not been attempted with the animation codebase. Running multiple jobs on the Xeon Phi to take fuller advantage of all the cores runs into memory constraints due to the limited amount of onboard RAM. As the hardware evolves over time, and code optimization continues, this may in future become a more interesting target architecture.

FIGURE 4.7: Evaluation of a character graph over a range of frames on four cores. The lower set of four runs show the frame rate over time without an affinity set, while the upper four runs show the performance with an affinity set. Note that not only is the overall frame rate ~10% higher with an affinity set, the frame rate is also much more consistent over the frame range, leading to a better animator experience.

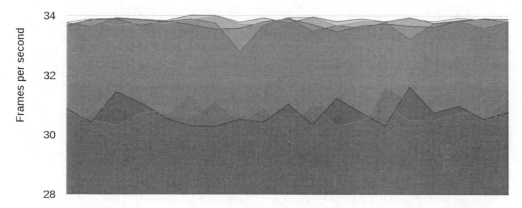

Carefully test on different hardware platforms and explore system settings for maximum performance.

4.8   Production Considerations

The previous sections relate primarily to the R&D work of building a parallel engine. Equally important are the production considerations that relate to the use of this engine. Integrating the new dependency graph engine into a feature animation pipeline required a number of significant changes to the character rigging process, namely:

- The character rigs needed to be rearchitected to integrate into the new animation tool and the engine.

- All custom nodes had to be written in C++ instead of in scripting languages like Python.

- Character systems needed to be optimized for parallel computation.

We discuss the challenges and efforts surrounding these three production changes in the following sections.

4.8.1 Character Systems Restructure

We realized that our underlying character systems needed to be rearchitected to work in the new interactive animation environment built on top of the graph engine. Most of the graph nodes used to construct our character setups had to be rewritten to be threadsafe and to integrate with the engine interfaces. In revamping the character systems, many existing nodes were discarded and new ones with different requirements were written in their place. Given that the codebase has been written over a span of many years, such a rewrite is a major undertaking.

4.8.2 No More Scripted Nodes

Riggers often write custom graph nodes to handle unique rigging challenges. Typically, custom nodes were written in a proprietary scripting language or in Python for ease of authoring. These nodes are relatively simple to write and integrate nicely into the production codebase. However, as mentioned earlier, the new graph evaluation engine requires all nodes to be written in C++ for optimum performance. This transition has been difficult for production, although clearly necessary.

We provided training programs for riggers to transition from writing script-based nodes to building C++ equivalents. We also developed a training curriculum to spread knowledge of writing threaded and threadsafe code for all potential node authors.

4.8.3 Optimizing for Maximum Parallelism

One of the interesting transitions required, which was in hindsight obvious but not considered initially, was that riggers had to become familiar with multithreading not just at a coding level, but also when it comes to building the rigs themselves. Dependencies between nodes in the graph need to be expressed in a way that allows as much of the graph as possible to run in parallel. No matter how well the engine itself scales, it can only extract from a graph the parallelism that the graph authors, that is, the riggers, have put into the system.

Previously, to optimize character setups, riggers used profiling tools to identify bottlenecks in individual graph nodes and then worked to address performance issues in these nodes. This approach is still necessary, but is no longer sufficient with a highly multithreaded graph since the ordering and dependency between nodes becomes a very large factor in the overall performance. There were new concepts that needed to be considered, in particular, the concept of the critical path.

The *critical path* is the most expensive serial chain of nodes in the graph. The overall runtime of the graph is limited by the critical path runtime. A goal for optimization therefore is to try to reduce the cost of the critical path, either by removing nodes from the path or by optimizing nodes along it. A corollary to this is that there is less benefit to optimizing nodes that are not on the critical path since, to first approximation, those nodes do not directly affect the graph runtime (although of course those nodes do consume compute resources that might otherwise be used to speed evaluation of nodes along the critical path).

Since riggers have limited time to spend on optimization, it is important that this time be used effectively. There was significant frustration early on when optimization efforts did not seem to yield the expected speedups. This turned out to be due to optimizations being applied to expensive nodes that were not on the critical path. As a result, it became apparent that we needed a tool which could provide relevant information on the graph performance characteristics, including the critical path, to the riggers.

This was a requirement that is readily apparent in hindsight, but which we did not anticipate, so the tool was developed and delivered to riggers relatively late, at a point where many of the characters for the first production show had already been substantially built and were thus no longer open to significant changes. This meant that characters on the first show were not as fully optimized as they could have been, but it also means that we expect future shows to have increasingly optimized characters. Expressing parallelism in rigs is a new and very important skill for riggers, one that we expect them to become more skilled at over the years.

4.9 Threading Visualization Tool

In this section, we describe the tool that was built to show the parallelism in the graph. We discuss this tool in some depth because this was and continues to be an extremely important part of the optimization process (and also because it allows us to show some pretty pictures which have been sadly lacking up to this point).

The tool is designed to allow riggers to visualize data flow and node evaluation in the graph. Riggers can identify which components of their character are running in parallel, where graph serialization bottlenecks occur, and where unexpected dependencies exist between parts of the rig. The tool also highlights the critical path. This is the most time consuming chain of serially dependent nodes in the graph, and so determines the best possible runtime of the graph when it is running in parallel (Figure 4.8).

The average concurrency metric is a very useful value as it gives a simple easily understood metric to indicate the parallelism in a rig. When comparing similar characters we expect similar levels of concurrency, and outliers attract special attention to detect potential problems in the rigs that limit scalability.

Over time we are learning how to build scalable characters in this new environment, but this is an ongoing process. Here are some of the strategies we have developed to optimize multithreaded character rigs:

- Focus primarily on nodes along the critical path.

- Identify expensive nodes that are bottlenecks and internally optimize these nodes as well as move their execution to a more parallel location within the graph.

- Identify a section of the graph that is serial and work to parallelize this area of the rig.

- Identify groups of nodes that are used repeatedly in the graph and rewrite them as a single custom node. This reduces the overall number of nodes in the graph and therefore minimizes thread scheduling overhead relative to time spent in node evaluation itself.

We are able to collect before/after statistics and compare them in the visualizer to give immediate feedback to the author on the benefits of their optimizations to the overall character runtime profile, as in Figure 4.9.

We have utilized a combination of the above described optimization approaches to successfully improve performance of character setups. The following section describes some real-world production examples that highlight the optimization process in action.

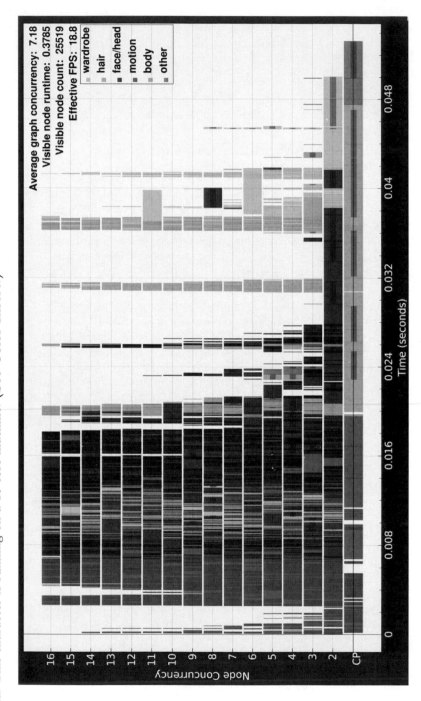

FIGURE 4.8: The threading visualization tool enables riggers to investigate bottlenecks within the graph. The vertical axis shows concurrent nodes in flight for various parts of the characters. The horizontal axis is time. Each block is a single node in the graph. Nodes with internal parallelism are displayed with a horizontal bar through them. Different components are drawn in different colors (e.g., body, face, wardrobe, and hair—see the Color Insert for actual colors). The average concurrency reported only represents graph parallelism and does not include node parallelism. The bottom row of nodes are the nodes on the critical path. This character is running on a 16 core machine. **(See Color Insert.)**

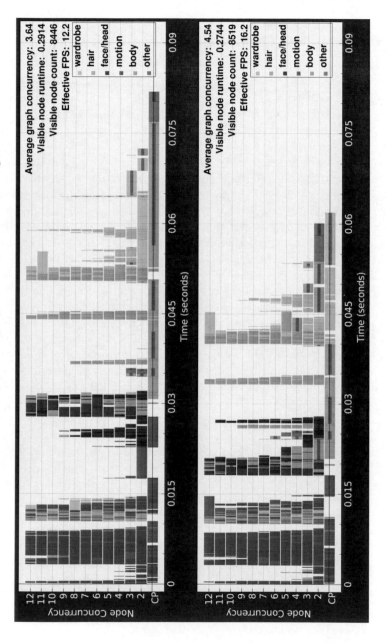

FIGURE 4.9: Mode to compare two profiles to check benefits of optimizations.

4.10 Rig Optimization Case Studies

This section reviews real-world optimization performed on character rigs to illustrate the process of tuning a character for optimum performance.

4.10.1 Case Study 1: Quadruped Critical Path Optimization

In this case we show the graph visualizations used to identify and fix bottlenecks within a quadruped character (Figure 4.10). We first identify a problematic chain of serial nodes along the critical path (the long chain of nodes up to 0.02 seconds in the figure). This represents the character's motion system for 12 claws (three claws per foot). Upon closer inspection, a node that concatenates joint hierarchies was used extensively in this chain but was not efficiently coded.

The second figure represents the rig after R&D had optimized the hierarchy concatenation code. Note that the serial path has been shortened but there is no change in the graph structure or parallelism. Next we look at the claw deformation system, identified by the lighter colored nodes. We note that the graph here shows a small degree of parallelism. Riggers rewired the claw system so that the claws deformed more concurrently. Riggers had separately noticed one very expensive node, displayed at the top of the middle graph, and had optimized it (before having access to this tool, which was at that point still under development).

The third figure shows the results of these two optimizations. The lighter colored claw deformation code path has shrunk due to the extra parallelism. However, note that the second change, to optimize the expensive node, which seemed like an obvious optimization candidate, did not improve the overall runtime at all. This is because that particular node was not on the critical path. This demonstrates the importance of focusing efforts on the critical path of the graph, and the value of having such a tool available to riggers so they can make informed choices about where best to focus their limited optimization efforts.

4.10.2 Case Study 2: Hair Solver

In this example (Figure 4.11), the riggers took an initial chain of nodes that implemented the hair system in a mostly serial manner and reworked the dependencies to allow different parts of the hair system to run in parallel. The same amount of work is performed, but in a much shorter overall runtime. Since the hair system computes at the end of the graph when nothing else is evaluating, the serial dependencies in the system greatly limit potential performance, and parallelism is a large win.

4.10.3 Case Study 3: Free Clothes!

Figure 4.12 shows the moment when for many of us the benefits of the threaded graph evaluation system finally became dramatically real. The top graph shows the motion and deformation system for a character. The bottom graph shows the same character with the addition of rigged clothing. This clothing is an expensive part of the overall character, nearly 25% of the total graph evaluation cost, but because it was attached to the torso it was able to compute in parallel with the limbs of the character. Since the critical path ran through the character body rather than the clothing, this meant that effectively the clothing evaluation was almost free when running the character by itself, only 3% slower than the same character without clothing.

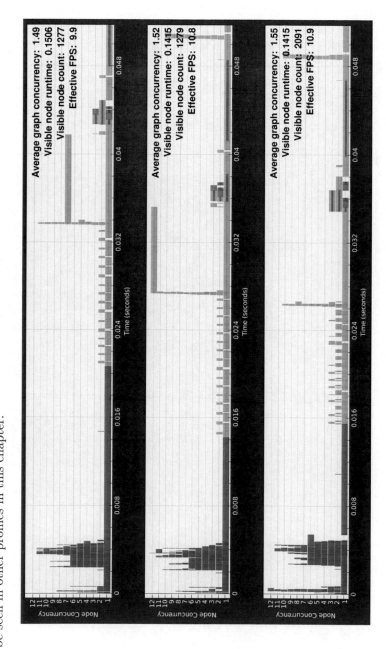

FIGURE 4.10: Example showing the process for optimizing a quadruped character. Note that the overall time for evaluation of the frame is reduced at each stage. Also note the relatively poor overall scaling. This profile is from an early stage in rig parallelism work from the rigging department. As optimization proceeded the parallelism of the character improved significantly, as can be seen in other profiles in this chapter.

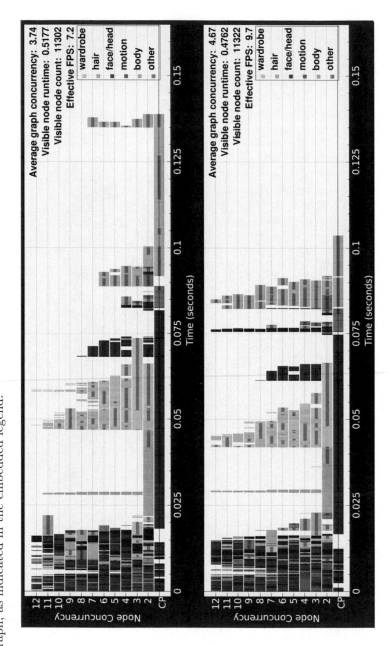

FIGURE 4.11: The top profile shows the initial hair system implementation, the bottom shows the same workload with dependencies expressed between nodes in a way that allows more parallel execution. The hair nodes are the nodes at the end of the graph, as indicated in the embedded legend.

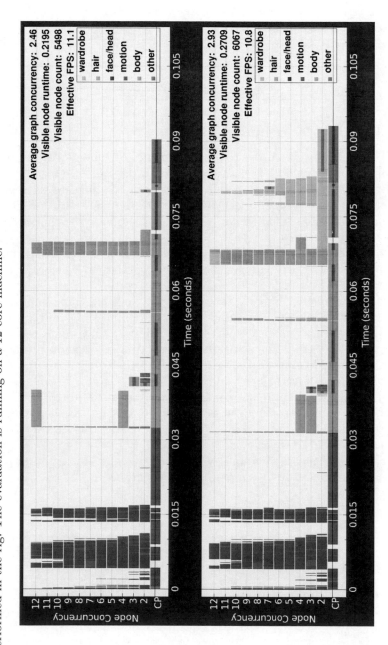

FIGURE 4.12: The top graph shows a character with motion and deformation systems, the bottom graph shows the addition of rigged clothing. Note that the overall runtime increases only marginally although there is a significant amount of extra work being performed in the rig. The evaluation is running on a 12 core machine.

We have been happy to see that this tool is now often open on a rigger's workstation as they are working on their rigs, the ultimate compliment showing that they now consider it an invaluable part of their character development process.

> *Provide tools to production users to allow them to visualize performance bottlenecks in the systems they create. This can reduce dependency of production on R&D by allowing production to take ownership of the optimization process.*

4.11   Overall Performance Results

As of early 2014, we were able to hit performance benchmarks of 15–24 fps for interactive posing of complete full-fidelity hero characters in the animation tool on HP Z820 16 core Sandy Bridge workstations with 3.1 GHz clock speeds, which are the standard deployment systems for animators. The fps benchmarks represent the execution of a single character rig without simulations running live (which would evaluate the character graph repeatedly through a range of frames).

One question is how much benefit is obtained from node threading versus graph threading. Figure ?? shows the performance of a rig with either node or graph threading disabled, and shows that most of the performance benefits come from graph level threading rather than node level threading, proving the value of the threaded graph implementation over simply threading individual nodes. In addition, once graph threading is enabled the benefits of node threading are diminished further since threads that would have evaluated a single node in parallel are now often dedicated to evaluating other nodes in the graph, leading to lower scaling for individual nodes.

The above results have since improved, and hero characters are now typically showing an overall scaling of 7–8× from a combination of node and graph-level parallelism, with a couple of outliers still languishing at ∼5.5×, while one best case hero character has reached 10× speedup on the 16 core systems. Preliminary testing with 20 core Ivy Bridge machines shows this same character achieving a 12× speedup, from 1.9 fps to 23 fps.

Further improvements to graph-level scaling are expected on future productions as riggers continue to gain expertise in parallel optimizations.

4.12   Limits of Scalability

Considerable effort was spent in optimizing both the rigs and the nodes themselves to attempt to improve scalability. As indicated in the previous section, we are approaching 8× scaling on 16 core machines, which is a good result, but one has to ask if it is possible to do better. Core counts will only continue to increase, and a simple application of Amdahl's law tells us that 8× on a 16 core machine will only give us 10× on a 32 core machine.

We investigated possible hardware limitations, for example, memory bandwidth, but this does not appear to be a factor with our rigs. Instead it appears that the scalability limits at this point are simply due to the amount of parallelism inherent in the characters themselves. We do expect to improve rig parallelism as riggers gain expertise, but fundamentally there

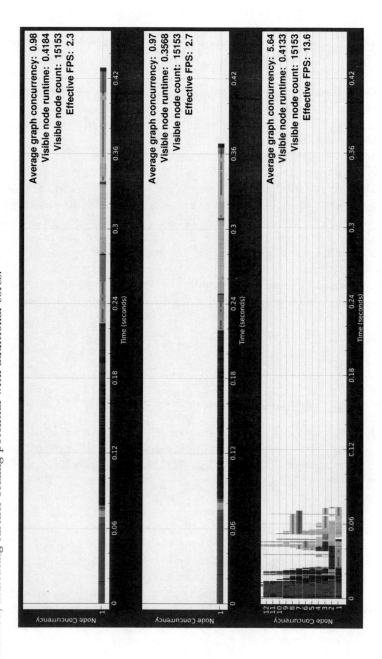

FIGURE 4.13: A demonstration of different levels of parallelism in a graph evaluation on a 12 core machine. The top run has both node and graph threading disabled. The middle run has node threading enabled but graph threading disabled. There is a 1.35× speedup for this case. The bottom run has both node and graph threading enabled. There is an additional 4.2× scaling in this case, for an overall 5.7× total speedup with a hero biped character. Note that all 12 cores are being used for parts of the evaluation, indicating further scaling potential with additional cores.

is a limit as to how much parallelism is possible to achieve in a human or simple animal rig, and we appear to be close to those limits.

Figure 4.14 shows one way to improve scaling, which is to have multiple characters in a scene. This is a common occurrence in real shots, and we are finding that overall scaling is indeed improved as the complexity of the scene increases. Of course, the overall runtime of the scene can still be slow, but at least the extra benefits of parallelism become more effective in such cases.

A second approach is to evaluate multiple graphs in parallel. The main use case for this would be computing multiple frames concurrently. For animation without simulations, where frames are independent, we have tested workflows where frame N and N+1 are triggered as independent concurrent graph evaluations. What we find is that overall throughput increases significantly although, as expected, the latency for any particular frame to compute is increased as it has to compete against evaluation of other graphs (Figure 4.15). Although this may not be ideal during user interactivity, since computation of adjacent frames will slow down the frame the artist is viewing, this approach is a good one for batch evaluation of frame ranges where the goal is to process as many frames as possible in the shortest time. Furthermore, the total scaling is very close to the machine limits, over $14\times$ in some cases on a 16 core machine (Figure 4.16). This means not only is current hardware being utilized to its fullest extent, without hitting memory bandwidth limits, but there is hope for further scaling with future machines that have higher core counts. Indeed, we have seen with 20 core Ivy Bridge systems that scaling has continued as expected based on an extrapolation of the 16 core Sandy Bridge results.

An obvious downside to this approach is the increased memory consumption due to storage of multiple independent graph states. This is a significant problem with large complex rigs.

4.13 Summary

The new evaluation engine delivered well over an order of magnitude speedup in comparison to the existing in-house animation tool, and also offers performance higher than third-party commercial tools can currently deliver. This allows productions to significantly increase the level of complexity and realism in upcoming productions, while simultaneously enabling a fluidity of workflow for animators by giving them much more interactivity even for heavy production character rigs.

Implementing the parallel graph evaluation engine was a significant effort (the project took 4 years) but the final results are proving to be worthwhile to animators, and we expect the tool to continue to scale in performance as rigs increase in complexity and hardware core counts rise, which was the long-term goal of the project.

One of the unanticipated requirements of parallel graph evaluation is that riggers need to develop significant new skills to be able to build and optimize character rigs in such an environment, which is a long-term learning process. Providing high-quality tools to enable them to do this is a critical requirement for success.

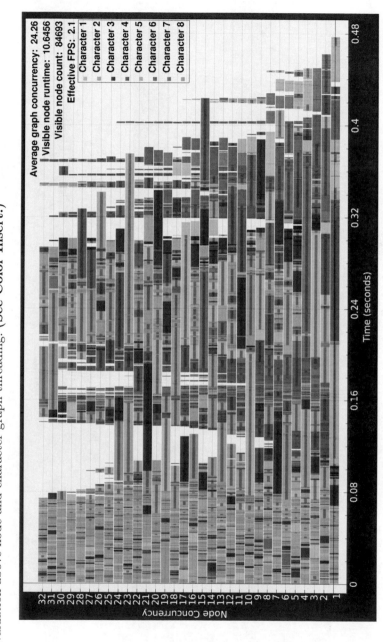

FIGURE 4.14: Evaluation of a single frame of animation for eight independent hero characters on a 32 core machine. The various shades represent different characters. All the characters evaluate concurrently, exhibiting an additional layer of parallelism in scene evaluation above node and character graph threading. **(See Color Insert.)**

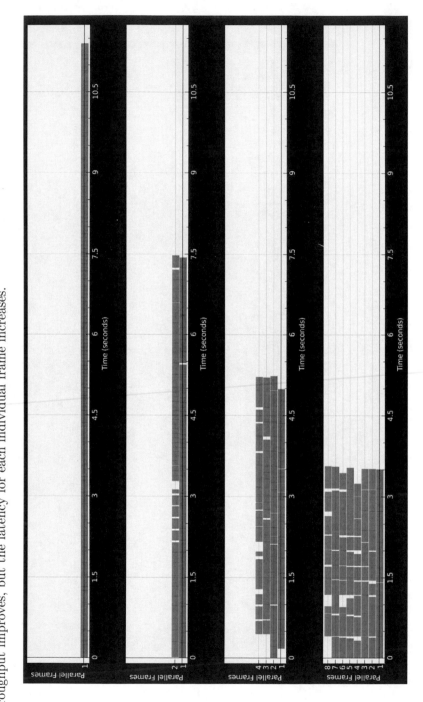

FIGURE 4.15: Multiple graph evaluations for 100 frames of playback. The top view shows each frame being evaluated consecutively, each box is one frame. The lower panels show two, four, and eight concurrent graphs, respectively. Note that the overall throughput improves, but the latency for each individual frame increases.

FIGURE 4.16: Multiple graph evaluation for six different hero characters. The lower bars show regular scaling from node and graph threading, the upper bars show the additional scaling from computing multiple graphs concurrently. Overall scaling is ~12–14× on a 16 core machine. Note that the graph needs to be read carefully. Although the upper and lower bars are similar sizes, the lower bars (graph threading) show on average a 7× speedup while the upper bars (multiple graphs) give a ~2× additional speedup.

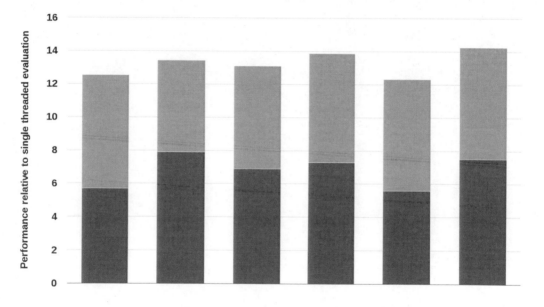

Chapter 5

Fluids: Simulation on the CPU

Ronald Henderson

DreamWorks Animation

5.1   Motivation 111
5.2   Programming Models 112
    5.2.1   Everything You Need to Get Started 114
    5.2.2   Example: Over 114
    5.2.3   Example: Dot Product 115
    5.2.4   Example: Maximum Absolute Value 117
    5.2.5   Platform Considerations 118
    5.2.6   Performance 119
5.3   Fluid Simulation 120
    5.3.1   Data Structures 120
    5.3.2   Smoke, Fire, and Explosions 122
        5.3.2.1   Advection Solvers 124
        5.3.2.2   Elliptic Solvers 126
    5.3.3   Liquids 128
        5.3.3.1   Parallel Point Rasterization 132
5.4   Summary 136

In this section, we look at the practical issues involved in introducing parallel computing for tool development in a studio environment with a focus on fluid simulation. We talk about the hardware models that programmers must now target for tool delivery, common visual effects platforms, libraries, and other tools that developers should be familiar with in order to be more productive, and considerations for key algorithms and how those relate to important application areas.

5.1   Motivation

Parallel computing is a requirement. Since microprocessor clock rates have stopped increasing, the only way to improve performance (outside of regular optimization or algorithmic improvements) is by exploiting parallelism. The good news is that parallel computing can offer dramatic speedups over existing serial code, and with modern programming models and a little practice you can quickly see impressive results.

The two dominant hardware platforms for deploying parallel programs at the moment are shared memory multicore CPUs and massively parallel GPUs. Table 5.1 shows the hardware in use at DreamWorks Animation (DWA) for our production tools over the past several years. This reflects the industry trends of increasing parallelism, increasing memory capacity,

Model	Deployed	Cores	RAM	Speed	Video Card	VRAM
HP 9300	2005	4	4 GB	2.2 GHz	NVIDIA FX 3450	512 MB
HP 9400	2006	4	4/8 GB	2.6 GHz	NVIDIA FX 3500	512 MB
HP 8600	2008	8	8 GB	3.2 GHz	NVIDIA FX 5600	1.5 GB
HP z800 (white)	2009	8	8 GB	2.93 GHz	NVIDIA FX 4800	1.5 GB
HP z800+ (gold)	2010	12	12 GB	2.93 GHz	NVIDIA FX 4800	1.5 GB
HP z800+ (red)	2011	12	24 GB	2.93 GHz	NVIDIA FX 5000	2.5 GB
HP z820	2012	16	32 GB	3.10 GHz	NVIDIA FX 5000	2.5 GB

TABLE 5.1: Hardware used for production computing at Dream-Works Animation from 2008–2013. Note that the processor speed has been flat or decreasing while the processor counts go steadily up.

and flat or decreasing processor clock rates. These numbers are for desktop hardware, but the hardware deployed in our data centers for batch simulation and rendering has followed a similar evolution. In addition, we maintain special clusters of machines with up to 32 cores and 96 GB memory as part of our simulation farm dedicated to running parallel jobs.

When developing software tools for film production, obviously we have to consider the hardware available to run those tools. By raw count, CPU cores represent 98% of the available compute capacity at the studio, and GPUs about 2%. For this reason, along with the flexibility to write tools that perform well across a wide variety of problem sizes, shared memory multiprocessors are by far the dominant hardware platform for internal development.

This chapter is organized as follows. First, we look at programming models for writing parallel programs, focusing on OpenMP and Threading Building Blocks (TBB). Next, we look at issues around understanding and measuring performance. And finally, we look at case studies for the most common algorithms used for fluid simulation.

5.2 Programming Models

Two programming models have dominated development at DWA since we started pushing parallel programming into a much wider portion of the toolset: OpenMP and TBB.

The first wave of software changes in the areas of simulation and volume processing used OpenMP, a tasking model that supports execution by a team of threads. OpenMP is easy to incorporate into an existing codebase with minimal effort and disruption, making it attractive for legacy applications and libraries. It requires compiler support, but is currently available for most modern compilers and even multiple languages (C, C++, and Fortran). As we developed more complex applications and incorporated more complex data structures, the limitations of OpenMP became more problematic and we moved to TBB. TBB is a C++ library that supports both regular and irregular parallelism. TBB has several advantages, in particular superior support for dynamic load balancing and nested parallelism. It should work with any modern C++ compiler and does not require any special language support, but requires a more intrusive change for an existing codebase.

Here is a quick summary of these two programming models from McCool, Robison, and Reinders [46]:

OpenMP

- Creation of teams of threads that jointly execute a block of code

- Support for parallel loops with a simple annotation syntax

- Support for atomic operations and locks

- Support for reductions with a predefined set of operations (but others are easy to program)

Threading Building Blocks (TBB)

- Template library supporting both regular and irregular parallelism

- Support for a variety of parallel patterns (map, fork-join, task graphs, reduction, scan, and pipelines)

- Efficient work-stealing load balancing

- Collection of threadsafe data structures

- Efficient low-level primitives for atomic operations and memory allocation

Early versions of TBB required writing functors and specialized classes in order to schedule work with the TBB task model. However, with the addition of lambda expressions in the C++11 standard, the syntax for writing such expressions is much easier and dramatically simplifies the task of incorporating TBB into an application or library.

We also make extensive use of the Intel Math Kernel Library (MKL) [34], a collection of high-performance kernels for linear algebra, partial differential equations, fast Fourier transforms (FFTs), and vector math. Note that MKL uses OpenMP as its internal threading model and has basic support for controlling the number of threads used by its internal functions.

In general, there are no major problems mixing these programming models in the same library or even the same application as long as you avoid nested parallelism that might lead to oversubscription. Because of the growing need to compose parallel algorithms in both third-party and proprietary applications, we have adopted TBB as our standard parallel programming model. Although you can mix these models, there may be platform-specific performance considerations. For example, OpenMP uses a spin-wait for worker threads that finish a parallel region early in order to reduce the latency of restarting threads between fine-grained parallel regions. The default time can be as long as 200 ms. If you mix TBB and OpenMP in the same application, this can show up as a significant overhead when an OpenMP parallel region finishes. You can control this in the Intel implementation using `kmp_set_blocktime()` and should consider setting the block time to zero before entering a parallel region if you know there will be no additional work for OpenMP threads.

If you need to mix threading models in the same application, pay close attention to any performance issues at the boundaries. Some threading runtimes (such as OpenMP) implement strategies to reduce runtime latency that backfire when switching execution models.

5.2.1 Everything You Need to Get Started

The vast majority of changes required to introduce parallelism using OpenMP are covered by the following pragmas:

```
#pragma omp parallel_for
#pragma omp parallel reduction(op : variable)
#pragma omp critical
#pragma omp flush
```

The first two are for specifying parallel loops and reductions, and the second two are for handling critical sections and reductions that are not covered by one of the built-in operators. A critical section will be executed by at most one thread at a time and is useful for avoiding race conditions. A flush forces synchronization of a thread-local variable across all threads and can be useful before a critical section that requires updates between thread-local and shared variables.

The most common usage patterns in TBB also involve parallel loops and reductions. One of the nice benefits of writing algorithms with TBB is that the need for critical sections and atomic variables largely disappears, even for complex production code, but support is provided just in case. The roughly analogous functions in TBB are the following:

```
tbb::parallel_for
tbb::parallel_reduce
```

The syntax for calling these functions can be a little odd if you have not used them before, but is easily explained with a few examples. TBB also offers hooks for critical sections and synchronization using:

```
tbb::mutex
tbb::atomic
```

If you are a good parallel programmer with TBB you probably will not need these.

5.2.2 Example: Over

Our first example is for a simple parallel loop to compute a linear combination of two vectors with an alpha channel for blending. This is a common operation in image and volume processing given by:

$$u \leftarrow (1 - \alpha)u + \alpha v$$

Here is an implementation in OpenMP:

```
inline void
omp_over(const size_t n, float* u,
        const float* v, const float* alpha)
{
#pragma omp parallel_for
    for (size_t i = 0; i < n; ++i) {
        u[i] = (1.f - alpha[i]) * u[i] + alpha[i] * v[i];
    }
}
```

It is easy to read the serial implementation and all we added was the pragma to specify the loop to execute in parallel. OpenMP will split this loop and execute each subrange using a team of threads.

Here is the same function implemented in TBB:

```
inline void
tbb_over(const size_t n, float* u,
         const float* v, const float* alpha)
{
  tbb::parallel_for(
    tbb::blocked_range<size_t>(0, n),
    [=](const tbb::blocked_range<size_t>& r)
    {
      for (size_t i = r.begin(); i < r.end(); ++i) {
        u[i] = (1.f - alpha[i]) * u[i] + alpha[i] * v[i];
      }
    }
  );
}
```

This is a little more complicated but still quite readable. This form of `tbb::parallel_for` takes a range of work to be scheduled and a function representing the task to be executed. We are using a lambda expression to keep the syntax compact, but you could also use a function pointer. These two implementations should have similar if not identical performance.

5.2.3 Example: Dot Product

The next example is for a simple reduction common to linear algebra and iterative methods like conjugate gradient iteration. The dot product is defined as:

$$u \cdot v = \sum_{i=0}^{n-1} u_i v_i$$

The implementation in OpenMP can be written using one of the built-in reduction operators:

```
inline float
omp_dot(const size_t n, const float* u, const float* v)
{
    float result(0.f);
#pragma omp parallel reduction(+: result)
    {
#pragma omp for
        for (size_t i = 0; i < n; ++i) {
            result += u[i] * v[i];
        }
    }
    return result;
}
```

In this example, a private copy of `result` is created for each thread. After all the threads execute they will add their value to the copy of `result` owned by the master thread. There is a relatively small number of built-in reduction operators, but we will look at how to code around any missing built-in reduction operators in the last example below.

Here is the equivalent function in TBB:

```
inline float
tbb_dot(const size_t n, const float* u, const float* v)
{
  return tbb::parallel_reduce(
    tbb::blocked_range<size_t>(0, n),
      0.f,
      [=](tbb::blocked_range<size_t>& r, float sum)->float
      {
        for (size_t i = r.begin(); i < r.end(); ++i) {
            sum += x[i] * y[i];
        }
        return sum;
      },
      std::plus<float>()
      );
}
```

Note that `tbb::parallel_reduce` requires two functors: one for the task to be executed and a binary reducer function that combines results to create a final value. TBB can execute using a binary tree to reduce each subrange and then combine results, or it can chain subranges if one task picks up additional work and combines it with intermediate results. The initial value of `sum` in the functor executed by each task could be zero or could be the result from reducing another subrange, but you cannot assume it is zero! Failing to handle this correctly is a common bug in TBB applications.

> *The task functor supplied to* `tbb::parallel_reduce` *takes a second argument, which is the* initial value *of the reduction for the current subrange. Pay close attention to handling this argument correctly.*

TBB combines the results of each subrange depending on the order that threads complete. For operations like the dot product that are sensitive to accumulated round-off error this can lead to non-deterministic results. In this case, you can accumulate the sum in double precision (which might help). TBB also includes an alternative `tbb::parallel_deterministic_reduce` function that always combines subranges using a binary tree. It may have a slightly lower performance, but guarantees that the order of operations in the reduction is identical for a given number of threads.

> *Ideally, a parallel algorithm will be deterministic for any number of worker threads. If this is not possible because of machine or algorithm limitations, for example, sensitivity to roundoff error or order of operations, then try to be deterministic for a fixed number of workers.*

5.2.4 Example: Maximum Absolute Value

Let's look at one final example of a reduction that cannot be implemented with an OpenMP built-in operator: the maximum absolute value of all elements in an array. Note that this calculation should be fully deterministic and the results are independent of the order of operations in carrying out the individual comparisons.

Here is one possible implementation in OpenMP:

```
inline float
omp_absmax(const size_t n, const float* u)
{
    float vmax(0.f);
#pragma omp parallel
    {
        float tmax(0.f);
#pragma omp for
        for (size_t i = 0; i < n; ++i) {
            const float value = std::abs(u[i]);
            if (value > tmax) tmax = value;
        }
#pragma omp flush(vmax)
#pragma omp critical
        {
            if (tmax > vmax) vmax = tmax;
        }
    }
    return vmax;
}
```

Here we have a thread-local variable (`tmax`) that is used to compute the maximum value for each thread, and a global maximum (`vmax`) that is updated inside a critical section. The pragma `flush(vmax)` forces a synchronization before the start of the final reduction.

You might be tempted to write this using a shared array where each thread stores its result in a unique element of the array and the main thread does a final calculation of the max once all worker threads complete. To set this up you need to know the number of threads to allocate the array and an ID for each thread to know what index you should use to store the thread-local result. Avoid patterns like this. Anything requiring a call to `omp_get_num_threads()` or `omp_get_thread_id()` can almost certainly be written more efficiently. TBB does not even offer such a feature.

> *Avoid implementations that make explicit reference to the number of worker threads or a specific thread ID. Such implementations are fragile when running in different environments and might not be portable across different threading models.*

The implementation of a maximum absolute value in TBB is essentially the same as the dot product example but with the specific methods for the reduction and combiner functions:

```
inline float
tbb_absmax(const size_t n, const float* u)
{
  return tbb::parallel_reduce(
    tbb::blocked_range<size_t>(0, n)
    0.f,
    [=](tbb::blocked_range<size_t>& r, float vmax)->float
    {
      for (size_t i = r.begin(); i < r.end(); ++i) {
        const float value = std::abs(u[i]);
        if (value > vmax) vmax = value;
      }
      return vmax;
    },
    [](float x, float y)->float { return x < y ? y : x; }
  );
}
```

We can take advantage in the combiner of the fact that all intermediate results are guaranteed to be greater than or equal to zero, so there is no need for a further check of the absolute value. In general, this method will have better scaling than the OpenMP version because it avoids the synchronization.

5.2.5 Platform Considerations

Tools used within the visual effects industry rarely run as stand-alone systems. Instead they are generally integrated into one or more extensible Digital Content Creation (DCC) platforms where they run in conjunction with other tools for animation, model generation, texture painting, compositing, simulation, and rendering. Software developers need to be aware of the difference between writing a stand-alone application that controls all memory and threading behavior, and writing a plugin for a larger environment.

Two common commercial platforms used at DWA are Houdini (Side Effects Software) and Maya (Autodesk). The good news is that generally speaking there is no problem writing plugins for either system that take advantage of threading using either of the programming models discussed above. In fact, both Maya and Houdini use TBB internally for threading and so this programming model integrates particularly well.

Houdini 12 introduced a number of convenience functions that wrap TBB to make parallel programming directly using the Houdini Development Kit (HDK) more developer friendly. SideFX also reorganized their geometry library to be more parallel and SIMD-friendly, with the result that parallel programming with the HDK can be quite efficient. For more details see Chapter 2, Houdini: Multithreading Existing Software.

In general, we structure code into libraries that are independent of any particular DCC application and plugins that isolate application-specific changes. Library code should never impose specific decisions about the number of threads to execute. We had problems with early library development using TBB where the scheduler was being reinitialized to a different thread pool size inside library functions. Since the scheduler is shared, this had the unintended side effect of changing performance of other unrelated code. It might be reasonable to introduce library code that switches to a serial implementation below some problem size where threading is not expected to produce any benefit, but any finer grained control of threading behavior inside a library function will be problematic when used in different applications.

Keep library code independent of thread count and leave the control of resources to the hosting application.

5.2.6 Performance

There are a few important concepts related to measuring and understanding performance for parallel applications.

Speedup compares the execution time of solving a problem with one "worker" versus P workers:

$$\text{speedup} = S_p = T_1/T_p, \tag{5.1}$$

where T_1 is the execution time with a single worker.

Efficiency is the speedup divided by the number of workers:

$$\text{efficiency} = \frac{S_p}{P} = \frac{T_1}{PT_p}. \tag{5.2}$$

Ideal efficiency would be 1 and we would get the full impact of adding more workers to a problem. With real problems this is never the case, and people often vastly overestimate parallel efficiency. Efficiency is a way to quantify and talk about the diminishing returns of using additional hardware for a given problem size.

Amdahl's Law relates the theoretical maximum speedup for a problem where a given fraction, f, of the work is inherently serial and cannot be parallelized, placing an upper bound on the possible speedup:

$$S_P \leq \frac{1}{f + (1 - f)/P}. \tag{5.3}$$

In real applications this can be severely limiting since it implies that the maximum speedup possible is $1/f$. For example, an application with $f = 0.1$ (90% of the work is perfectly parallel) has a maximum speedup of only 10. Practical considerations like I/O can often be crippling to performance unless they can be handled asynchronously. To get good parallel efficiency we try to reduce f to the smallest value possible.

Gustafson-Barsis' Law is the related observation that large speedups are still possible as long as problem sizes grow as computers become more powerful, and the serial fraction is only a weak function of problem size. In other words, f is not only a function of the algorithm or implementation, but also the problem size N. Scalability often improves with larger problems because the serial fraction of execution time gets smaller, that is, $f(N) \to 0$ as $N \to \infty$. This is often the case, and in visual effects it is not uncommon to solve problems that are $1000\times$ larger than what was considered practical just 5 years ago.

Asymptotic complexity is an approach to estimating how both memory and execution time vary with problem size. This is a key technique for comparing how various algorithms are expected to perform independent of any specific hardware.

Arithmetic intensity is a measure of the ratio of computation to communication (memory access) for a given algorithm. Memory continues to be a source of performance limitations for hardware and so algorithms with low arithmetic intensity will exhibit poor speedup even if they are perfectly parallel. The examples shown earlier of dot products and simple vector operations all have low arithmetic intensity, while algorithms like FFTs and dense matrix operations tend to have higher arithmetic intensity.

Try to start any algorithm development with expectations for asymptotic complexity and parallel efficiency, and then measure your performance on real hardware to make sure your implementation matches expectations.

5.3 Fluid Simulation

For the remainder of this chapter we will look at case studies for two simulation problems: algorithms for simulating smoke, fire, and explosions; and algorithms for simulation liquids. These are closely related but use different data structures and present different challenges for scalability.

5.3.1 Data Structures

Data structures can have a big impact on the complexity and scalability of a given algorithm. For the case studies in this chapter there are three data structures of particular importance: particles, volumes, and sparse grids.

Particles are one of the most general ways to represent spatial information. In general, particles will have common physical properties such as position and velocity, but they are often used to carry a large number of additional attributes around for bookkeeping. Houdini 12 provides a flexible API for managing general point attributes organized into a paged data structure for each attribute type. It is a great implementation to study as a balance of flexibility and performance.

Volumes represent an organization of data into a contiguous $N = N_x \times N_y \times N_z$ segment of memory. Data is stored in *volume elements* or *voxels*. Data can be read and written to the volume at an arbitrary (i, j, k)-coordinate as long as the indices are in bounds. Volumes can be implemented using simple data structures in C++ or using common libraries such as `boost::multiarray`. Normally, a volume will have a spatial transform associated with it to place the voxels into world space, allowing the world space position of any voxel to be computed without explicitly storing any position data. For dense data, the elimination of explicit positions is where the storage efficiency comes from relative to particles. If memory is allocated contiguously then operations on a volume can take place in an (i, j, k)-index space or by treating the voxel data like a single array of length N. Volumes support a simple form of data decomposition by partitioning work along any dimension (i, j, or k) or the entire index range N.

Dense volumes can cause problems with data locality since points close in index space may be far apart in physical memory, but this is often still the most convenient memory layout for simple problems.

Sparse Grids are a hybrid of particles and volumes. A sparse grid is a data structure that can store information at an arbitrary (i, j, k)-coordinate but only consumes memory proportional to the number of stored values. In order to achieve this a sparse grid might be organized into tiles that are allocated on demand, typically tracked with some other data structure like an octree, B-tree, or hash table. Houdini volumes are organized in this way, and the open source Field3D library provides both tiled and sparse volumes [66].

In this chapter, we will use OpenVDB [49] as a reference sparse grid data structure, shown schematically in Figure 5.1. OpenVDB uses a B+tree to encode the structure of the grid. This is a shallow binary tree with a large fan-out factor between levels. Voxel data is stored in leaf nodes organized into 8^3 tiles with a bit mask indicating which voxels have been set. Internal nodes store bit masks to indicate whether any of their children contain filled values. The root node can grow as large as memory requires in order to accommodate an effectively infinite index space. Data in an OpenVDB grid is spatially coherent, meaning that neighbors in index space are generally stored close together in physical memory simply because of the organization into tiles. See Museth [48] for more details on the advantages of this data structure.

FIGURE 5.1: (Top) Schematic of the OpenVDB data structure for sparse volumes [48] and (bottom) a typical cloud model stored as a sparse volume. The data structure consists of a tree starting with a *root node*, one or more *internal nodes*, and finally *leaf nodes* that store the volume data, for example, density. Existing values can be accessed in parallel, but inserting new values is not threadsafe. However, OpenVDB supports a number of important parallel algorithms. **(See Color Insert.)**

Sparse grids are important for achieving the memory savings required for high-resolution simulations and volumetric models. The cloud model shown in Figure 5.1 has an equivalent dense volume of $N = 16384 \times 2048 \times 1024$, or about $N \approx 35$ billion voxels. Models at this resolution would be impractical to store with dense volumes. However, sparse volume data structures present some interesting challenges and opportunities for parallel computing. Writes to an OpenVDB grid are inherently not threadsafe since each write requires (potentially) allocating tiles and updating bit masks for tracking. In practice, we can implement many parallel operations either by preallocating result grids on a single thread or by writing results into a separate grid per thread and then merging the final results using a parallel reduction. This is more efficient than it sounds because often entire branches of the B+tree can be moved from one grid to another during a reduction with simple pointer copies (as opposed to data copies). If branches of the tree do collide then a traversal is triggered that ultimately may result in merging individual leaf nodes. Reads from an OpenVDB grid are always threadsafe and parallel computations can be scheduled by iterating over active

FIGURE 5.2: Volume rendering of a large dust cloud simulated with a resolution of $N = 1200 \times 195 \times 500$ along with a final frame from the movie *Megamind* [65]. **(See Color Insert.)**

voxels or active tiles. The latter is generally most efficient since each tile represents up to 512 voxels. Optimized implementations of these operations are supported in the OpenVDB library along with many examples of basic kernels for simulation and volumetric processing.

5.3.2 Smoke, Fire, and Explosions

Fluid simulation is an important category of effect, representing as much as 23–35% of the shot work in feature films at DWA from 2008–2013. Figure 5.2 shows an example of a large-scale destruction shot from the movie *Megamind*, and Figure 5.3 shows additional examples of a simulated torch fire and pyroclastic dust from *The Croods*. These effects are produced by Flux, our general purpose fluid simulation framework [32]. Flux uses adaptively resized dense grids to store simulation variables such as velocity, force fields, and active scalars representing smoke, temperature, and so forth, and incorporates a number of algorithms that are of general use for simulated transport problems.

Motion in the system is determined by solving a modified form of the incompressible Navier-Stokes equations:

$$\nabla \cdot \vec{u} \;=\; D \tag{5.4}$$

FIGURE 5.3: (Top) Simulated torch fire and (bottom) high-resolution pyroclastic dust and destruction from *The Croods*. **(See Color Insert.)**

$$\frac{\partial \vec{u}}{\partial t} + (\vec{u} \cdot \nabla)\vec{u} \quad = \quad -\frac{1}{\rho}\nabla p + \nu\nabla^2\vec{u} - \gamma\vec{u} + \vec{F} \tag{5.5}$$

where $\vec{u}$ is the fluid velocity, ρ is the fluid density, p is the pressure, ν is the kinematic viscosity, and γ is a momentum dissipation rate per unit mass. The field $D(\vec{x}, t)$ is a divergence control term used to create local sources and sinks of velocity. The field $\vec{F}(\vec{x}, t)$ represents an arbitrary force per unit mass. We simultaneously solve for some number of scalar fields ϕ_i using the general transport system given by:

$$\frac{\partial \phi_i}{\partial t} + (\vec{u} \cdot \nabla)\phi_i \quad = \quad \mu_i\nabla^2\phi_i - \gamma_i\phi_i + E_i \tag{5.6}$$

where the constants γ_i and μ_i describe the dissipation and diffusion of ϕ_i, respectively, and may be defined separately for any scalar field. The field $E_i(\vec{x}, t)$ controls emission or absorption of ϕ_i.

The scalar fields ϕ_i may represent smoke, temperature, fuel, color components, or any other quantity that an artist wishes to animate, and the framework allows an arbitrary number of such fields to be animated simultaneously. The values of these fields animated over time are the primary output of the system.

We integrate the fluid equations in the following stages:

$$\vec{u}^{(0)} = \text{advect}(\vec{u}^n, \Delta t, \vec{u}^n) + \Delta t \vec{F}^n \tag{5.7}$$

$$\vec{u}^{(1)} = \text{compose}(\vec{\mathbf{u}}^{(0)}, \vec{\mathbf{U}}_{\text{coll}}, \alpha_{\text{coll}}) \tag{5.8}$$

$$\vec{u}^{(2)} = \vec{u}^{(1)} - \Delta t \frac{1}{\rho} \nabla p \tag{5.9}$$

$$\vec{u}^{n+1} = \vec{u}^{(2)} + \nu \Delta t \nabla^2 \vec{u}^{n+1} - \gamma \Delta t \vec{u}^{n+1} \tag{5.10}$$

Taking the divergence of Equation (5.9) and requiring that $\vec{u}^{(2)}$ satisfy the divergence specified in Equation (5.4) gives the following Poisson equation for the pressure:

$$\nabla^2 p = \frac{\rho}{\Delta t} \left[\nabla \cdot \vec{u}^{(1)} - D \right] \tag{5.11}$$

In the case of $D = 0$, this is a variant of the method of fractional steps with the diffusion and dissipation handled in the last stage [40, 38]. Diffusion requires the solution of a similar elliptic problem:

$$(\nabla^2 - \frac{1 + \gamma \Delta t}{\nu \Delta t}) \vec{u}^{n+1} = -\frac{1}{\nu \Delta t} \vec{u}^{(2)} \tag{5.12}$$

Once the velocity field $\vec{u}^{n+1}$ is known, we can solve the transport equations for each scalar field using a similar integration scheme:

$$\phi_i^{(0)} = \text{advect}(\phi_i^n, \Delta t, \vec{u}^{n+1}) + \Delta t E_i \tag{5.13}$$

$$\phi_i^{(1)} = \text{compose}(\phi_i^{(0)}, S_i, \alpha_i) \tag{5.14}$$

$$\phi_i^{n+1} = \phi_i^{(1)} + \mu_i \Delta t \nabla^2 \phi_i^{n+1} - \gamma_i \Delta t \phi_i^{n+1} \tag{5.15}$$

The transport system is integrated independently for each scalar field ϕ_i. Note that the algorithms for integrating the fluid velocity and scalar transport are identical with the exception of Equation (5.9). This symmetry is deliberate and emphasizes that the fluid and transport algorithms are built from the same set of basic solvers.

The function advect($\phi, \Delta t, \vec{u}$) must implement some algorithm to integrate the homogeneous advection equation:

$$\frac{\partial \phi}{\partial t} + (\vec{u} \cdot \nabla)\phi = 0 \tag{5.16}$$

over a time step Δt. Possible choices for this implementation are described below.

The function compose (u, v, α) provides an important form of artistic control as it allows direct modification of the simulation state during each time step. Common operations include methods like "over," which are covered in Section 5.2.1, but others are possible. For simplicity, the integration scheme above is written for a single set of input volumes, but this is trivially extended to multiple input volumes.

5.3.2.1 Advection Solvers

We implement advect($q, \Delta t, \vec{u}$) using a family of semi-Lagrangian advection schemes. These methods have the common characteristic that they can be made unconditionally stable with respect to the time step Δt either by construction or through the application of an appropriate limiting technique.

We provide support for first order semi-Lagrangian [61], semi-Lagrangian with 2-stage and 3-stage Runge-Kutta schemes for path tracing, a modified MacCormack scheme with a local minmax limiter [59], and Back and Forth Error Compensation and Correction (BFECC) [20, 39]. All of these methods have linear complexity in the number of grid points, but may differ in overall cost by a factor of two to five depending on the number of interpolations required. They are easily parallelizable and show linear speedup with increasing numbers of workers for sufficiently high resolution. Methods like BFECC are attractive for fluid simulation because they are unconditionally stable and simple to implement.

Here is a straightforward implementation of BFECC using OpenMP. We start with a method that implements first-order semi-Lagrangian advection:

```
void advectSL(const float dt,
              const VectorVolume& v,
              const ScalarVolume& phiN,
              ScalarVolume& phiN1)
{
  const Vec3i res = v.resolution();

  // phi_n+1 = L phi_n

#pragma omp parallel_for
  for (size_t x = 0; x < res.x(); ++x) {
    for (size_t y = 0; y < res.y(); ++y) {
      for size_t z = 0;  z < res.z(); ++z) {
        const Vec3i coord(x, y, z);
        const Vec3s velocity = v.getValue(coord);
        const Vec3s pos = Vec3s(coord) - dt * velocity;
        phiN1.setValue(coord, sample(phiN, pos));
      }
    }
  }
}
```

We interpolate values from one grid and write them to another. Clearly, there is no contention on writes and we can thread over the grid dimension that varies slowest in memory. BFECC is then built from three applications of this function:

```
void advectBFECC(const float dt,
                 const VectorVolume& v,
                 const ScalarVolume& phiN,
                 ScalarVolume& phiN1,
                 ScalarVolume& work1,
                 ScalarVolume& work2)
{
    // Local notation
    ScalarVolume& phiHatN1 = work1;
    ScalarVolume& phiHatN  = work2;
    ScalarVolume& phiBarN  = work2;

    // phi^_n+1 = L phi_n
    advectSL(dt, v, phiN, phiHatN1);

    // phi^_n = L^R phi^_n+1
    advectSL(-dt, v, phiHatN1, phiHatN);
```

```
// phiBar_n = (3 phi_n - phi^n ) / 2

#pragma omp parallel_for
    for(size_t i=0; i< phiN.size(); ++i) {
        phiBarN.setValue(i, 1.5f*phiN.getValue(i) -
                              0.5f*phiHatN.getValue(i)));
    }

    // phi_n+1 = L phiBar_n
    advectSL(dt, v, phiBarN, phiN1);

    // Apply limiter
    limit(v, phiN, phiN1);
}
```

The function `limit()` applies some rule to deal with any newly created extrema in the advected scalar in order to guarantee that all new values are bounded by values at the previous time step. The middle step can treat the grids like flat arrays since the operation is independent of position.

In Figure 5.4, we show speedup measurements for solving the linear advection equation (5.16). We advect an initial scalar field in the shape of a smoothed sphere through a velocity field computed from curl noise [7]. Most of the work is in the `sample()` method, and here we just use trilinear interpolation. The equivalent implementation in TBB is straightforward, and in this figure we compare the speedup behavior of the two programming models to confirm that for large problems they have essentially identical performance. From this set of measurements we can also determine that this implementation performs like an equivalent ideal implementation with $f = 0.025$, which allows us to predict the maximum speedup and parallel efficiency for different configurations. This serial fraction is higher than you might expect from looking at the implementation. It reveals what might be a hidden fragment of serial code inside the `limit()` function or simply the overhead of the threading runtime.

5.3.2.2 Elliptic Solvers

Note that Equations (5.10), (5.11), and (5.15) can all be written in the form:

$$(\nabla^2 - \lambda^2)\phi = f \tag{5.17}$$

where λ^2 is a constant. In general, we need to solve this with either Dirichlet ($\phi = g$) or Neumann ($\vec{n} \cdot \nabla \phi = h$) boundary conditions applied to grid points on the external faces of the domain. For $\lambda > 0$, this is referred to as the Helmholtz equation, and for $\lambda = 0$ the Poisson equation. Solving this equation for a discrete volume amounts to solving a large, sparse linear system, and selecting the method to use for this step has a critical impact on performance of the overall framework.

The solution techniques most commonly invoked in the computer graphics literature are the conjugate gradient method (CG) and multigrid (MG). Both are iterative techniques that require no explicit representation of the matrix. For constant-coefficient problems like the ones required here, we can also consider techniques based on the FFT. This is a direct method that takes advantage of the fact that the Helmholtz equation can be solved independently for each Fourier mode. A common misconception about FFT-based methods is

FIGURE 5.4: Speedup curve for scalar advection on a grid with $N = 512^3$ grid points using the BFECC advection kernel. The dashed line shows the theoretical speedup for an algorithm with a serial fraction of $f = 0.025$. Performance was measured on a desktop system with dual Intel Xeon Processors E5-2687W (20M Cache, 3.10 GHz) using up to 16 computational threads.

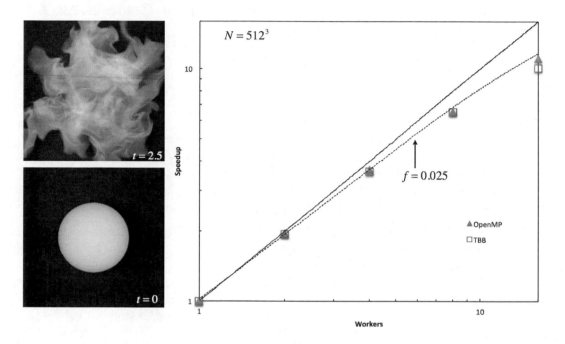

Algorithm	Type	Serial Time	PRAM Time
SOR	Iterative	$N^{3/2}$	$N^{1/2}$
CG	Iterative	$N^{3/2}$	$N^{1/2} \log N$
Multigrid	Iterative	N	$(\log N)^2$
FFT	Direct	$N \log N$	$\log N$
Lower Bound		N	$\log N$

TABLE 5.2: Asymptotic complexity for several common methods used to solve the discrete Poisson problem [16].

that they are restricted to problems with periodic boundary conditions, but by using appropriate sine or cosine expansions they can be used to solve problems with general boundary conditions. A good overview of all three methods is available in the scientific computing literature [56], with additional details on MG available from Briggs et al. [8].

No serial method can be faster than $O(N)$ since it must visit each grid point at least once. MG is the only serial method that achieves this scaling. On an idealized machine with $P = N$ processors, scaling depends on the amount of parallelism that can be exploited in the algorithm. The lower bound is $O(\log N)$ because this is the minimal time to propagate information across the domain via parallel reduction. The FFT-based solver is the only method that achieves this scaling. CG is slower than the best method by a factor of $N^{1/2}$ in both cases and will not be considered further. The key observation is this: for large problems the optimal serial algorithm is MG, while the optimal parallel algorithm is an FFT-based solver.

However, these estimates are only for the overall scaling. Actual performance will depend on the details of the hardware platform. As a benchmark problem we compute the solution to the Poisson problem with zero Dirichlet boundary conditions on the unit cube. Times are measured on a workstation with dual Intel Processors X5670 (12M cache, 2.93 GHz), which support up to 12 hardware threads.

The MG solver is compiled using the Intel 12 vectorizing Fortran compiler with optimization level 3. The MG solver uses a W(2,1) cycle with a vectorized Gauss-Sidel iteration for residual relaxation at each grid level [2]. MG iterations are limited to five complete cycles, which is enough to reduce the relative change between fine grid iterations to less than 1×10^{-5} in all cases reported. Fine grid resolution is restricted to powers-of-two multiples of a fixed coarse grid resolution. FFT-based solution timings use the Helmholtz solver interface in the Intel Math Kernel Library [34]. This interface provides a "black box" solver for the Helmholtz equation on grids with arbitrary resolutions using prime factorization, but is most efficient for power-of-two grid points. This is a direct technique that produces the solution to machine precision in a fixed number of operations independent of the right-hand side and therefore has no iteration parameters. Both implementations use OpenMP for shared memory parallelism [53].

In Figure 5.5, we show the measured solve times for the above benchmark case for problem sizes from $N = 16^3$ to $N = 1024^3$, which covers the problem sizes of practical interest for visual effects production. Both methods scale as expected with problem size, but the FFT-based solver is almost an order of magnitude faster for a given number of grid points. In fact, the FFT-based solver produces a solution to machine precision in less time than a single MG cycle. Figure 5.6 shows the parallel speedup for both solvers, and as expected the FFT-based solver also has much better parallel efficiency. Note that the MG solve times and parallel efficiencies reported here are consistent with the recent work of McAdams et al. [45] for similar problem sizes and hardware.

These measurements confirm that even for a relatively small number of processing cores there is a significant performance advantage to using the FFT-based solver over MG. Although the MG solver can be applied to a much more general class of elliptic problems, it is an order of magnitude more expensive. They also confirm that the FFT-based technique has better parallel scaling and efficiency, as expected. Since all of the elliptic solves required in this framework are by design suitable for the use of FFT-based techniques, this is the method used exclusively. This includes the solution to the pressure Poisson problem, and the implicit diffusion step for both fluid velocity and scalar transport. This is the single most important choice affecting performance of the fluid integration algorithm.

Measure performance over a range of problem sizes in order to estimate parallel scalability and identify any bottlenecks that appear at large or small N.

5.3.3   Liquids

Liquid simulation is closely related to the techniques that we use for smoke and fire, but with the additional complication of free surface boundary conditions and the need to explicitly track a surface. In most cases the objective of a liquid simulation is to produce a highly detailed surface representation, with little or no regard for the bulk flow above or beneath the surface. Figure 5.7 shows a close-up of a detailed liquid surface and a full

FIGURE 5.5: Comparison of solve times for the Poisson equation with N total grid points using MG and FFT solution techniques. The solid curves confirm the expected asymptotic scaling. Runtimes are measured on a workstation with dual Intel Xeon Processors X5670 using 12 computational threads.

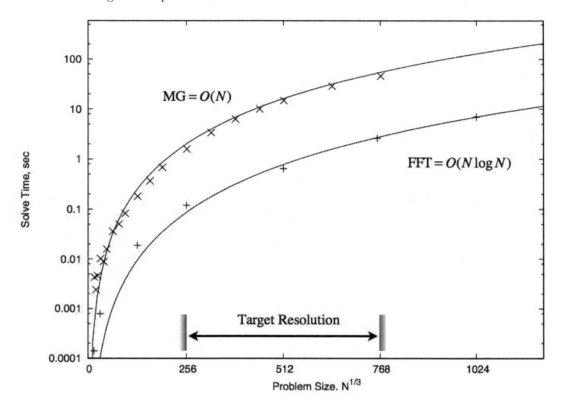

production render from *The Croods* to illustrate the basic challenge. This focus on the thin region marking the interface means that the data structures and algorithms used for liquid simulation can be quite different from the techniques discussed in Section 5.3.2.

Multiple approaches are possible, but the most popular is to use a hybrid particle and grid-based method. These are generally variants of the marker-in-cell or particle-in-cell (PIC) approaches that originated in the early work on compressible flow [31, 30]. These methods were adapted for some of the first systems used in computer graphics for animation and film production [25, 26]. One of the more recent algorithmic changes to find its way into computer graphics is the Fluid Implicit Particle (FLIP) method, introduced to overcome some of the problems with numerical dissipation observed in simpler advection algorithms [5, 67, 6].

The data model in these approaches is as follows. Particles are used to represent the liquid, and a sparse grid is used as an intermediate data structure to perform operations such as pressure projection or viscous diffusion that run more efficiently on the grid. This is shown schematically in Figure 5.8. Sparse grids are important because the grid data representing a liquid typically covers a highly irregular or highly localized region of space. In addition to the algorithms discussed above that must run efficiently on a grid (diffusion, pressure projection), we also need to consider efficient methods for transferring information between the particle and grid representations of fields like velocity.

FIGURE 5.6: Parallel speedup for the FFT-based Poisson solver (top) and MG Poisson solver (bottom) for various grid resolutions.

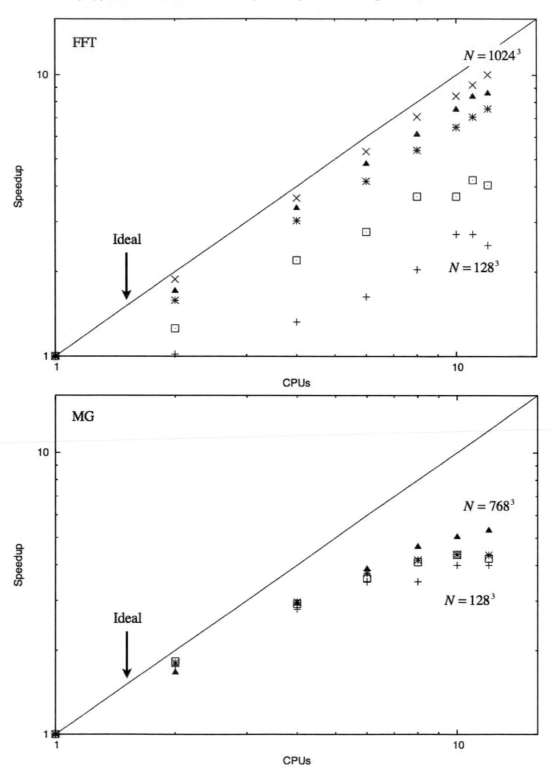

FIGURE 5.7: (Top) Surface details of a simulated liquid integrated with a surrounding procedural ocean surface, and (bottom) production shot from *The Croods* with character integration and final lighting [9]. **(See Color Insert.)**

The mathematical model for liquids is identical to the equations of motion given in Equations (5.4)–(5.5), but the time integration algorithm is quite different. We start with a set of particles with known positions and velocities $(x_p, \vec{u}_p)$ representing the current state of the liquid. We then compute the corresponding values on a grid:

$$\vec{u}_m = \sum_{p=1}^{N} W(x_m - x_p)\vec{u}_p, \tag{5.18}$$

where W is a smoothing kernel. In practice, W will be compact so each particle will only influence a small set of neighboring grid points, and is often implicitly tied to the voxel size h of the grid. We then run similar stages as above except for velocity advection:

$$\vec{u}^{(0)} = \vec{u}_m, \tag{5.19}$$

$$\vec{u}^{(1)} = \vec{u}^{(0)} + \Delta t \vec{F}^n, \tag{5.20}$$

$$\vec{u}^{(2)} = \vec{u}^{(1)} - \Delta t \frac{1}{\rho} \nabla p, \tag{5.21}$$

FIGURE 5.8: Schematic of the data structure used for liquid simulations. We maintain a hybrid data structure using both particle data $(x_p, \vec{u}_p)$ and sparse grid data $(x_m, \vec{u}_m)$, where h is a fixed voxel size.

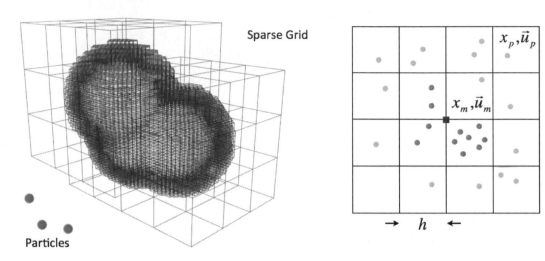

$$\vec{u}^{(3)} \quad = \quad \vec{u}^{(2)} + \nu \Delta t \nabla^2 \vec{u}^{(3)} - \gamma \Delta t \vec{u}^{(3)}. \tag{5.22}$$

Finally, we add the interpolated velocity difference $\Delta U = \vec{u}^{(3)} - \vec{u}^{(0)}$ to the velocity at each particle position and use an ordinary differential equation solver to get new particle positions, taking into account any collisions or other desired particle behaviors.

In the above time integration algorithm we still need to solve elliptic equations for the pressure and viscous diffusion steps. However, these will now need to be solved on a highly irregular domain with more complex boundary conditions than we considered before. In our internal implementation we use CG iteration with an Incomplete Cholesky preconditioner for these elliptic systems [6]. This has limited parallelism, but for moderate resolution this is not the bottleneck for performance. In our internal implementation with systems having a grid resolution of $N = O(10^6)$ particles, pressure projection only represents about 15% of the total simulation time. For higher resolution this may not be the case, and other techniques based on CG or MG preconditioning may be preferred [45].

5.3.3.1   Parallel Point Rasterization

Evaluating Equation (5.18) turns out to be the performance bottleneck in our liquid solver, representing about 40% of the overall simulation time. We refer to this problem as *point rasterization* or *point splatting*. The general problem is to compute the interpolation of some field value ϕ_p defined at irregular particle locations x_p onto the regular grid points x_m:

$$\phi_m = \sum_{p=1}^{N} W(x_m - x_p)\phi_p.$$

We can implement this method in two ways, which we will refer to as *gather* or *scatter* based on the pattern of data access.

The gather approach is to iterate over the grid points, find the overlapping particles based on the specific choice of W, and then sum their contributions exactly as written above. We *gather* the value of several particle locations into a single grid point. If we know the location of each grid point then we should be able to compute the field value ϕ_m in parallel with no locking. There are a few challenges with this approach. If the grid is sparse and created dynamically from the current set of particles, then we may not know the necessary grid points in advance. Even if we know the grid points, we need a fast method to locate all nearby particles. This can be implemented using an acceleration structure such as a k-dimensional tree, but we need to either construct or update this acceleration structure at the beginning of each time step. We can write the pseudocode for this operation as follows:

```
for each grid point m:
  for each particle i in neighborhood(x_grid[m]):
    phi_grid[m] += W(x_grid[m] - x_pa[i]) * phi_pa[i]
```

The scatter approach is to iterate over the particles, find the overlapping grid points, and then sum the contribution of the particle into each grid point. We *scatter* the contribution of each particle onto all overlapping grid points. This has several advantages. Computing the location of the overlapping grid points is trivial, usually some fixed number of grid points along each axis depending on W. We do not need to construct or maintain an acceleration data structure. However, many nearby particles can contribute to the same grid points, so we need some strategy for either separating particles to prevent overlap or locking access to the grid values to prevent overwriting previous results. We can write the pseudocode for this operation as follows:

```
for each particle i:
  for each grid point m in neighborhood(x_pa[i]):
    phi_grid[m] += W(x_grid[m] - x_pa[i]) * phi_pa[i]
```

The inner loop in these two approaches is the same, but the order of the outer loops is reversed and the implications for good parallel performance are dramatically different. Because they can be implemented with minimal locking, implementation patterns based on gather are generally preferred for parallel computing [46]. However, in this case we have an elegant implementation of the scatter approach using TBB and OpenVDB.

The basic strategy is to create a separate sparse grid for each thread and rasterize a subrange of particle velocities into that grid, then use a binary reduction to combine results from each subrange into a single output. This is shown schematically in Figure 5.9, where we illustrate rasterizing a subrange of particles on two independent threads. As mentioned above, OpenVDB supports fast operations to combine grids that take advantage of its tree structure. The reduction can be performed with minimal work in areas of the grids that do not overlap, and areas that do overlap the reductions can still be processed pair-wise in parallel. The OpenVDB library provides optimized implementations of various reduction kernels to support these types of operations.

We can express the entire operation using a simple TBB reduction. Here is the parallel implementation of the point rasterization algorithm for particle velocities:

```
class PaToGrid
{
  const PaList& mPa;    // Input locations and velocities
  VectorGrid& mV;       // Output grid velocities

public:
  PaToGrid(const PaList& pa, VectorGrid& v)
      : mPa(pa), mV(v) {}
  PaToGrid(const PaToGrid& other, tbb::split)
```

```
     : mPa(other.mPa), mV(other.mV.copy()) {}

  // Rasterize particle velocities into grid v

  void operator()(const tbb::blocked_range<size_t>& r)
  {
      for (size_t i = r.begin(); i < r.end(); ++i) {
          const Vec3s pos = mPa.getPos(i);
          const Vec3s vel = mPa.getVel(i);
          scatter(mV, pos, vel);
      }
  }

  // Merge grids from separate threads

  void join(const PaToGrid& other) {
      openvdb::tools::compSum(mV, other.mV);
  }
};

// Execute particle rasterization
PaToGrid op(pa, v);
tbb::parallel_reduce
  (tbb::blocked_range<size_t>(0, pa.size()), op);
```

Note that we have hidden the inner rasterization loop (the loop over grid points) in the function scatter(). The implementation details are not important to understand the parallel implementation. The function openvdb::tools::compSum() is a built-in reduction method

FIGURE 5.9: Schematic of parallel point rasterization into separate grids for threads T_0 and T_1, and then a final reduction to combine the results. In OpenVDB, areas with no overlap on separate threads can be combined without any data copies, but even overlapping areas can be processed pair-wise in parallel.

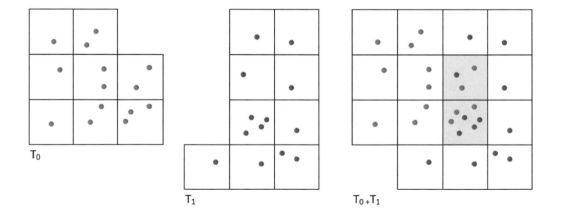

that combines two grids by summing the values of any overlapping grid points. The above approach allows the rasterization to execute without the need for any locks.

Performance will also be affected by the choice of the smoothing kernel W. We will consider two of the common smoothing kernels defined in the literature: a low-order B-spline (BSP2) and the M_4' function (MP4) [47]. The BSP2 kernel is defined as

$$B_2 = \begin{cases} 0 & \text{if } r > 1 \\ 1 - r & \text{if } 1 \geq r \end{cases}$$

where $r = |x_m - x_p|/h$ is the normalized distance from the particle to the grid point. Using this kernel, a particle only affects only the neighboring $2 \times 2 \times 2 = 8$ grid points. The MP4 kernel is defined as

$$M_4' = \begin{cases} 0 & \text{if } r > 2 \\ \frac{1}{2}(2 - r^2)(1 - r) & \text{if } 1 \leq r \leq 2. \\ 1 - \frac{5}{2}r^2 + \frac{3}{2}r^3 & \text{if } 1 \geq r \end{cases}$$

Using this kernel, a particle affects $4 \times 4 \times 4 = 64$ grid points and each kernel weight is more expensive to compute. These kernels provide different levels of accuracy for interpolating particle data onto the grid. In general, more accurate kernels require spreading particle contributions over a wider set of grid points. These kernels are interesting to compare because of the differences in arithmetic complexity associated with processing each particle.

Figure 5.10 shows speedups for a benchmark problem with $N = 446$ million points rasterized into a grid with a final effective resolution of more than 800^3. The particle positions are randomly distributed within a spherical region with an average overlap of about 10 particles per voxel, similar to the target density used for liquid simulations. Note that the scaling for the MP4 kernel is significantly better ($f = 0.04$) than the simpler BSP2 kernel ($f = 0.18$), a result of the higher arithmetic complexity associated with this kernel. The BSP2 kernel is limited by memory bandwidth and only achieves a maximum speedup of $S \approx 5$, which is also about the maximum speedup we observe for our internal liquid simulation framework using BSP2. Scalability can impact the choice of which approach is ultimately more efficient. For example, at $P = 1$ the simpler BSP2 kernel runs $10\times$ faster than MP4, but at $P = 32$ they practically break even.

Parallel scalability may determine the optimal method to use for simulation algorithms. Serial algorithms that seem impractical because of higher arithmetic complexity may have better scalability and ultimately be the best choice for multicore systems.

The above benchmark, with points scattered randomly, is a worst case for this algorithm because it maximizes the amount of overlap in the independent grids created on each thread. It should be possible to improve performance by ordering particles to minimize overlap, but the overhead of maintaining particle order must be balanced against any improvement in parallel scalability. Exploring these options as well as comparing to equivalent gather-type implementations is a subject of future work.

FIGURE 5.10: Speedup curve for velocity rasterization from $N = 446$ million points into a $N = 836^3$ (effective resolution) sparse grid using a high-order (MP4) and low-order (BSP2) kernel. Runtimes are measured on a workstation with dual Intel Xeon Processors E5-2687W (20M Cache, 3.10 GHz) using up to 16 computational threads.

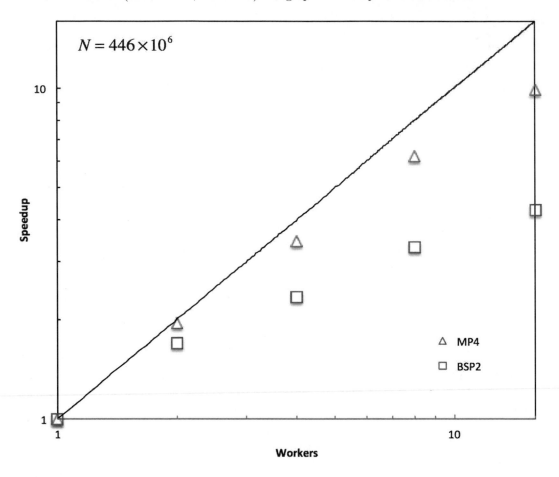

5.4 Summary

We have reviewed some of the history and current hardware choices driving algorithm and tool development at DreamWorks Animation. We presented case studies of computational kernels for fluid simulation to illustrate the relationship between hardware, algorithms, and data structures.

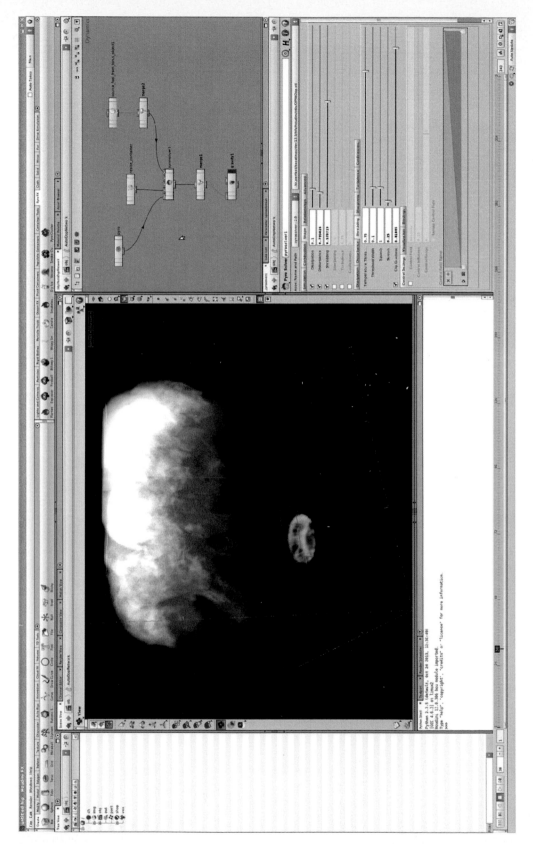

FIGURE 2.1: Screenshot of a simulation running in Houdini.

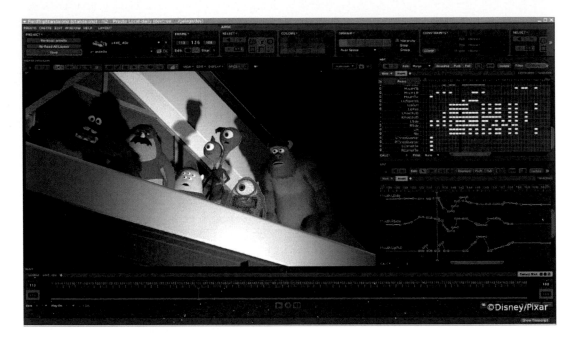

FIGURE 3.1: Screenshot of a session in Presto, Pixar's proprietary animation system. Presto provides an integrated environment that supports rigging and animation workflows, among others. The editors shown here (the spline editor and the spreadsheet editor) are commonly used for animation. Chapter 3 describes Presto's execution system, which is responsible for posing the characters and other such computations at interactive rates.

FIGURE 4.1: Animator working interactively on a character in Premo.

FIGURE 4.2: Detail from a still frame from the DreamWorks movie *How to Train Your Dragon 2*, showing character animation generated using the parallel dependency graph engine LibEE running in Premo. This is the first movie to be released that was animated using this engine.

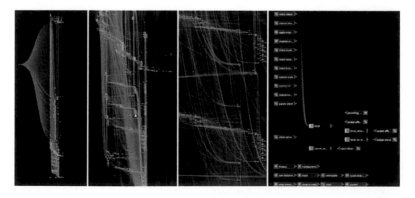

FIGURE 4.3: A typical hero character graph. The leftmost panel is the full graph. Each panel to the right is a zoomed-in region showing a small part of the graph view to the left of it. This graph has over 100k nodes.

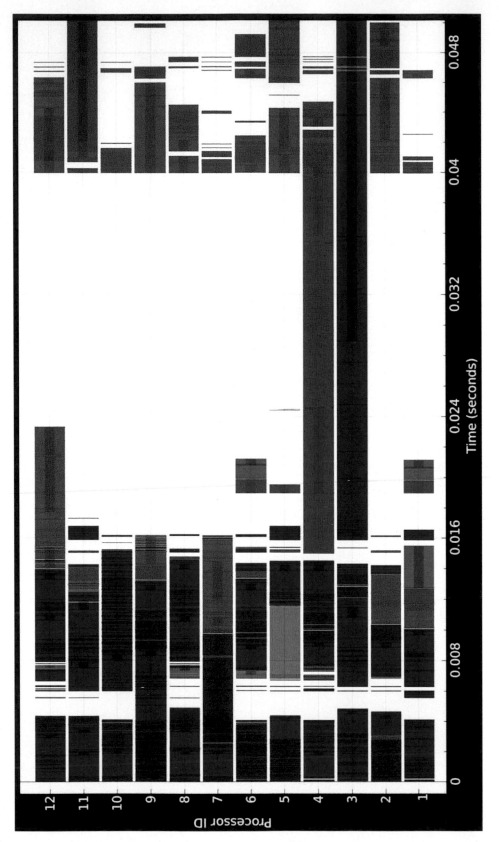

FIGURE 4.4: Tasks plotted against processor ID for a 12 core system. Note the two chains of nodes on cores 3 and 4, respectively, between 0.016s and 0.04s. These nodes have a consistent color along each chain, indicating they are from the same part of the character, and closer inspection shows that they are serially dependent. Because of this dependency they are explicitly treated as a single TBB task and so scheduled on the same processor core, thereby maximizing cache reuse along the chain.

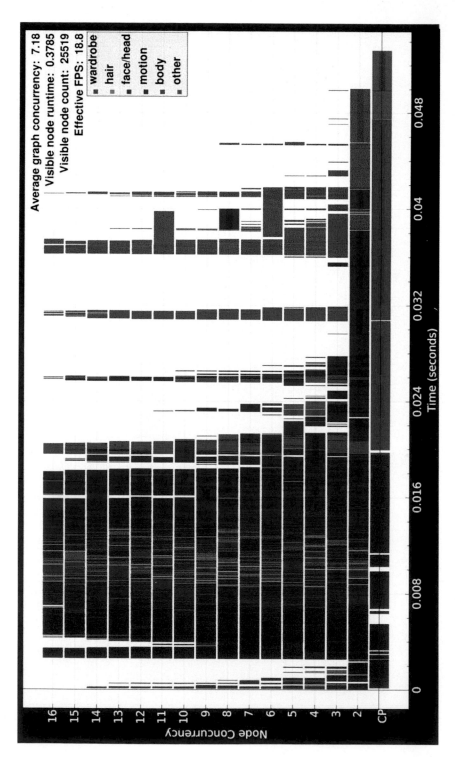

FIGURE 4.8: The threading visualization tool enables riggers to investigate bottlenecks within the graph. The vertical axis shows concurrent nodes in flight for various parts of the characters. The horizontal axis is time. Each block is a single node in the graph. Nodes with internal parallelism are displayed with a horizontal bar through them. Different components are drawn in different colors (e.g., body, face, wardrobe, and hair). The average concurrency reported only represents graph parallelism and does not include node parallelism. The bottom row of nodes are the nodes on the critical path. This character is running on a 16 core machine.

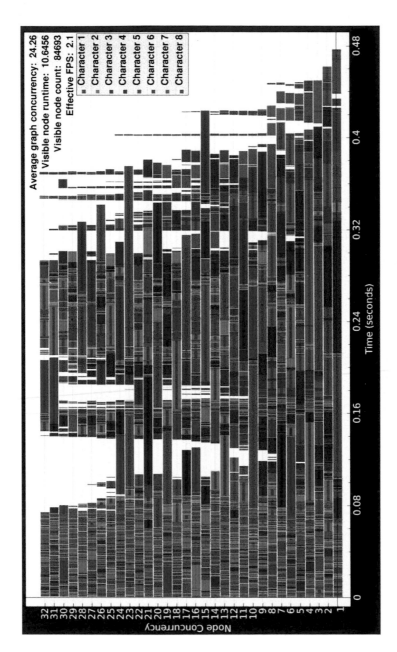

FIGURE 4.14: Evaluation of a single frame of animation for eight independent hero characters on a 32 core machine. The various shades represent different characters. All the characters evaluate concurrently, exhibiting an additional layer of parallelism in scene evaluation above node and character graph threading.

FIGURE 5.1: (Top) Schematic of the OpenVDB data structure for sparse volumes [49] and (bottom) a typical cloud model stored as a sparse volume. The data structure consists of a tree starting with a *root node*, one or more *internal nodes*, and finally *leaf nodes* that store the volume data, for example, density. Existing values can be accessed in parallel, but inserting new values is not threadsafe. However, OpenVDB supports a number of important parallel algorithms.

FIGURE 5.2: Volume rendering of a large dust cloud simulated with a resolution of $N = 1200 \times 195 \times 500$ along with a final frame from the movie *Megamind* [68].

FIGURE 5.3: (Top) Simulated torch fire and (bottom) high-resolution pyroclastic dust and destruction from *The Croods*.

FIGURE 5.7: (Top) Surface details of a simulated liquid integrated with a surrounding procedural ocean surface, and (bottom) production shot from *The Croods* with character integration and final lighting [9].

FIGURE 6.21: Bullet Physics rigid body benchmark, 112k box stack on a GPU simulated in 70 ms/frame.

FIGURE 6.22: Bullet Physics GPU rigid body benchmark, 64k boxes colliding with a concave trimesh, simulated in 100 ms/frame.

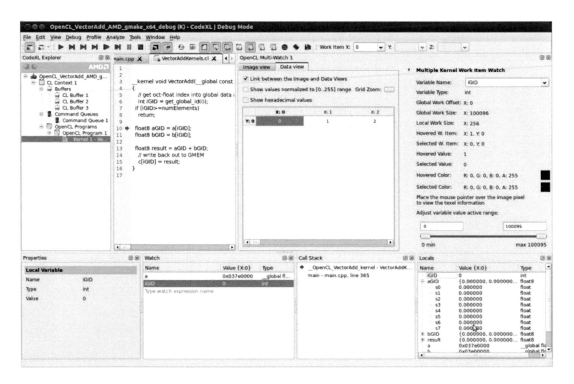

FIGURE 6.23: AMD CodeXL tool used to debug an OpenCL kernel under Linux. It enables the inspection of variables, adding of breakpoints, and stepping through a kernel. You can select any of the active work items.

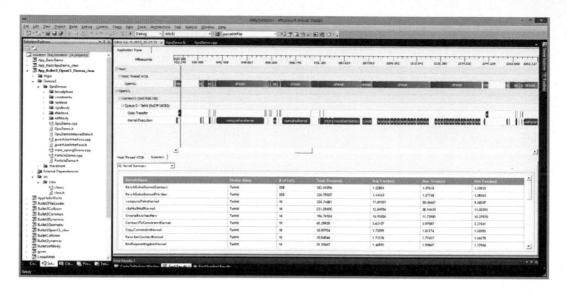

FIGURE 6.24: AMD CodeXL tool used to profile an OpenCL kernel under Windows in Microsoft Visual Studio.

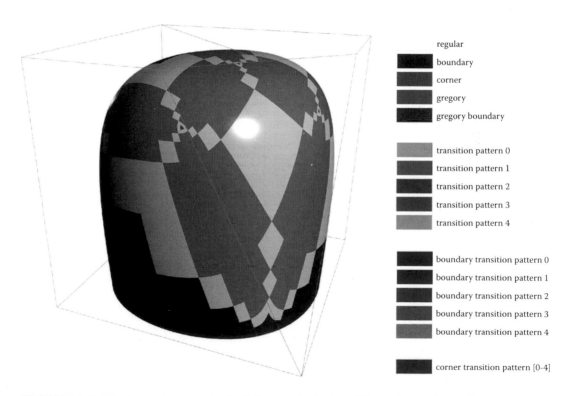

regular
boundary
corner
gregory
gregory boundary

transition pattern 0
transition pattern 1
transition pattern 2
transition pattern 3
transition pattern 4

boundary transition pattern 0
boundary transition pattern 1
boundary transition pattern 2
boundary transition pattern 3
boundary transition pattern 4

corner transition pattern [0-4]

FIGURE 7.25: Adaptive topological feature isolation. The color coding illustrates how the different types of patches are used to isolate boundaries or extraordinary vertices.

FIGURE 7.28: Wireframe showing the triangles generated by the GPU tessellation unit. Fractional patch tessellation allows for a continuous screen-space level of detail without cracks at the patch boundaries.

FIGURE 7.34: Mudbox sculpture showing analytical displacement with GPU hardware tessellation for interactive animation. Color and displacement textures are stored in the Ptex format.

Chapter 6

Bullet Physics: Simulation with OpenCL

Erwin Coumans

Bullet Physics

6.1		Introduction	138
	6.1.1	Rigid Body Dynamics Simulation	138
	6.1.2	Refactoring before the Full Rewrite	139
6.2		Rewriting from Scratch Using OpenCL	140
	6.2.1	Brief OpenCL Introduction	140
	6.2.2	Exploiting the GPU	142
	6.2.3	Dealing with Branchy Code/Thread Divergence	143
	6.2.4	Serializing Data to Contiguous Memory	144
	6.2.5	Sharing CPU and GPU Code	144
	6.2.6	Precompiled Kernel Caching	145
6.3		GPU Spatial Acceleration Structures	145
	6.3.1	Reference All Pairs Overlap Test	146
	6.3.2	Uniform Grid	147
	6.3.3	Parallel 1-Axis Sort and Sweep	148
	6.3.4	Parallel 3-Axis Sweep and Prune	149
	6.3.5	Hybrid Approaches	150
	6.3.6	Static Local Space AABB Tree	150
6.4		GPU Contact Point Generation	151
	6.4.1	Collision Shape Representation	151
	6.4.2	Convex 3D Height Field Using Cube Maps	152
	6.4.3	Separating Axis Test	153
	6.4.4	Sutherland Hodgeman Clipping	153
	6.4.5	Minkowski Portal Refinement	154
	6.4.6	Contact Reduction	154
6.5		GPU Constraint Solving	155
	6.5.1	Equations of Motion	155
	6.5.2	Contact and Friction Constraint Setup	155
	6.5.3	Parallel Projected Gauss-Seidel Method	156
	6.5.4	Batch Creation and Two-Stage Batching	157
	6.5.5	Non-Contact Constraints	158
	6.5.6	GPU Deterministic Simulation	159
	6.5.7	Conclusion and Future Work	159

6.1 Introduction

Bullet Physics is an open source real-time 3D collision detection and multi-physics library, in particular, for rigid body simulation. Bullet is being used by game developers and movie studios, and is being integrated into 3D modeling and authoring tools such as Maya, Blender, Cinema 4D Houdini, and many others. In the visual effects industry it is common to use large-scale rigid body simulation especially in destruction scenes, such as in Figure 6.1.

Bullet 3.x includes a rigid body simulator that is written from scratch to execute entirely on the GPU using OpenCL. This chapter discusses the efforts to make the simulator suitable for massively multithreaded systems such as GPUs. It is also possible to execute certain stages on a CPU and other stages on an OpenCL GPU.

Although OpenCL is used, most of it can be applied to projects using other GPU compute languages, such as NVIDIA CUDA and Microsoft DirectX11 Direct Compute. As seen in Figure 6.21 (see Color Insert), a high-end desktop GPU can simulate a hundred thousand stacked rigid bodies at interactive rates of 10 to 30 frames per second. The full source code is available as open source at `http://github.com/erwincoumans/bullet3`.

Before this rewrite, we have been optimizing the single threaded performance of Bullet 2.x and refactoring the existing code toward multithreading for multicore CPU. We will briefly discuss those efforts, before going into detail about the rewrite from scratch.

6.1.1 Rigid Body Dynamics Simulation

The dynamics of rigid bodies can be simulated by computing the velocities and positions according to several laws of physics. In this chapter we focus on moving objects in the range of a few millimeters to a few meters, where the Newton laws are applicable as described in 6.5.1. The simulation of rigid bodies is trivial for the special case of a few bodies freely floating in space without object interaction and external forces: we would just update the world transform for each object in parallel. In general, we are interested in object interaction, such as resting and colliding contacts between bodies. Figure 6.2 shows some stages that a rigid body simulator executes.

Aside from the update of object transforms, each stage has its own challenges moving from single threaded execution to parallel execution. A naive approach could compute all $O(n^2)$ potential object-object interactions, but only a few of those interactions lead to actual contact points. To determine the potential number of overlapping pairs of objects we make use of spatial acceleration structures as discussed in Section 6.3. For each pair

FIGURE 6.1: Destruction simulation.

FIGURE 6.2: Rigid body pipeline.

Rigid Body Pipeline

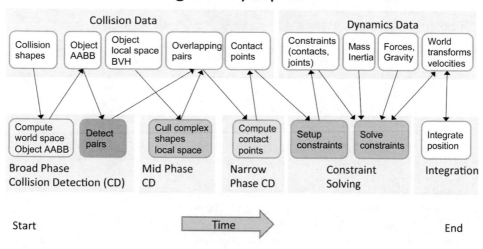

of potential overlapping objects we determine if the objects are actually overlapping and generate contact points. Section 6.4 discusses how we deal with multithreaded contact point generation on the GPU. Finally, Section 6.5 deals with the handling of contacts through contact constraints, as well as joint constraints between objects on the GPU.

6.1.2 Refactoring before the Full Rewrite

Bullet 2.x is written in modular C++ and its API was primarily designed to be flexible and extendible, rather than optimized for performance. The C++ API allows users to derive their own classes and to select or replace individual modules that are used for the simulation. A lot of refactoring work has been done to optimize its single-threaded performance, without changing the API and public data structures.

- Reduce the amount of dynamic memory (de)allocations, for example, using memory pools
- Use efficient acceleration structures to avoid expensive computations
- Incrementally update data structures instead of computing from scratch
- Precompute and cache data so that results can be reused
- Optimize the inner loops using SSE and align data along cache lines

Around 2006, we started optimizing Bullet 2.x for Playstation 3 Cell and its SPU processors. This required some refactoring and we reused some of this effort toward a basic multithreaded version that was cross-platform using pthreads and Win32 Threads.

We created several tests to benchmark the performance of CPU, multithreaded CPU, and Cell SPUs. Each of the tests highlights the performance of different parts of the rigid body simulator.

Three thousand falling boxes test the performance of the box-box collision detection and the contact constraint solver. One thousand stacked boxes test contact quality in collision detection and constraint solver, as well as optimizations for near-resting situations. One

FIGURE 6.3: Obsolete CPU performance benchmarks.

hundred and thirty-six ragdolls test the constraint stability and performance, as well as capsule primitive collision detection. One thousand convex hulls test the convex polyhedra. Unlike primitives, such as box and sphere, convex hulls are harder to optimize. One thousand convex hulls against a concave triangle mesh: concave triangle meshes are usually used for 3D world environments, buildings, bridges, and so forth.

Those older benchmarks are not well suited for the OpenCL GPU rigid body pipeline: there is not enough work to keep all the GPU threads busy and the overhead of the OpenCL launch will negate the benefits. Therefore, we created larger-scale benchmarks, two of them are shown in Figures 6.21 and 6.22 (see Color Inserts for both).

6.2 Rewriting from Scratch Using OpenCL

Once we figured out that the API, algorithms, and data structures were not suitable for GPU we started a pure OpenCL implementation from scratch.

6.2.1 Brief OpenCL Introduction

With OpenCL, we can target not only devices such as GPUs, but CPUs as well. The OpenCL device is initialized from a host, using the CPU and main memory running the operating system as shown in Figure 6.4.

The OpenCL code that runs on the device is called a kernel. OpenCL kernel code looks very similar to regular C code. Such kernel code needs to be compiled using a special compiler, that is usually provided by the device vendor. This is similar to graphics shader compilation, such as GLSL, HLSL, and Cg.

FIGURE 6.4: Host and OpenCL device.

To get access to OpenCL we need at minimum the OpenCL header files, and some way to link against the OpenCL implementation. Various vendors such as AMD, Intel, NVIDIA, and Apple provide an OpenCL software development kit, which provides those header files and a library to link against. As an alternative, we also added the option to dynamically load the OpenCL dynamic library and import its symbols at runtime. This way, the program can continue to run without using OpenCL in case the OpenCL driver is missing.

Let's start with a very simple example (Listing 6.1) that shows the conversion of some simple code fragment into an OpenCL kernel.

```
typedef struct
{
    float4      m_pos;
    float4      m_linVel;
    float4      m_angVel;
    int         m_collidableIdx;
    float       m_invMass;
} Body;

void    integrateTransforms (Body* bodies, int numBodies, float timeStep)
{
    for (int nodeID = 0;nodeID<numBodies;nodeID++)
    {
        if( bodies[nodeID].m_invMass != 0.f)
        {
            bodies[nodeID].m_pos +=  bodies[nodeID].m_linVel * timeStep;
        }
    }
}
```

Listing 6.1: C99 code snippet for integrateTransforms.

When we convert this code into an OpenCL kernel it looks like Listing 6.2:

```
__kernel void    integrateTransformsKernel( __global Body* bodies,
const int numBodies, float timeStep)
{
    int nodeID = get_global_id(0);
    if( nodeID < numBodies && (bodies[nodeID].m_invMass != 0.f))
    {
        bodies[nodeID].m_pos +=  bodies[nodeID].m_linVel * timeStep;
    }
}
```

Listing 6.2: OpenCL kernel for integrateTransforms.

We need to write some host code in order to execute this OpenCL kernel. Here are typical steps for this host code:

- Initialize OpenCL context and choose the target device
- Compile your OpenCL kernel program
- Create/allocate OpenCL device memory buffers
- Copy the Host memory buffer to the device buffer
- Execute the OpenCL kernel
- Copy the results back to Host memory

The OpenCL API is very low level, so we created a simple wrapper to match our coding style and to make it easier to use. This was a good learning experience. We also added additional features for debugging, profiling, and unit testing in the wrapper. This wrapper does not hide the OpenCL API, so at any stage we can use plain OpenCL.

FIGURE 6.7: Uniform grid.

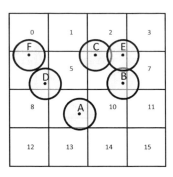

Some work is involved in making it efficient to iterate over objects in its own cell and neighboring cells. Once each object has its cell index assigned, we can sort all objects based on the cell index. We can use a parallel radix sort for this sort. Each cell will store an index to the first object in its cell and the number of objects. This information can be gathered using a prefix scan on the sorted object array. All operations to build and use the uniform grid are embarrassingly parallel so the performance is very good on GPU. We can use it as a reference for other algorithms. The main limitations of the uniform grid is that it cannot deal with objects that are larger than the cell size.

6.3.3   Parallel 1-Axis Sort and Sweep

To overcome the object size limitation of the uniform grid, it is possible to use a different spatial sort. One way is to project the AABB begin- and end-points onto a single world space axis. Each object can search for an AABB overlap in an interval that overlaps its own begin- and end-points as shown in Figure 6.8.

The actual implementation of the 1 axis sort and sweep is similar to the brute-force one described in detail in the book, *Real-Time Collision Detection* [23]. Instead of sweeping along the entire axis, we can terminate once we encounter a begin- or end-point that is larger than our own extents on this axis. We have made various improvements, also documented in more detail by Liu et al. [42]. All work items in a work group access similar data, so we can cache it in local memory. Every time a new pair is added, we need to use a global atomic to append it to the global array of potential overlapping pairs. We can reduce the amount of global atomic operations by caching all new pairs within a work group in local memory, and appending them to global memory in a batch.

FIGURE 6.8: Projected AABB intervals.

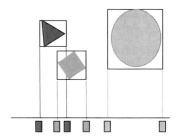

FIGURE 6.9: Sequential incremental 3-axis sweep and prune.

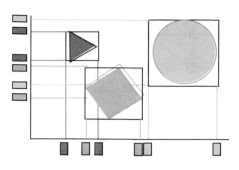 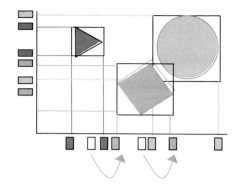

6.3.4 Parallel 3-Axis Sweep and Prune

The sequential 3-axis sweep and prune broad phase pair search algorithms incrementally updates the sorted AABBs for each of the 3 world axes in 3D as shown in Figure 6.9. We sort the begin and end-points for each AABB to their new position, one object at a time, using swap operations. We incrementally add or remove pairs during those swap operations. This exploits spatial and temporal coherency: in many cases objects do not move a lot between frames. This algorithm is difficult to parallelize due to data dependencies: globally changing data structure would require locking.

We modify the 3D axis sweep and prune algorithm to make it more suitable for GPU, while keeping the benefits of the incremental pair search during the swaps. Instead of performing the incremental sort and swap together, we perform the sorting in parallel as one stage, and perform the swaps in a separate stage using read-only operations.

We maintain the previous sorted axis and compare it with the updated sorted axis. Each object can perform the swaps by traversing the previous and current sorted elements, without modifying the data as shown in Figure 6.10.

Although unusual, we can detect rare degenerate cases that would lead to too many swaps in the 3-axis sweep and prune (SAP) algorithm, and do a fallback to another broad phase. Such fallback is not necessary in most practical simulations. Still, generally it can

FIGURE 6.10: Parallel 3-axis sweep and prune.

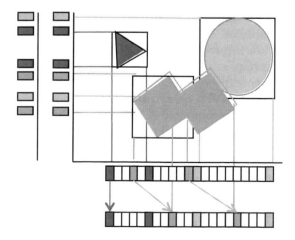

each stage executes its own kernel. The splitting introduced temporary data that is output of the previous stage and input of the next stage. As we preallocated this temporary data, we needed to make some estimate on the size, introducing some artificial limitations.

The heuristic of using a single clipping face from each object works well for low-polygon shapes such as tetrahedra, cubes, and pyramids. In certain cases, such as nearly co-planar faces, small, or degenerate faces, the heuristic can fail to generate contact points. It is possible to use more than a single clipping face from each object, as described in the book, *Game Physics Pearls* [4]. Instead, we implemented an additional algorithm called Minkowski Portal Refinement.

6.4.5 Minkowski Portal Refinement

The Minkowski Portal Refinement algorithm [35] can compute the separating axis, penetration depth, and deepest contact point more efficiently for complex convex hulls. Porting the basic implementation to OpenCL ended up being trivial. The OpenCL kernel is still more complex than most OpenCL devices can process, so we had to split up the algorithm into multiple stages.

The Minkowski Portal Refinement algorithm provides a single contact point, penetration depth and contact normal. A single contact point is often not sufficient to maintain a stable resting pose.

One way to collect multiple points is using a contact cache. The idea is to maintain a contact point cache for each overlapping pair of objects over multiple simulation frames. Whenever we find a new contact point, we check if the point is already in the cache and replace it or add the new point. Also, we need to make sure to remove points from the cache that are not suitable anymore. To maintain a persistent contact cache, we keep a contact cache index for each overlapping pair. Depending on the algorithm used to find the overlapping pairs, we need to keep track of this index.

Another way of collecting multiple points is by combining MPR with contact clipping. The performance of MPR is very attractive, in particular for complex convex shapes with many vertices, faces, and edges.We can use MPR to compute the separating normal, instead of using SAT, and then use the contact clipping algorithm. We found that in some cases the contact normal generated by MPR is not the best separating normal. This becomes a problem when using this normal for the contact clipping algorithm: when we pick the wrong candidate faces to perform clipping, the contact points can have very deep penetration, causing instability.

6.4.6 Contact Reduction

The contact clipping algorithm can generate a lot of contact points. For better performance, we reduce the number of contacts between two convex polyhedra to a maximum of four points. We always keep the contact point with the deepest penetration, to make sure the simulation gets rid of penetrations. We keep three other contact points with maximum or minimum projections along two orthogonal axes in the contact plane. When using the cube map approach, it is common to generate many contact points, so it is useful to optimize the contact reduction for the GPU SIMD architecture within a Compute Unit using local shared memory. The 2D convex hull approximation computes the maximum and minimum extends in a few directions, involving a dot product over all vertices. We can perform this dot product in parallel using all threads in a Compute Unit, and then compute the maximum and minimum using the built-in atomic max and min operator of OpenCL. When using the incremental contact cache or contact clipping algorithm there are usually not enough contact points to benefit from using such SIMD optimization.

6.5 GPU Constraint Solving

6.5.1 Equations of Motion

The dynamics of rigid bodies can be simulated by computing the velocities and positions according to the three Newton laws of motion:

1. The velocity of a body remains unchanged unless acted upon by a force.
2. The rate of change of momentum of a body is equal to the applied force.
3. For every force there is an equal and opposite force.

For a rigid body where all mass is located at a single point at its center of mass, also known as particle or point mass, the equation of motion is obtained by applying Newton's second law:

$$F = ma \tag{6.1}$$

where F is the force, m is the mass and a is the acceleration. If the mass is not centered in a single point, but distributed in space, we can use the Euler extension that adds a rotational component to Newton's second law:

$$\tau = I\dot{\vec{\omega}} + \vec{\omega} \times I\vec{\omega} \tag{6.2}$$

where τ is the torque and I is the 3-by-3 inertia matrix and $\times$ represents the vector cross product.

6.5.2 Contact and Friction Constraint Setup

When a pair of objects collide, we need to satisfy the non-penetration constraints. We can apply forces or impulses to change the velocity of the objects so that the objects will not interpenetrate. For a single contact point we need to apply an impulse so that the projection (dot product) of the relative velocity onto the contact normal is non-negative ($v.n >= 0$) as shown in Figure 6.18. For a particle with all the mass at the center, the relationship between impulse, change in velocity, and mass is $imp = m * \Delta v$.

FIGURE 6.18: Single contact point collision impulse.

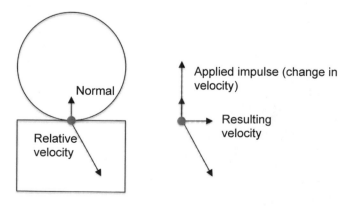

FIGURE 6.19: Multiple contact constraints.

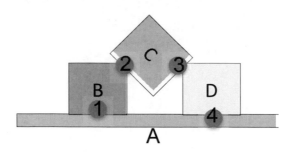

The constraint impulses or forces for multiple contact points can be computed simultaneously using a constraint solver using a numerical method to solve this linear complementarity problem. A popular numerical method for this purpose is the iterative projected Gauss-Seidel algorithm.

```
for (i = 0; i <numRows; i++)
{
    delta = 0.0f;
    for (j = 0; j <i; j++)
        delta += A(i,j) * x[j];
    for (j = i+1; j<numRows; j++)
        delta += A(i,j) * x[j];
    x [i] = (b [i] - delta) / A(i,i);
}
```

Listing 6.9: Gauss-Seidel solver inner loop.

6.5.3   Parallel Projected Gauss-Seidel Method

If we look at the projected Gauss-Seidel algorithm we can see that the individual constraint rows can access the same elements in the x vector because the contact constraints 1, 2, 3, and 4 shown in Figure 6.19, are shared by bodies A, B, C, and D.

To avoid the read/write conflict to the same memory address from different threads, we could use synchronization but that would become a performance bottleneck. Instead, constraint rows can be processed in parallel if they do not share the same body. A preparation step called batching will fill the batches of the constraint rows, so that all the constraint rows in the same batch do not share the same body. That way we can solve all the constraint rows in a batch in parallel. The host will enqueue the solveSingleContact kernel from Listing 6.10 once for each batch, and repeat this for each Gauss-Seidel iteration. If the number of batches is large, say 20 to 30 batches, and we have a large number of Gauss-Seidel iterations, say 20 iterations, we end up with 400 to 600 kernel enqueue operations. This kernel enqueue launch overhead can become a bottleneck for certain problem sizes and GPUs. To reduce the number of kernel enqueue operations, we created a way to deal with the synchronization between the batches within the solver kernel as shown in Listing 6.11. The main idea is that all the threads within a Compute Unit are processing constraint rows with the same batch index. Using a barrier we can guarantee that all the threads are finished processing the constraint rows in the current batch. At that stage the first thread in the work group will increment the batch index and all the threads will repeat this until all the batches are processed.

```
__kernel void solveSingleContactKernel(__global Body* gBodies,
                    __global Shape* gShapes,
                    __global Constraint4* gConstraints,
                     int cellIdx,
                     int batchOffset,
                     int numConstraintsInBatch
                    )
{
        int index = get_global_id(0);
        if (index < numConstraintsInBatch)
        {
                int idx=batchOffset+index;
                solveContactConstraint( gBodies, gShapes, &gConstraints[idx] );
        }
}
```

Listing 6.10: Solve a single contact kernel.

```
void batchSolveKernelContact(__global Body* gBodies,
                    __global Shape* gShapes,
                    __global Constraint4* gConstraints,
                    __global int* gN,
                    __global int* gOffsets,
                     int maxBatch,
                     int cellBatch,
                     int4 nSplit
                    )
{
    //left out some initialization for clarity
        . . .

        barrier(CLK_LOCAL_MEM_FENCE);

        int idx=ldsStart+lIdx;
        while (ldsCurBatch < maxBatch)
        {
                for(; idx<end; )
                {
                        if (gConstraints[idx].m_batchIdx == ldsCurBatch)
                        {
                                        solveContactConstraint( gBodies,
                                                gShapes,
                                                &gConstraints[idx] );
                                idx+=64;
                        } else
                        {
                                break;
                        }
                }
                barrier(CLK_LOCAL_MEM_FENCE);

                if( lIdx == 0 )
                {
                        ldsCurBatch++;
                }
                barrier(CLK_LOCAL_MEM_FENCE);
        }
}
```

Listing 6.11: Solve all the batches contact kernel.

6.5.4 Batch Creation and Two-Stage Batching

The flood fill algorithm to fill batches with constraint rows so that they do not share a body is sequential. In many cases, it is suitable to perform this batch creation on the host CPU as shown in Listing 6.12.

```
while( nIdxSrc ) {
    nIdxDst = 0;        int nCurrentBatch = 0;
    for(int i=0; i<N_FLG/32; i++) flg[i] = 0; //clear flag
    for(int i=0; i<nIdxSrc; i++)      {
        int idx = idxSrc[i];
        assert( idx < n );
        //check if it can go
        int aIdx = cs[idx].m_bodyAPtr & FLG_MASK;
        int bIdx = cs[idx].m_bodyBPtr & FLG_MASK;
        unsigned int aUnavailable = flg[ aIdx/32 ] & (1<<(aIdx&31));
        unsigned int bUnavailable = flg[ bIdx/32 ] & (1<<(bIdx&31));
        if( aUnavailable==0 && bUnavailable==0 )    {
            flg[ aIdx/32 ] |= (1<<(aIdx&31));
            flg[ bIdx/32 ] |= (1<<(bIdx&31));
            cs[idx].getBatchIdx() = batchIdx;
            sortData[idx].m_key = batchIdx;
            sortData[idx].m_value = idx;
            nCurrentBatch++;
            if( nCurrentBatch == simdWidth ) {
                nCurrentBatch = 0;
                for(int i=0; i<N_FLG/32; i++) flg[i] = 0;
            }
        }
        else   {
            idxDst[nIdxDst++] = idx;
        }
    }
    swap( idxSrc, idxDst ); swap( nIdxSrc, nIdxDst );
    batchIdx ++;
}
```

Listing 6.12: Sequential batch creation on the host CPU.

The batch creation itself is a sequential process and it requires additional effort to parallelize the batch creation into multiple Compute Units. It is possible to parallelize the process across the threads in a single Compute Unit using synchronization within the Compute Unit. In order to use more than one Compute Unit, we can add a first coarse-grain splitting that allows us to safely distribute constraint rows among multiple Compute Units. A uniform grid can provide such splitting based on spatial distribution: as long as objects are smaller than the grid cell size, we can process non-neighboring cells in parallel on different Compute Units. In other words, the cells with the same letter as shown in Figure 6.20 can be processed in parallel on different Compute Units. More details are available in a SIGGRAPH 2011 sketch [29] and in the chapter "Two-Level Constraint Solver" of the *GPU Pro 5* book [22].

FIGURE 6.20: Uniform grid to split batches.

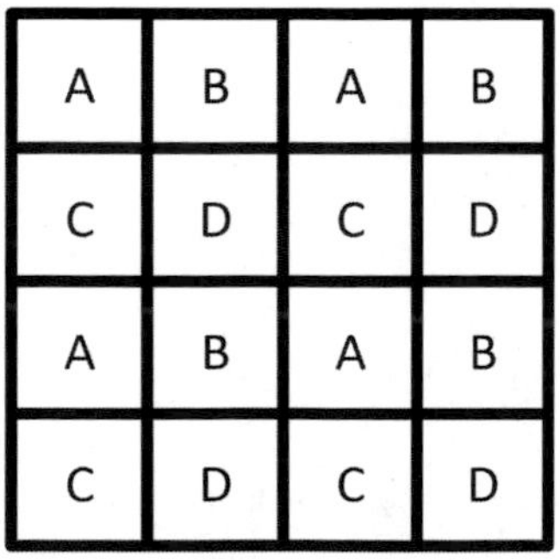

A	B	A	B
C	D	C	D
A	B	A	B
C	D	C	D

6.5.5 Non-Contact Constraints

Aside from contact constraints, it is possible to attach two bodies using joints that restrict the degrees of freedom between the two attached bodies. For each degree of freedom that is removed by the joint, a separate constraint row needs to be solved by the constraint solver. For example, a fixed joint would remove all 6 degrees of freedom between the two attached bodies. A hinge joint removes 5 degrees of freedom, and a ball-socket joint removes 3 degrees of freedom. In order to allocate the right amount of temporary memory such as the constraint rows, we split the constraint setup in two stages.

First, each constraint reports the required number of constraint rows. Using the parallel prefix sum we can accumulate this data so that we can preallocate all constraint rows and the offset for each constraint. In the second stage, all joints can initialize their own constraint rows in parallel.

It is common for constraints to be the same over multiple simulation frames. This means that the batching is the same as well, so we can cache the constraint row batches from the previous frame, unless there is a change in constraints.

6.5.6 GPU Deterministic Simulation

The work items and Compute Units in a GPU are executed in parallel, and the order in which work items are executed can be different each time. This non-determinism, or lack of consistency, can affect the results. For instance, if the pair search appends pairs using an atomic increment operation, there is no guarantee that pairs are inserted in the same order.

If we have a different order of overlapping pairs and contact points, we may also have a different order of contact constraints. The projected Gauss-Seidel algorithm produces slightly different results, if the constraint rows are solved in a different order. Those small differences accumulate over time and result in totally different results. If we want exactly the same results each time we run the simulation (on the same hardware/compiler) we need to make sure that the order is always the same.

We can sort the overlapping pairs, or contact points, using a parallel radix sort. In a similar way, we need to sort the output that is generated during parallel tree traversals for complex concave collision shapes.

6.5.7 Conclusion and Future Work

The results of the OpenCL rigid body pipeline of Bullet Physics are encouraging for further OpenCL GPU work. There are still many features in the original Bullet 2 version that need to be implemented in OpenCL, such as

- Hybrid CPU and GPU simulation
- Object (de)activation
- Continuous collision detection
- Continuous physics response
- User callbacks
- Ray intersection testing
- Two-way interaction with cloth, fluid, and other simulation methods, and so on

The software is all open source and can be built on Windows, Linux, and Mac OSX. It will work well on a high-end desktop GPU, such as AMD Radeon HD7970 or NVIDIA 680 GTX. The download location is `http://github.com/erwincoumans/bullet3`.

FIGURE 6.21: Bullet Physics rigid body benchmark, 112k box stack on a GPU simulated in 70 ms/frame. **(See Color Insert.)**

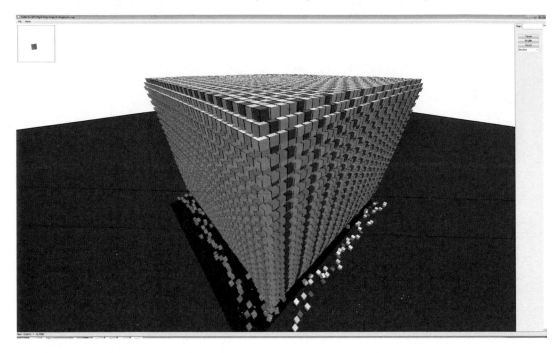

FIGURE 6.22: Bullet Physics GPU rigid body benchmark, 64k boxes colliding with a concave trimesh, simulated in 100 ms/frame. **(See Color Insert.)**

FIGURE 6.23: AMD CodeXL tool used to debug an OpenCL kernel under Linux. It enables the inspection of variables, adding of breakpoints, and stepping through a kernel. You can select any of the active work items. **(See Color Insert.)**

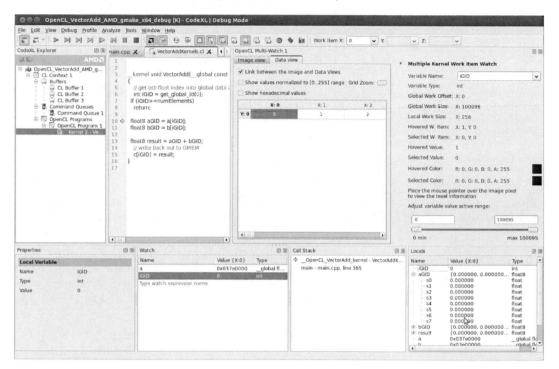

FIGURE 6.24: AMD CodeXL tool used to profile an OpenCL kernel under Windows in Microsoft Visual Studio. **(See Color Insert.)**

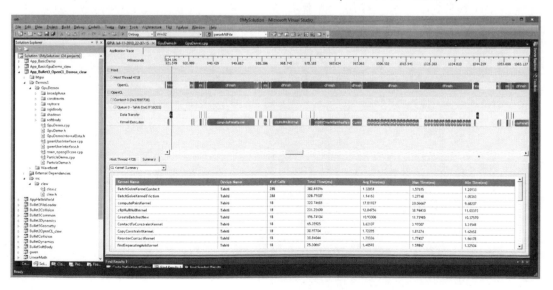

Chapter 7

OpenSubdiv: Interoperating GPU Compute and Drawing

Manuel Kraemer

Pixar Animation Studios

7.1		Representing Shapes	164
	7.1.1	Why Fast Subdivision?	165
	7.1.2	Legacy	165
	7.1.3	OpenSubdiv	166
7.2		The Control Cage	166
	7.2.1	Patches and Arbitrary Topology	166
	7.2.2	Topological Data Structures	167
	7.2.3	Manifold Surfaces	167
	7.2.4	The Limit Surface	168
7.3		Uniform Subdivision	169
	7.3.1	Implementing Subdivision Schemata	169
7.4		Serializing the Mesh Representation	170
	7.4.1	Case Study: Subdividing a Pyramid	170
	7.4.2	Generating Indexing Tables	170
	7.4.3	Preparing for Parallel Execution	172
7.5		Transition from Multicores to Many-Cores.	173
	7.5.1	Streaming Multiprocessors and SIMT	173
	7.5.2	Practical Implementation with OpenCL	174
7.6		Reducing Branching Divergence	175
	7.6.1	Sorting Vertices by Type	176
	7.6.2	Further Vertex Sorting	176
7.7		Optimization Trade-Offs	179
	7.7.1	Alternative Strategy: NVIDIA Dynamic Parallelism	179
	7.7.2	Alternative Strategy: Vertex Stencils	180
	7.7.3	Memory Bottlenecks	181
7.8		Evaluating Our Progress	182
7.9		Fundamental Limitations of Uniform Subdivision	183
	7.9.1	Exponential Growth	184
	7.9.2	Geometric Fidelity	184
	7.9.3	Animating Subdivision Surfaces	185
	7.9.4	Better, Faster, Different	185
7.10		Feature-Adaptive Subdivision	186
	7.10.1	GPU Hardware Tessellation	186
	7.10.2	Catmull-Clark Terminology	187
	7.10.3	Bi-Cubic Patch Representation	188
	7.10.4	Feature-Adaptive Subdivision	189
7.11		Implementing the GPU Rendering Engine	190

7.11.1   Bi-Cubic Bspline Patches with GLSL 191
    7.11.1.1   Handling Surface Boundaries 192
    7.11.1.2   Handling Patch Transitions 193
    7.11.1.3   "End" Patches 194
7.11.2   Mitigating Drawing Overheads 196
7.12   Texturing 197
7.12.1   Displacement Mapping 198
7.13   Conclusion 199

7.1   Representing Shapes

The geometric representation of surfaces and closed volumes is one of the cornerstones of computer graphics. The oldest, and still ubiquitous, modeling method is the polygonal mesh. Polygons, however, are very poor at representing smooth surfaces, where many faces are required in order to approximate the desired shape.

The advent of modern industrial manufacturing processes has exacerbated the need for a reliable representation of smoothed curves. This eventually led automobile engineer Pierre Bézier to replace his unreliable mechanical spline drafting tools with a mathematical tool: a set of polynomial interpolation equations.

Bézier surfaces are far superior to polygon meshes in many ways: they are more compact, easier to manipulate, and have much better continuity properties. They can also easily approximate the common parametric surfaces such as spheres and cylinders. Bézier's piecewise polynomial patches were eventually generalized with the introduction of the non-uniform rational B-splines (NURBS).

However, despite all these advantages, patch surfaces still remain difficult to work with. Because their topology is limited to rectangles, modeling simple everyday life organic shapes becomes a challenge. This changed with the introduction of recursive subdivision refinement algorithms such as the Catmull-Clark scheme depicted in Figure 7.1.

Unlike polygon meshes, the mathematics of subdivision meshes guarantee the smooth continuity of curved surfaces, but without the topological limitations of NURBS and other patch representations. This gives modelers the flexibility they need to represent a wide range of both organic and manufactured shapes. These key advantages, coupled with the fact that existing polygonal modeling tools can be used to create the control cage meshes, have ensured a ubiquitous adoption of subdivision surfaces in the graphics pipelines of the visual effects and animation industries.

FIGURE 7.1: Recursive subdivision of a polyhedron.

7.1.1 Why Fast Subdivision?

Despite being ubiquitous, the manipulation of subdivision surfaces in interactive applications is still challenging though. One common problem is that the surface is typically not fully drawn because of limited computational performance. As a consequence, the polygonal control hull that is represented to the user is only an approximation, and it is offset from the actual smooth surface.

This geometric approximation makes it difficult to see exact contact, like fingers threading a needle, or hands touching a cheek. It also makes it difficult to see poke-throughs in cloth simulation, if both the character's body and clothing are only approximations. Further, these problems can be amplified, when one character is much larger than another, for instance, or when unequally subdivided faces cause approximation errors to be magnified. All these limitations hinder the creative processes and turn what should be fluid and intuitive interactions into exercises in frustration.

In practice, digital content creation software such as Maya or Pixar's proprietary Presto animation system can take up to 100 milliseconds to subdivide a character of 30,000 polygons to the second level of subdivision (creating about half-a-million polygons). Being able to perform the subdivision refinement operations in less than 5 milliseconds would allow the user to interact with the smooth, accurate limit surface at all times.

7.1.2 Legacy

Pixar's original Marionette animation software has been instrumental in pioneering many of the subdivision research landmarks in a lineage that started with Ed Catmull [12] in the late 1970s. The first practical implementation to be used in production was developed for Jan Pinkava's *Geri's Game* in 1997 [17]. Figure 7.2 shows the original wireframe control mesh that gave Geri his very distinctive look. The Catmull-Clark subdivision surface primitive was eventually added to the commercial release of PhotoRealistic Renderman in version 3.8 in 1998.

FIGURE 7.2: Wireframe of Geri's head.

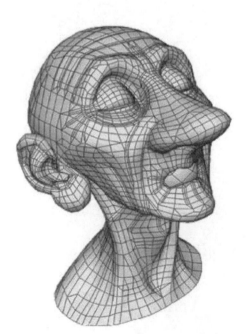

Each generation of the software since then has seen complete rewrites, and has built upon new experiences gleaned in the process of making animated feature films. This includes the addition of new features as well as numerous optimizations.

However, until recently, implementations have been mostly single threaded and the complex subdivision algorithms have been executed exclusively on the CPU. The recent emergence of programmable GPU architectures spurred new research and saw Pixar partnering with Microsoft in order to produce the first full implementation of the Catmull-Clark subdivision algorithm on GPU [52]. This feature-adaptive subdivision algorithm has become the backbone of the OpenSubdiv project.

7.1.3   OpenSubdiv

The OpenSubdiv initiative represents the fifth iteration of subdivision code deployed within Pixar's proprietary software tools. Unlike previous generations of closed-source efforts, for the first time in its history, the studio has made the code publicly available as a set of open-source libraries. Our latest source has been released under the Apache 2.0 license and all of the OpenSubdiv project development is managed under GitHub.com revision control. The entire community can access the latest features and bug fixes at the same time as they are rolled out to Pixar's own animation productions. In addition, Pixar is also licensing the use of its subdivision patents.

Our API implements high performance subdivision surface evaluation on massively parallel CPU or GPU architectures. We have optimized our code paths for drawing deforming surfaces with static topology at interactive frame rates. The resulting limit surfaces are intended to fully match Pixar's Renderman specification, with allowances made for the inherent constraints of IEEE floating-point arithmetic precision.

OpenSubdiv is only an API: it does not directly provide any tools that can be used to author digital assets. However, we do hope that the availability of quality display code will facilitate its integration into many third-party applications, and into digital content creation tools in particular. Our goal is to enable a fully featured and reliable authoring end-to-end toolchain in order to facilitate the use of subdivision primitives in graphics pipelines.

7.2   The Control Cage

Subdivision surfaces are controlled by specifying a coarser piecewise linear polygon mesh. This mesh is often also referred to as the control mesh or the control cage. A very large part of the difficulties behind efficiently evaluating smooth surfaces lies in the topological properties of the control mesh.

Each stage involved in the creation of a digital asset imposes a different set of constraints. The interactive editing requirements of a modeling application are somewhat different from a motion editing tool or an off-line image renderer. Therefore, the data structures we use to represent the mesh are critical to the efficiency of the smooth surface calculations.

7.2.1   Patches and Arbitrary Topology

Bi-cubic patch surfaces are very powerful because they offer the guarantee of a constant smoothness across the shape they describe. However, we run into some very hard problems when we try to apply them on to models of arbitrary topology: geometric primitives as

FIGURE 7.3: Half-edges data structure.

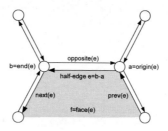

simple as a mug with a handle are difficult to describe with a single non-degenerate B-Spline patch. Unfortunately, these types of free-form surfaces are extremely common in everyday life, a trend which is unsurprisingly mirrored within our virtual worlds.

This particular geometric limitation is eventually what motivated animators to migrate from Bézier and NURBS tools to subdivision surfaces. However, in order to represent these free-form shapes, we need to carefully pick a data structure that can accommodate a wider topological range than the two-dimensional set that parametric patches are constrained to.

7.2.2 Topological Data Structures

Many topological representations have been developed over the years, giving us several candidates to choose from. In its current implementation, OpenSubdiv uses a modified half-edge data structure (see Figure 7.3): the Hbr namespace layer stands for "hierarchical boundary representation." This set of topology classes can represent connectivity between faces, edges, and vertices across multiple levels of subdivision, which is the "hierarchical" part of the name. The "boundary" part of the representation stems from the way Hbr attempts to optimize the storage of discontinuous vertex data, such as unwrapped texture coordinates with seams (what we call "face-varying primitive variable data").

Half-edge data structures are a reasonable compromise between memory usage and speed. Quad-edges would allow for better traversal performance, but they generally require significantly more storage space, which can very quickly become a major hurdle when implementing an off-line renderer, for instance.

7.2.3 Manifold Surfaces

However, both half-edge and quad-edge representations are limited to manifold topology. Excluding non-manifold features means that we need to eliminate certain geometric configurations, such as an edge that is being shared by more than two faces (see Figure 7.4). In practice, this should be a reasonable limitation, since the vast majority of volumes and surfaces used in production should indeed be manifold.

FIGURE 7.4: Non-manifold fan.

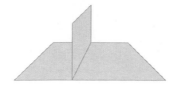

There is, however, a legitimate case to be made for also supporting non-manifold geometry in some special cases. While winged-edges data structures would be able to accommodate any manifold, they require even more storage space than quad-edges. As a potential solution, we are investigating a new simplicial complex "edge-bundles" data structure as a replacement for our current half-edge based Hbr. This new representation would be able to accommodate non-manifold topology, but also allow for easier node traversals and comparable memory requirement.

This is certainly a very ambitious feature list, but OpenSubdiv gives us an ideal sandbox to experiment with such blue-sky research. This particular project will likely require the formulation of an intermediate topological representation, which has several indirect benefits. For instance, it would give us the flexibility to allow client-code to easily substitute their own custom high-level topological representations, which could reduce the difficulty of transitioning from a legacy codebase. It would also allow us to optimize our internal data structures to take advantage of the property that refinement of a face can only produce quad sub-faces (or triangles). While it is an open problem on our roadmap, we have already begun to take the incremental steps necessary to deploy a comprehensive solution.

7.2.4   The Limit Surface

The limit surface is the continuous surface produced by iteratively applying an infinite number of times the subdivision refinement process to the control mesh. Figure 7.5 shows the gradual convergence of a coarse control mesh toward the ideal limit curve. In practice though, using legacy single-threaded software, we can only realistically subdivide a surface two or three times before the process becomes unwieldy.

From a mathematical standpoint, evaluating the limit of subdivision surfaces can be equivalent to analytically evaluating spline patches, with some consideration for singularities around extraordinary vertices. It can be shown that the Catmull-Clark limit surfaces are C^2 continuous everywhere, except at the parametric location of extraordinary vertices, where they are at least C^1 continuous. Compared to NURBS surfaces, the parametric continuity of subdivision surfaces is much more limited, and is often insufficient for the more rigorous needs of the manufacturing and engineering industries. The "less than perfect" smoothness of subdivision limit surfaces, however, appears to be sufficient for all practical applications within the gaming and visual effects fields.

Although we are introducing it early in this chapter, the concept of a limit surface is pivotal to the manipulation of parametric topological representations. While we are going to focus on an approach that produces a discretized approximation first, we will eventually show later how using the analytical expression of the limit surfaces allows us to break from the restrictions of this first approach.

FIGURE 7.5: Successive subdivision iterations.

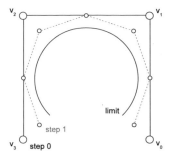

FIGURE 7.6: Two iterations of uniform subdivision.

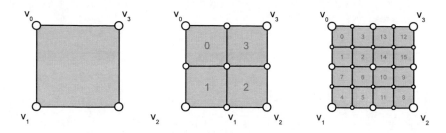

7.3   Uniform Subdivision

It is fairly easy to visualize how we can discretely approximate a smooth surface by recursively evaluating the subdivision algorithm over each polygonal face of the control mesh (see Figure 7.6). With each iteration the generated quads or triangles converge closer to the smooth limit surface. The number of levels of subdivision necessary to achieve an acceptable surface will depend both on the topology and the precision requirements of the application. In this section, we are going to explore how subdivision rules are applied and find properties that we can take advantage of for a parallel implementation.

7.3.1   Implementing Subdivision Schemata

Several subdivision schemas have been developed over the years but the bulk of modern animation work is performed using the Catmull-Clark schema [12]. The other schema that sees some use in production was developed by Charles Loop [11] and is optimized for meshes made of triangular faces only. At Pixar, Loop subdivision is often seen applied to geometry that requires heavy procedural animation or physical simulation, such as character garments.

The Hbr code layer in OpenSubdiv supports both schemas, and their implementation is very similar. We have abstracted the differences by inheriting classes from a common *HbrSubdivision* ancestor (Listing 7.1).

```
template <class T> class HbrSubdivision {
    ...
    virtual HbrVertex<T>* Subdivide(HbrMesh<T>* mesh, HbrFace<T>* face)=0;
    virtual HbrVertex<T>* Subdivide(HbrMesh<T>* mesh, HbrHalfedge<T>* edge)=0;
    virtual HbrVertex<T>* Subdivide(HbrMesh<T>* mesh, HbrVertex<T>* vertex)=0;
    ...
};
```

Listing 7.1: HbrSubdivision class.

The "Subdivide" virtual methods generate new HbrVertex vertices. The vertices are then connected into half-edge cycles through the HbrHalfedge and HbrFace classes, which allows for easy navigation of neighboring topology.

Furthermore, in Hbr, we also connect child and parent vertices to each other, as well as faces and sub-faces. These connections allow us to implement vertical traversals of sub-components by using indexed paths. We use this path indexing system to implement a variety of local hierarchical editing features.

While this highly interconnected data structure is very elegant and allows for easy traversals with a single thread, it presents many challenges. In a parallel environment, each thread would have to protect every vertex, face, and half-edge node in order to maintain the coherence of the data structure under parallel modification. Such an algorithm would obviously scale very poorly, so we have to find a solution to reduce the inter-dependency of our data structures.

7.4 Serializing the Mesh Representation

While relatively straightforward on a CPU, a GPU implementation requires the ability to manipulate topological neighborhood information from a large number of threads with absolutely no concurrency. Fortunately, we can take advantage of the fact that most typical meshes are animated using articulation techniques that keep their topology invariant (and so do semi-sharp creases and most other authored edits). Once we have refined the topology of the mesh to a given level, we can then serialize our interconnected half-edge data structures into precomputed tables that will guide a set of simpler computation kernels.

7.4.1 Case Study: Subdividing a Pyramid

Let's look at an example: Figure 7.7 shows a four-sided pyramid mesh and the vertices from the first level of subdivision.

With the Catmull-Clark schema, a subdivided vertex can be one of three types: the child of a face, an edge, or another vertex as show in Figure 7.8. The data dependency of the subdivision scheme dictates that the face-vertices must be computed first, then edge-vertices, and last vertex-vertices. However, within each category, the blending computations do not rely on any inter-dependent data, so we can safely execute these computations in parallel.

7.4.2 Generating Indexing Tables

In the paper "Feature-Adaptive GPU Rendering of Catmull-Clark Subdivision Surfaces" [52], Nießner et al. propose the serialization scheme reproduced in Figure 7.9. While they use this scheme to refine the mesh adaptively, we can also use it to refine meshes uniformly.

FIGURE 7.7: One subdivision iteration applied on a pyramid.

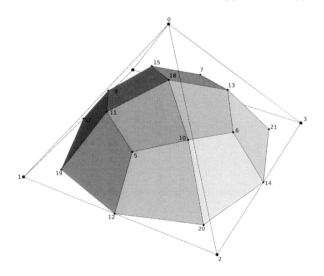

FIGURE 7.8: The child vertices created from a regular quad face.

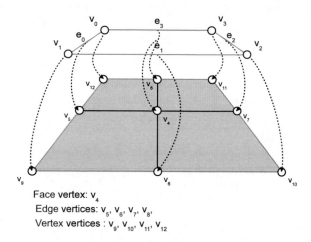

Face vertex: v_4
Edge vertices: v_5, v_6, v_7, v_8,
Vertex vertices : v_9, v_{10}, v_{11}, v_{12}

We keep the primitive vertex data in a single linear buffer shown in column (A) of Figure 7.9. The vertex data assigned from the coarse vertices is located at the front, and the successive refinement iterations keep pushing back the interpolated elements from children vertices. Even though this buffer sustains both read and write operations, there should be no contention or broken dependencies because the vertices are sorted by type in the buffer.

The bulk of the tabular data describes vertex neighborhood topological information and the indices of the vertices connected to the vertex being subdivided. This information is

FIGURE 7.9: Subdivision tables for the pyramid of Figure 7.7: (A) is the vertex buffer, (B) contains topology information, (C) provides the edge and vertex sharpness, and (D) are indices which point into the vertex buffer.

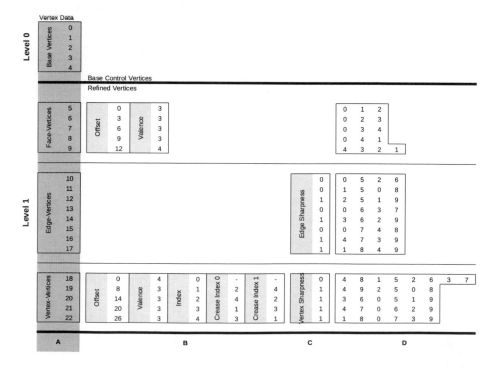

held in columns (B) and (D) of Figure 7.9. These items are supplemented with sub-tables that contain crease sharpnesses (column (C)) or hierarchical edits (not shown in figure).

This serialization of our topological data allows us to interpolate the vertex data buffer without execution dependencies, thus enabling many parallel threads to work concurrently.

7.4.3   Preparing for Parallel Execution

With both the topology tables and vertex data ready, we now turn to the details of the implementation of our compute kernels. We will use the face-vertex subdivision rule as a narrower case-study. Although face-vertices are specific to the Catmull-Clark scheme, this rule is the easiest to implement: the kernel is reduced to simply averaging the data from all the vertices from the parent face. We do not have to concern ourselves with logic accounting for boundaries or semi-sharp creases here.

```
template <class U> void
FarCatmarkSubdivisionTables<U>::computeFacePoints(
    int offset, int tableOffset, int start, int end, void * clientdata ) const {

    assert(this->_mesh);

    U * vsrc = &this->_mesh->GetVertices().at(0),
      * vdst = vsrc + offset + start;

    for (int i=start+tableOffset; i<end+tableOffset; ++i, ++vdst ) {

        vdst->Clear(clientdata);

        int h = this->_F_ITa[2*i  ],
            n = this->_F_ITa[2*i+1];
        float weight = 1.0f/n;

        for (int j=0; j<n; ++j) {
            vdst->AddWithWeight( vsrc[ this->_F_IT[h+j] ], weight, clientdata );
            vdst->AddVaryingWithWeight( vsrc[ this->_F_IT[h+j] ], weight, clientdata );
        }
    }
}
```

Listing 7.2: Face-points CPU compute kernel.

Listing 7.2 shows a single-thread C++ implementation of the OpenSubdiv face-point compute kernel (note that the templated class is an abstract vertex class). In our serialization prepass, we saved the following tabular data:

- The indices of the points in the face: the (D) column in Figure 7.9, which corresponds to the _F_IT member of the table structure in Listing 7.2.

- The topology of the face: the (B) column in Figure 7.9, which corresponds to the _F_ITa element of the table structure in Listing 7.2. The only topological element required in this case is the valence of the parent face.

  However, since these kernels will be executed in many-core environments, we also store offsets to the vertex indices of the _F_IT table, to avoid having to share an incremental counter across cores or threads.

- Finally, in order to support semi-sharp creases, the edge and vertex kernels also need access to the sharpness tag data, which is accounted for in column (C) of Figure 7.9.

Converting the kernel from Listing 7.2 to any given multithreaded environment is now much simpler: all we have to do is distribute the *"for"* loop over the processing cores. All the data inter-dependencies have been removed, in both the scattering and gathering directions.

7.5 Transition from Multicores to Many-Cores.

Before jumping directly into the GPU code implementation of our kernel, we should take a quick look at some of the broad strokes of our intended target micro-architecture. By design, CPU and GPUs are optimizing for very different configurations of code execution and energy efficiency.

Figure 7.10 shows a rough characterization of the amount of real estate apportioned between processing, execution flow control, and data access patterns between a typical CPU and GPU. This comparison reveals some fundamental differences in their approach to data processing.

The first obvious difference is the amount of available Arithmetic Logic Units (ALU): where a CPU typically has a small number of physical cores, the GPU has thousands. Conversely, where the GPU only dedicates a small portion to L2 caching, the CPU adds proportionately very large amounts of cache. Finally, CPUs tend to have very complex control logic circuitry.

Consequently, we expect CPU architectures to be optimized for the execution of a relatively lower number of threads, obviating memory latency through larger data caches. CPUs also use complex embedded logic in an effort to preempt conditional branches and attempt to execute instructions out-of-order as much as possible.

On the other hand, GPU architectures optimize for high computational throughput instead, dedicating most of their resources to simpler ALUs, but at the cost of being much more sensitive to memory latency. Rather than minimizing latency, we try to *"hide"* it instead, mostly by switching computations from other execution threads. Ultimately, the many-core model has the highest theoretical throughput as well as the best energy efficiency.

However, depending on the application, leveraging this optimal throughput is not always possible without a radical paradigm shift. We will show why subdivision surface algorithms fall in the latter category and how we were able to partially overcome these limitations.

7.5.1 Streaming Multiprocessors and SIMT

From our coarse comparison of CPUs and GPUs, we still need to break down the core architecture of GPUs a little further and describe stream processing. This concept relies on the implementation of SIMT kernel execution: single instruction, multiple threads (very similar to SIMD). SIMT kernels only exploit a limited form of parallel execution, where multiple ALUs execute an instruction in parallel, but without direct allocation, synchronization, or

FIGURE 7.10: Comparison of CPU and GPU architectures.

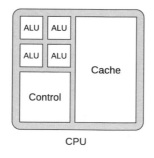

CPU

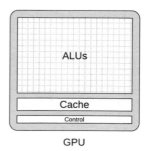

GPU

FIGURE 7.11: Streaming multiprocessors with multiple processing cores.

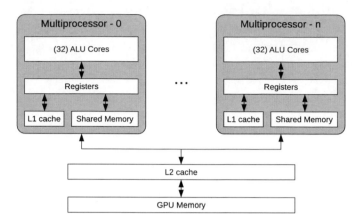

communication between each ALU. Given a *stream* of data, a given kernel instruction is applied to each element by a different core.

Reflecting this paradigm, modern GPU architectures group ALU cores into discrete blocks of streaming multiprocessors (Figure 7.11). The language varies slightly between hardware vendors: NVIDIA literature labels the Streaming Multiprocessor (*"SM"*) units accessed through CUDA *"Warps,"* while AMD groups its Compute Units (*"CU"*) within *"Wavefronts"* of threads. Specifications are similarly different, with an NVIDIA *Fermi* SM containing 32 cores, while the equivalent ATI chip usually has more CUs, but with fewer cores each (16).

Despite these fine-grain differences, the overall constraints imposed by the SIMT architecture paradigm are fundamentally similar:

- Instructions are issued per Warp.

- Data dependent instructions stall the entire Warp.

- The execution context can switch quickly between stalled Warps: an SM can have many active Warps.

- We should try to hide memory latency by increasing the number of active threads until the memory bus is saturated.

7.5.2   Practical Implementation with OpenCL

We can now look at the OpenCL implementation of the kernel in Listing 7.3 as an illustration of the portability of our algorithm. Beyond the language syntactical differences, we can identify how the code maps fairly naturally to SIMT execution:

- In this CL compute kernel we do not have the luxury of a templated vertex class that can specialize the implementation of the *AddWithWeight()* and its AddVarying-WithWeight() blending methods. We had to translate these from an object oriented programming style to a functional one, because our compute kernels work exclusively on linear buffers of interleaved vertex data.

```
__kernel void computeFace(__global struct Vertex *vertex,
                          __global struct Varying *varying,
                          __global int *F_IT,
                          __global int *F_ITa,
                          int vertexOffset, int tableOffset,
                          int start, int end) {

    int i = start + get_global_id(0) + tableOffset;
    int vid = start + get_global_id(0) + vertexOffset;

    struct Vertex dst;
    struct Varying dstVarying;
    clearVertex(&dst);
    clearVarying(&dstVarying);

    int h = F_ITa[2*i];
    int n = F_ITa[2*i+1];

    float weight = 1.0f/n;

    for (int j=0; j<n; ++j) {

        int index = F_IT[h+j];
        AddWithWeight(&dst, &vertex[index], weight);

        if(varying) {
            AddVaryingWithWeight(&dstVarying, &varying[index], weight);
        }
    }
    vertex[vid] = dst;
    if (varying) {
        varying[vid] = dstVarying;
    }
}
```

Listing 7.3: Face-points OpenCL compute kernel.

- Another noticeable difference is that we allocated local variables to accumulate the weighted data (*"dst"* and *"dstvarying"*). At the end of the kernel these variables are copied back into the destination buffer. This strategy allows the compiler to use the faster local registries of a given compute core during the blending iteration loop. This reduces the need to write the data back to its final destination in GPU's main memory into a single operation. This pattern helps tremendously in hiding the inherent latency of memory accesses in GPU architectures, where a very large number of cores are all competing for scarce memory bus bandwidth.

7.6 Reducing Branching Divergence

Because each thread block is executed in the SIMT mode described above, all threads within a block execute the same instruction of the kernel at the same time. Branching divergence is when one or more threads in a given Warp are dynamically branching into a different code path as the result of a data-dependent condition. The Warp will execute each code branch in sequence, with only a subset of the threads active. The threads that are on a different code branch are temporarily deactivated, and will reconverge once all the paths have been completed. Branching divergence can substantially slow down the execution of our subdivision kernels and should obviously be mitigated as much as possible. In practice, we need to reduce dynamic conditions in our kernel code to an absolute minimum. The following sections detail the strategies that we implemented in the various OsdCompute kernels.

FIGURE 7.12: Several kernels executing in sequence.

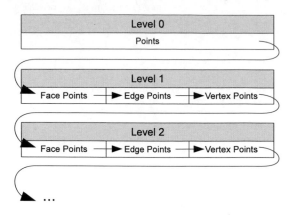

7.6.1 Sorting Vertices by Type

In Section 7.4.1 we showed how subdivided vertices can be sorted based on their progenitor (face, edge, or vertex). Each of these three categories requires the blending of vertex data from a different number of parent vertices using different weights.

If we implemented all the subdivision rules in a single kernel and used conditional branching to select the correct rules, we would be executing distinct vertex interpolations from over 30 different possibilities, depending on the local topology of the vertex. The problem in this case stems from SIMD execution in Warps locking all the cores until all the code paths have been executed: statistically, the average child vertex is the result of interpolating somewhere between 7 or 8 parent vertices. However, the odds of traversing many of the topological configurations in a large Warp of 32 vertices are significant enough that we would regularly be immobilizing threads for hundreds of instructions, waiting for each conditional sub-part of the kernel to be executed.

By reducing branching divergence, we can increase the efficiency of our computations, particularly when processing large batches of child vertices, as is the case in uniform subdivision. The simple solution is to split our algorithm in a subset of kernels and try to take advantage of the subdivision algorithm where possible.

The table in Figure 7.9 shows us an obvious classification based on the parent of the vertex being processed (face, edge, or vertex). We can start splitting our computations into a matching face-vertex kernel, edge-vertex kernel, and vertex-vertex kernel. If we presort the vertex data in the source buffer, we can then queue the execution of our sub-kernels into batches as shown in Figure 7.12.

7.6.2 Further Vertex Sorting

Looking at the vertex-vertices subdivision rules, the addition of semi-sharp creases introduces a fair amount of complexity. This kernel has to selectively apply one of four rules: Smooth, Dart, Crease, and Corner (for details, see DeRose [17]). These rules are evaluated and cached as a *mask* with each HbrVertex during the subdivision process. However, with the introduction of semi-sharp creases, the rules may also require to blend vertices from both the current and the parent subdivision level. This introduces the need for a second iteration of the kernel over the subset of vertices in the batch that have a fractional sharpness.

Figure 7.13 shows the combinations of masks and passes that are possible with the Catmull-Clark subdivision schema. This table shows that we can take advantage of the fact that several combinations can never occur in a mesh. Furthermore, both the Dart and

FIGURE 7.13: Combinations of subdivision rules.

Rules										
Pass 0	Dt	Sm	Sm	Dt	Sm	Dt	Sm	Cr	Co	Cr
Pass 1				Co	Co	Cr	Cr	Co		
Kernel Type										
Pass 0	B	B	B	B	B	B	B	A	A	A
Pass 1				A	A	A	A	A		
Vertex Rank	0	1	2	3	4	5	6	7	8	9

Smooth rules are equivalent from an interpolation standpoint. Based on these premises, we have decided to split our vertex-vertex kernel into two sub-kernels (creatively named *"A"* and *"B"*):

- Kernel A: Implements the Crease and Corner rules.
- Kernel B: Implements the Smooth and Dart rules.

Since the results of each execution pass are linearly interpolated, the order of execution is commutative. Figure 7.13 shows that by sorting our vertices based on interpolation rules, we can reduce the number of vertex compute batches that have to be launched to a worst-case maximum of 3:

1. Apply kernel B to the first 7 vertex ranks
2. Apply kernel A to ranks 3 to 7
3. Apply kernel A again to ranks 7 to 9

This vertex ranking system can be represented in a two-dimensional matrix (Figure 7.14) where the rows describe the rule *"mask"* of the parent vertex and the columns describe the rule *"mask"* of the child vertex. This matrix allows us to select the appropriate rank of our vertex-vertices, which in turn makes sorting their order of execution in the subdivision tables a fairly trivial step.

The results of this kernel reorganization can be seen in Listings 7.4 and 7.5. The Smooth/Dart rules kernel B is completely free of conditionals, while the Crease/Corner kernel A is reduced to a single remaining condition. With this arrangement, in the worst case scenario, a Warp can be held at most for the duration of the interpolation of the data of three vertices: specifically, in the case of a k_Crease mask, where we have to call the function *"AddWithWeight()"* three times, in order to interpolate three vertices. This represents a very significant improvement over the previous worst case scenario, where a Warp or a Wavefront could often be held up for the interpolation of tens of vertices on average.

FIGURE 7.14: Vertex ranking matrix.

Mask (n+1)	Mask (n)			
	0	1	6	4
	-	2	5	3
	-	-	9	7
	-	-	-	8

```
// multi-pass kernel handling k_Crease and k_Corner rules
template <class U> void
FarCatmarkSubdivisionTables<U>::computeVertexPointsA(
    int offset, bool pass, int tableOffset, int start, int end, void * clientdata ) const {

    assert(this->_mesh);

    U * vsrc = &this->_mesh->GetVertices().at(0),
      * vdst = vsrc + offset + start;

    for (int i=start+tableOffset; i<end+tableOffset; ++i, ++vdst ) {

        if (not pass)
            vdst->Clear(clientdata);

        int     n=this->_V_ITa[5*i+1],    // number of vertices in the _VO_IT array (valence)
                p=this->_V_ITa[5*i+2],     // index of the parent vertex
            eidx0=this->_V_ITa[5*i+3],     // index of the first crease rule edge
            eidx1=this->_V_ITa[5*i+4];     // index of the second crease rule edge

        float weight = pass ? this->_V_W[i] : 1.0f - this->_V_W[i];

        // In the case of fractional weight, the weight must be inverted since
        // the value is shared with the k_Smooth kernel (statistically the
        // k_Smooth kernel runs much more often than this one)
        if (weight>0.0f and weight<1.0f and n>0)
            weight=1.0f-weight;

        // In the case of a k_Corner / k_Crease combination, the edge indices
        // won't be null,  so we use a -1 valence to detect that particular case
        if (eidx0==-1 or (pass==false and (n==-1)) ) {
            // k_Corner case
            vdst->AddWithWeight( vsrc[p], weight, clientdata );
        } else {
            // k_Crease case
            vdst->AddWithWeight( vsrc[p], weight * 0.75f, clientdata );
            vdst->AddWithWeight( vsrc[eidx0], weight * 0.125f, clientdata );
            vdst->AddWithWeight( vsrc[eidx1], weight * 0.125f, clientdata );
        }
        vdst->AddVaryingWithWeight( vsrc[p], 1.0f, clientdata );
    }
}
```

Listing 7.4: Vertex-points compute kernel A.

```
// multi-pass kernel handling k_Dart and k_Smooth rules
template <class U> void
FarCatmarkSubdivisionTables<U>::computeVertexPointsB(
    int offset, int tableOffset, int start, int end, void * clientdata ) const {

    assert(this->_mesh);

    U * vsrc = &this->_mesh->GetVertices().at(0),
      * vdst = vsrc + offset + start;

    for (int i=start+tableOffset; i<end+tableOffset; ++i, ++vdst ) {

        vdst->Clear(clientdata);

        int h = this->_V_ITa[5*i  ],    // offset of the vertices in the _VO_IT array
            n = this->_V_ITa[5*i+1],     // number of vertices in the _VO_IT array (valence)
            p = this->_V_ITa[5*i+2];     // index of the parent vertex

        float weight = this->_V_W[i],
                 wp = 1.0f/(n*n),
                 wv = (n-2.0f)*n*wp;

        vdst->AddWithWeight( vsrc[p], weight * wv, clientdata );

        for (int j=0; j<n; ++j) {
            vdst->AddWithWeight( vsrc[this->_V_IT[h+j*2  ]], weight * wp, clientdata );
            vdst->AddWithWeight( vsrc[this->_V_IT[h+j*2+1]], weight * wp, clientdata );
        }
        vdst->AddVaryingWithWeight( vsrc[p], 1.0f, clientdata );
    }
}
```

Listing 7.5: Vertex-points compute kernel B.

FIGURE 7.15: Final execution sequence.

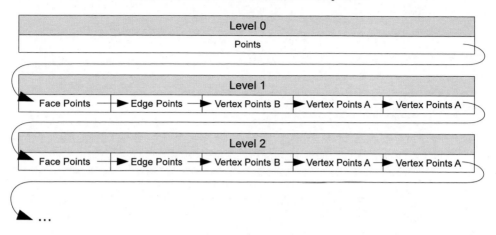

7.7 Optimization Trade-Offs

One major drawback of the methods we just described above is that, while we did optimize branching divergence, we did so at the cost of multiplying the number of compute kernel launches. Figure 7.15 shows the final execution sequence, using all the branching optimizations. Depending on the mesh topology, we are queuing up at least three times as many computation sequences for each level of subdivision. The worst-case scenario, when using semi-sharp creases, can trigger as many as five kernel launches for a given level.

Depending on the target platform and API, both CPU thread and GPU kernel queuing launches can incur varying level of penalties. Our choice of retaining one condition in the vertex-vertex kernel "A" is therefore a compromise that attempts to balance kernel execution time against launch overheads.

From our limited experimentations, it seems that we can dispatch up to about a hundred CUDA kernels on desktop hardware without serious degradation. By contrast, we have reports of OpenCL drivers on certain mobile platforms incurring tens of millisecond's worth of overhead for a single launch (the latter case was eventually attributed to some likely teething issues with the driver software, rather than hardware limitations). With this much variability between platforms, we are probably going to adapt our framework to allow the seamless integration of multiple computation strategies to best address the challenges of a given hardware or driver configuration.

7.7.1 Alternative Strategy: NVIDIA Dynamic Parallelism

For instance, with the recent release of the Kepler GK110 GPU architecture, NVIDIA introduced several new features, including one that could help address our particular problem of CUDA kernel execution overheads. NVIDIA calls the new feature *"Dynamic Parallelism,"* and it adds the capability for the GPU to generate and synchronize its own work queues. Figure 7.16 illustrates how a CUDA compute context could be taking advantage of this new feature.

In our current implementation, all the compute kernel launches are performed by a CPU-based thread. This thread has to wait for each CUDA kernel to complete until it synchronizes with the GPU and launches the next kernel.

FIGURE 7.16: Execution sequence without and with Dynamic Parallelism.

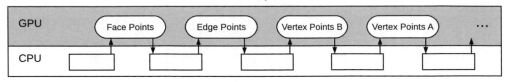

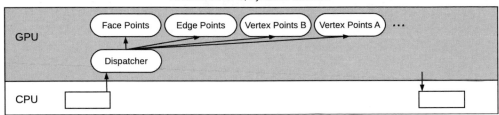

With Dynamic Parallelism instead, we would be able to set up a CUDA dispatcher thread that would launch and synchronize the execution of all our vertex compute kernels. Since those are dependent upon the completion of the previous kernel in the execution queue, we would not be gaining any additional execution parallelism. However, we might see some gains from the elimination of overheads due to frequent synchronization through software drivers. We have not quantified these gains yet, as we currently have no implementation that takes advantage of this new CUDA 5.0 feature. This strategy targets a very specific set of proprietary architectures and would not be extendable outside of the subset of compatible devices though.

7.7.2   Alternative Strategy: Vertex Stencils

Ultimately, the trade-offs between conditional branching and kernel launches are a limitation of the subdivision tables representation that we are using. Our serialization of the vertex neighborhood information is probably close to optimal from the point of view of memory size, but at the cost of retaining some data dependency.

Computing platforms with outlying performance envelopes will likely require more radical solutions. To meet this demand, we have added to the OpenSubdiv API a set of factories that can generate sets of precomputed vertex stencils, as an alternative to the serialized subdivision tables scheme. Stencils require slightly more memory and computations, but only require a single kernel launch with absolutely no conditional branching. Listing 7.6 shows the extreme simplicity of the stencil kernel.

We have begun the implementation of the *FarStencilTables* in the hope that it would give our API more flexibility in adapting our solution to these particular situations where overheads represent a relatively disproportionate portion of the computation sequences. Our preliminary parallel implementations with Intel's Threading Building Blocks (TBB) shows a lot of promise with the ability to process more than 5 million limit stencils per second on a hyperthreaded 16 cores CPU. We are expecting a future GPU counterpart to scale similarly well, although we are assuming that the same memory latency bottlenecks that are hindering the execution of our subdivision kernels will be even more apparent with the stencils kernel.

```
template <class T> void
FarStencilTables::_computeVertexStencil( T const *controlValues,
                                         float const * weights,
                                         T *values,
                                         int stride ) const {

    int const * index = &_indices.at(0);

    for (int i=0; i<GetNumStencils(); ++i) {

        // Zero out the result accumulators
        values[i].Clear();

        // For each element in the array, add the coefs contribution
        for (int j=0; j<_sizes[i]; ++j, ++index, ++weights) {
            values[i].AddWithWeight( controlValues[*index], *weights );
        }
    }
}
```

Listing 7.6: Stencil compute kernels.

Under the right circumstances, we anticipate that vertex stencils can be a very useful alternative to serialized subdivision tables. However, the stencils kernel does not really offer any intrinsic improvement over how the interpolations are performed by our more specialized kernels. We will have to look elsewhere to uncover more substantial gains.

7.7.3 Memory Bottlenecks

By reordering the vertex interpolations, we have reduced branching divergence, and managed to dramatically improve the efficiency of SIMD execution in Warps (or Wavefronts). These optimizations have brought up general core occupancy from 10% to a rough average around 30% on Fermi and Kepler hardware, where we were able to measure it. These numbers may seem low, but they are somewhat in line with the expectations of applications where the computational bandwidth is limited by large numbers of heterogenous data accesses: the vertex data is gathered in mostly semi-random patterns, which cause significant memory access latency.

This suggests that we should be able to achieve some further gains by reordering the vertex data accessed by our compute kernels to improve memory coalescing, as shown in Figure 7.17. We would want to organize the vertex data in a more optimal pattern, whereby vertices that are topologically close should be closely clustered in memory.

A variety of mesh striping techniques have been published that could be used [33]. Similar optimizations have more recently been seen in association with finite elements simulations

FIGURE 7.17: Coalesced global memory access.

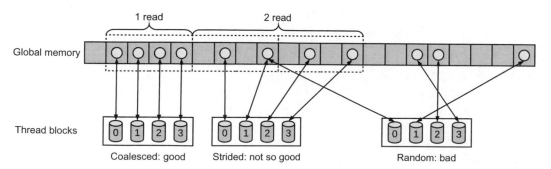

FIGURE 7.18: Kernel compute times for six uniform subdivision levels of a simple mesh.

API / CPU	Intel i7-4770k (Haswell) 4 cores @3.5 Ghz	Intel E5-2680 (IvyBridge) 2 x 8 cores @2.70 Ghz	Intel E5-2680 (IvyBridge) 2 x 8 cores @2.70 Ghz
C++ (single-thread)	120ms / 147ms **	188ms / 256ms	194ms / 278ms **
OpenMP	30ms / 52ms **	23ms / 88ms	N/A **
TBB	33ms / 56ms **	17ms / 80ms	20ms / 107ms **

** hyper-threading active

API / GPU	NVIDIA Quadro 5000 352 cores (Fermi)	ATI Radeon 7970 2048 cores (Tahiti)	NVIDIA GeForce 680 GTX 1536 cores (Kepler)
CUDA	15.9ms / 37ms	N/A	7 .8ms / 18ms
OpenCL	21.3ms / 41ms	N/A	9.7ms / 18.5ms
GLSL (compute)	16.7ms / 37ms	N/A	8.5ms / 18.5ms
HLSL (compute)	N/A	58.7ms / 69ms	N/A

used in engineering CAD. We would expect the performance gains from such strategies to be very dependent on the specific hardware architectures. Because they are fairly complex to engineer and not very portable, our team has not invested any resources yet into pursuing these avenues.

7.8   Evaluating Our Progress

Because our goal is to integrate OpenSubdiv into as many applications as possible, we did not just open-source our software, we also had to make it portable. Cross-platform support has been a critical part of our design choices from the beginning. Fortunately, the reduction of the subdivision rules into a set of very simple compute kernels has helped us tremendously in porting our code to a very large collection of APIs.

As of this writing, client-code that uses our *"OsdCompute"* module can select to deploy the execution through any of the following standards: OpenMP, TBB, GCD, OpenCL, CUDA, GLSL, and HLSL. This wide selection of APIs gives us access to most micro-architectures, as well as most operating systems.

Ease of portability, however, does not necessarily imply ease of optimization. While we did spend some time profiling our CUDA implementation with NVIDIA's Nsight tool for instance, most of the low-level optimizations have been provided by outside expert contributors, several of them being employed by hardware providers. Despite the fact that not all of our kernels have been optimized to an equal level, we are going to attempt to provide an objective benchmark.

Figure 7.18 shows a performance comparison between APIs where we apply the subdivision tables to an animated mesh. The refined geometry displayed consists of approximately

6 million refined vertices. We logged the runtime execution of our kernel batches as well as the total time of a displayed frame. Obviously, this scenario is somewhat subjective, as the topology of the selected mesh is far from offering a representative subset of real-world applications. With these caveats in mind, we can note the following trends:

- As expected, in single-thread mode, clock frequency prevails: a 3.5 Ghz Haswell out-performs a 2.7 Ghz IvyBridge almost linearly.
- Intel hyperthreaded strategies for core over-subscription appear to degrade perfor-mance slightly with TBB (unfortunately, we could not test the same with OpenMP).
- Comparing GPU to CPU compute time, a 16 cores Intel IvyBridge configuration almost keeps up with an NVIDIA Fermi generation GPU. This result is somewhat accidental though, as tests using larger batches of vertices give the GPU an increasing advantage. We attribute this trend to better amortization of GPU driver overheads.
- Some APIs perform slightly better than others: CUDA is slightly faster than OpenCL on an NVIDIA GPU, while TBB appears to scale slightly better than OpenMP with our code. However, these differences appear to be mostly marginal within a given class of API and hardware. The upside is that this allows other considerations to play a role in the decision process.
- When looking at total frame execution time though, a different picture emerges: we notice a very clear advantage to relocating the subdivision kernel computations to the GPU. Even when the CPU cores can match kernel execution time, the frame rates are nearly tripled when using CUDA instead of TBB. This severe disparity highlights the very high costs of streaming large amounts of data from main memory to a separate pool on board of a discrete compute device. Our CPU implementations have to move the entire buffer of subdivided vertices, while the GPU implementations only have to update the vertices of the control mesh. Bandwidth between main memory and GPU memory appears to be an extremely valuable commodity.

If the destination of the subdivision process is interactive display, interpolating the vertex data on the GPU becomes a fairly obvious choice. On the other hand, if the results are intended for general computing processes, the choice between CPU and GPU is far from being so clear-cut. The flexibility to easily switch from one to the other could eventually prove to be an extremely powerful advantage.

However, we did learn that regardless of API and languages, writing kernels that are well optimized to a particular micro-architecture requires expert knowledge, good profil-ing tools, and time. These resources being in general short supply, we would like to call out the generous contributions from domain experts within the open-source community. Their efforts allowed us to focus our attention on addressing some of the more fundamental limitations of our algorithms.

7.9 Fundamental Limitations of Uniform Subdivision

As we have been hinting above, it seems that despite multiple levels of optimizations, the performance of our subdivision tables scales somewhat poorly with the thousands of cores found in modern GPUs. The core occupancy readings from our profilers indicate that the root cause is memory coalescing. While occupancy is not a very reliable measure of the efficiency with which our code leverages the computational power of the hardware, it does

FIGURE 7.19: Geometric progression of subdivided polygons.

Primitive	Triangle	Quad	Pentagon
Level 0	3	4	5
Level 1	4 x 3 = 12	4 x 4 = 16	4 x 5 = 20
Level 2	4 x 12 = 48	4 x 16 = 64	4 x 20 = 80
Level 3	4 x 48 = 192	4 x 64 = 256	4 x 80 = 320
Level 4	4 x 192 = 768	4 x 256 = 1024	4 x 320 = 1280

hint that there is a better solution to be found yet. Addressing this fundamental problem should allow us to make some substantial improvements in performance and unlock the full potential of the thousands of cores in our GPUs. Let's start by identifying some of the obstacles that still remain in our way.

7.9.1 Exponential Growth

The most obvious problem with uniform subdivision is the exponential growth incurred for each iteration. Both the Catmull-Clark and Loop subdivision schemes quadruple the number of faces generated with each iteration. Figure 7.19 shows the number of sub-faces generated for a single face across multiple levels of subdivision. Approximating the limit surface by successive iterations of the subdivision algorithm is very much a brute-force approach.

Because this exponential growth is applied to both processing speed and memory consumption, few interactive applications to date have been able to manipulate or, even simply display, more than the first or second level of subdivision. Depending on the control cage, this can be a very coarse approximation indeed.

7.9.2 Geometric Fidelity

Because uniform subdivision of meshes is unable to scale beyond the first few iterations, it can only offer very limited fidelity with regard to the approximation of the limit surface it intends to describe.

By definition, we are subdividing the entire shape with the same density everywhere. However, in order to get a good approximation, the density of the mesh should be high enough to correctly smooth even the areas of high curvature.

Few practical shapes have a uniform complexity, so we are left with a compromise of either wasting a lot of geometry in relatively flat areas, or we have to sacrifice the quality of the surface in the areas with a lot of detail. Not surprisingly, these areas are often the most critical ones in the shape: fingers, facial features for characters, grips or handles for tools, and so on.

Furthermore, because the geometry being generated is composed of bilinear quads or triangles, it is not differentiable. Because of this, we cannot derive analytical tangents, resulting in unreliable surface normals, particularly in the area along edges with semi-sharp creases. The absence of reliable normal vectors imposes significant restrictions on shading: for instance, we cannot apply crack-free displacement maps under deformation, and we also have to contend with rendering artifacts appearing in specular and diffuse reflections.

FIGURE 7.20: Comparison of off-line and interactive assets.

Character Asset	Movie (off-line)	Game (interactive)
Topology	10^9 (micro-polygons)	10^6 (polygons)
Animation	100 bones + 100 blend shapes	50 bones
Rendering Time	7200 seconds	0.016 seconds (60 Hz.)

7.9.3 Animating Subdivision Surfaces

Our ambition is to allow artists to interact with a high-fidelity rendition of the limit surface, including advanced shading and lighting techniques.

As a practical exercise, Figure 7.20 compares several criteria in order to evaluate the overall complexity found in a typical production asset. In particular, this comparison emphasizes the differences of scale found between interactives and an off-line display system. The figures quoted in the off-line case are typical for a regular CG character or creature rendered and composited in any recent visual-effect movie. We compare the same elementary animation and rendering attributes to those of a high-quality avatar found in a MMORPG or first-person shooter running on current generation hardware. While not directly comparable, we expect both the complexity of the topology and the render time to differ by several orders of magnitude.

The important distinction between the two models, however, is that most interactive game engines perform animation tasks exclusively through bone articulation, which allows for direct GPU-based execution.

By contrast, typical feature film characters require much more fine-grained articulation controls, especially where subtle facial expressions are concerned. This requirement currently dictates the use of blend shapes and higher-order deformers to be layered over the simpler kinematic bone structures. As a direct consequence, as we have seen in other chapters, articulation computations are typically derived from complex dependency graphs, imposing data dependencies that currently limits evaluation to a much smaller pool of cores than is typically found on a GPU.

From these figures, it is obvious that we can only afford to apply complex and expensive articulation algorithms to the vertices of a coarser-control mesh. We propose instead to rely on the subdivision process in order to locally amplify the surface data displayed.

7.9.4 Better, Faster, Different

While we have shown that traditional uniform subdivision schemes can be executed concurrently on many-core architectures, unfortunately our implementation simply does not scale well enough to meet the ambitious requirements imposed by our goals for a smoother user experience. We need a solution that yields an accurate sampling of the surface limit, not just an approximation, and does it several orders of magnitudes faster still.

FIGURE 7.21: Discrete and fractional tessellation patterns.

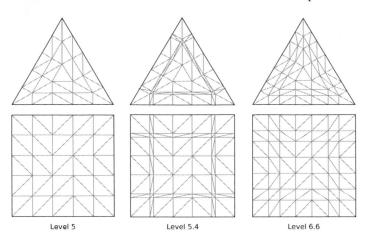

Level 5   Level 5.4   Level 6.6

7.10   Feature-Adaptive Subdivision

In order to move beyond the limitations of uniform subdivision, we are going to have to abandon the iterative refinement process that we have been using to converge toward the surface limit. Ideally, we also want to overcome the memory latency bottlenecks described earlier: we need to make a better use of the massively parallel architecture of modern GPUs if we are to achieve our target refresh rates. In addition, we have to retain all the features and extensions to the original definition of Catmull-Clark surfaces, exactly as they are currently supported in off-line rendering software such as Photorealistic Renderman (PRMan). Once again, we will turn to the intricacies of GPU micro-architectures.

7.10.1   GPU Hardware Tessellation

Despite the prevalence of subdivision surfaces use for digital content creation, real-time applications, and games in particular, still use almost exclusively triangle representations for their geometry. However, given the ubiquity of subdivision algorithms on the authoring side, graphics hardware vendors have recently started to add dedicated tessellation units to GPU architectures, with attending standardized APIs both in OpenGL and DirectX.

The new hardware tessellation units take parametric patches as input and execute programmable shaders to generate a triangulated mesh. The triangulation process is controlled by tessellation factors, which specify the number of vertices created on each edge of the patch. Tessellation factors can be fractional, which allows for smooth transition between discrete levels of tessellation, without popping artifacts between levels. Figure 7.21 shows the resulting tessellation patterns of several ratios on a triangular and square patch.

The main advantage of tessellation units is the ability to take a very compact parametric representation and generate very high densities of triangulated geometry directly on the chip. The triangles generated are also sent directly to the rasterizer. This configuration contributes to drastically reducing GPU memory I/O, thus maximizing the use of the computational capabilities of the parallel cores. Tessellation is possibly one of the best ways to leverage the strengths and energy efficiency of hybrid GPU architectures [58].

Being able to leverage the tessellation pipeline also gives us the control and flexibility to render continuous surfaces with a varying level of detail, for elements both close and distant

FIGURE 7.22: A regular and extraordinary vertex.

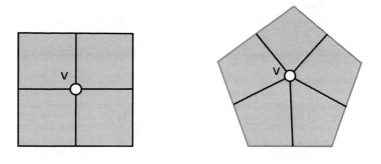

Regular vertex   Extraordinary vertex

FIGURE 7.23: Subdivision of regular and extraordinary faces.

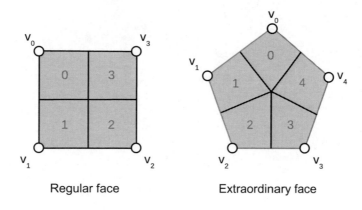

Regular face   Extraordinary face

from the view point. View-dependent level of detail allows us to decouple the tessellation from the iterative subdivision process.

However, this requires that we now find a way to express the topology of our meshes into a collection of parametric patches.

7.10.2 Catmull-Clark Terminology

Before diving into the details of the feature-adaptive algorithm, we will introduce some terminology specific to the Catmull-Clark subdivision scheme.

- The *valence* of a vertex is the number of incident edges to a vertex.

- A *regular vertex* is a vertex of valence 4, otherwise it is an *extraordinary vertex* (Figure 7.22).

- A *regular face* is a face with four regular vertices (Figure 7.23).

FIGURE 7.24: Bi-cubic patches around an extraordinary vertex.

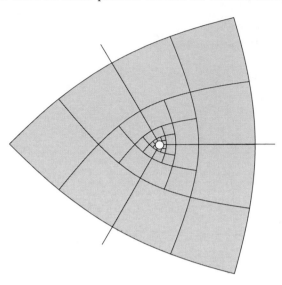

7.10.3   Bi-Cubic Patch Representation

As early as 1998, Jos Stam developed an algorithm to directly evaluate the limit of the parametric form of Catmull-Clark surfaces [60]. However, his method requires meshes comprising quad faces exclusively, with at most one extraordinary vertex each. Stam's technique also requires the evaluation of a heavily data-driven *eigen space transform* during the tessellation process, which makes the GPU implementation very impractical. The full direct analytical evaluation of the limit of a subdivision surface has remained an open problem until recently.

Fortunately, there is a property that we can leverage: by design, the limit surface of a Catmull-Clark subdivision can be described with an infinite collection of bi-cubic polynomial patches [19]. More specifically: the limit of a *regular* Catmull-Clark face can be represented with a single bi-cubic patch, while the area around extraordinary vertices requires the nesting of an infinity of patches. Figure 7.24 illustrates the recursive arrangement of nested patches isolating an extraordinary vertex.

We can also use adaptive feature isolation to handle other discontinuous topological features: we can isolate semi-sharp creases by nesting patches along creased edges. The number of subdivision steps required to isolate a semi-sharp crease is equal to the ceiling of its scalar sharpness value. Topological hierarchical edits are handled in a similar fashion, by iteratively generating patches around the edit location. The Color Insert for Figure 7.25 uses color coding to illustrate how the feature isolation patches are arranged around extraordinary features and boundaries.

While infinite patching would be a problem, the technique of adaptively patching around extraordinary vertices has been made practical with the application of several approximation schemes: Loop and Schaefer [43] first proposed "Approximate Catmull-Clark (ACC) Patches," and then introduced the use of Gregory patches [44] as a way of reducing the number of control vertices, while still retaining the continuity of the surface.

This research led to the implementation of the first feature-adaptive algorithm able to fully conform to the Renderman specification, as described by Nießner et al. [52].

FIGURE 7.25: Adaptive topological feature isolation. The color coding illustrates how the different types of patches are used to isolate boundaries or extraordinary vertices. **(See Color Insert.)**

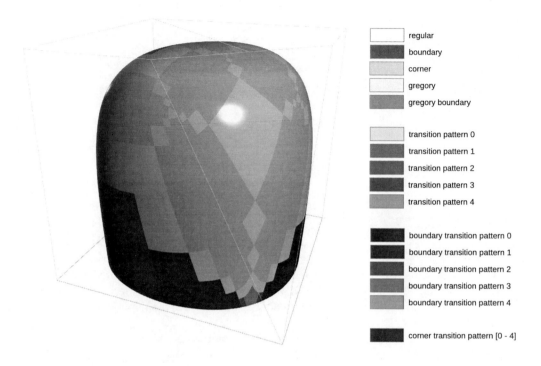

	regular
	boundary
	corner
	gregory
	gregory boundary
	transition pattern 0
	transition pattern 1
	transition pattern 2
	transition pattern 3
	transition pattern 4
	boundary transition pattern 0
	boundary transition pattern 1
	boundary transition pattern 2
	boundary transition pattern 3
	boundary transition pattern 4
	corner transition pattern [0 - 4]

7.10.4 Feature-Adaptive Subdivision

We can implement feature-adaptive GPU tessellation entirely as an extension of our existing uniform refinement code. The main difference is that instead of indiscriminately subdividing every face in the control cage mesh, we only seek faces with features that break surface continuity: extraordinary vertices, creases, or hierarchical edit tags. Using our CPU implementation of the Catmull-Clark subdivision scheme, we are going to isolate extraordinary locations with smaller and smaller sub-faces.

Once we have achieved the required level of isolation for each extraordinary feature, we traverse the resulting collection of faces and generate a list of patches. At the same time, we also gather the index of the vertices within the 1-ring that will constitute the control vertices of our bi-cubic patches. OpenSubdiv stores this information in a series of serialized *"Patch Tables,"* which can be found within its *"Far"* API layer.

Finally, we still need to generate subdivision tables, which we will use to recompute the position of all the patch control vertices every time the control mesh is deformed. The method is identical to that described previously for uniform subdivision, with the exception of the sparse set of points and patches.

The overall flow of the feature-adaptive algorithm is summarized in Figure 7.26. While the somewhat complex geometry analysis phase of topological feature isolation is executed entirely on the CPU, this cost is only incurred once and the resulting data can easily be cached. Once the subdivision and patch tables have been generated, the entire rendering process is executed on the GPU. The only bandwidth required between the devices is being used to update the small buffer containing the vertex data from the coarse control mesh.

FIGURE 7.26: Feature-adaptive display pipeline.

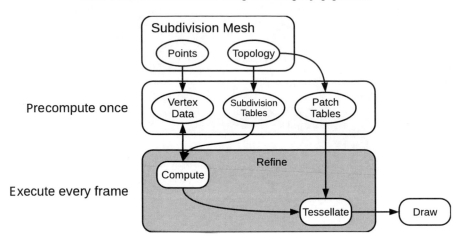

7.11 Implementing the GPU Rendering Engine

Unlike our table driven subdivision algorithm that relies on the flexibility of *"General Purpose"* computing platforms (GP-GPU), such as CUDA or OpenCL, to execute on a discrete device, tessellation can be implemented directly in the display system, using native rendering interfaces.

Modern GPUs break down shading operations into an assembly pipeline composed of multiple programmable shading stages. Figure 7.27 shows the shading pipelines for OpenGL and Microsoft's D3D APIs.

The naming conventions differ slightly in the literature, but fundamentally, the principles are the same: each shading stage corresponds to a frequency of execution of computations:

- The *Vertex Shader* is executed first and once for each vertex of the mesh.

- The *Geometry Shader* is executed once for each primitive drawn (triangle, quad, or patch).

- The *Fragment Shader* is executed at the very end on every pixel rendered and is executed most intensively.

With the advent of hardware tessellation, users have been given access to a new programmable primitive generator with the addition of two new stages: the *tessellation control* and *tessellation evaluation* stages with OpenGL 4.1, and the *hull* and *domain* shaders for D3D 11.

On the OpenGL side, the new shading stages are enabled with a new *GL_PATCHES* primitive mode that can be invoked with the draw calls from Listing 7.7.

```
glPatchParameteri(GL_PATCH_VERTICES, 16);
glDrawElements(GL_PATCHES, buffer_len, GL_UNSIGNED_INT, 0);
```

Listing 7.7: Application control.

FIGURE 7.27: GPU shader stages pipeline.

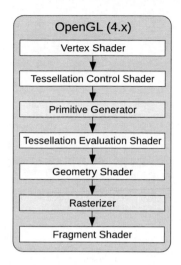 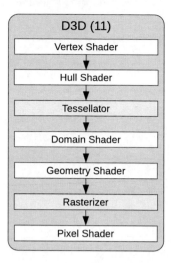

7.11.1 Bi-Cubic Bspline Patches with GLSL

We now have to implement the bi-cubic patch interpolation within this new shading pipeline. Listings 7.8 and 7.9 show a simplified version of our tessellation control and evaluation shaders corresponding to *"regular"* bi-cubic patches.

Notice how at the end of the tessellation control stage, the shader specifies the number of vertices generated on the inner and outer rings by setting the gl_TessEvalInner and gl_TessEvalOuter GLSL variables. This mechanism allows us to control dynamically the number of sub-triangles generated by the *Primitive Generator* for each individual frame: the *"GetTessLevel()"* function implements a screen-space metric based on the distance between the control vertices. While this feature is extremely powerful when integrated into a level-of-detail strategy, we will see that it can still be improved upon.

Both Listings 7.8 and 7.9 show nested loops where control vertices are being interpolated. These are not redundant computations: we apply a basis conversion in the tessellation control stage, where the control vertices are transformed into a Bézier form. The tessellation evaluation stage then interpolates these intermediate control vertices with Bézier polynomials (hidden in the *Univar4x4()* function).

We incur a small up-front cost for the basis conversion, but as the tessellation rate increases, the more compact Bézier interpolation allows us to amortize it by saving computations in the higher-frequency tessellation evaluation stage. This optimization technique is originally described by Loop and Schaefer [43].

The real-time render in Figure 7.28 (see Color Insert) displays the fractional patterns of triangles generated by the hardware tessellation engine with a yellow wireframe. In this image, the rate of tessellation is driven by the length of the edges of the patches projected in screen-space. We can adjust this metric to produce triangles with a generally consistent area of rendered screen pixels. If the metric is small enough, we can guarantee that the surface displayed is always sufficiently sampled to retain its smoothness, even under extreme close-ups. Conversely, because the sampling rate is related to the distance to the viewpoint, distant objects are automatically adjusted to a very sparse sampling rate, and become very cheap to render. In some ways, this method is similar to the screen-space dicing heuristics that the REYES rendering algorithm uses to generate micro-polygons.

We have now fleshed out the general structure of our hardware tessellation driven implementation, but there are still many details to attend to.

```
// Regular patch tess-control stage
uniform mat4 Q = mat4(
    1.f/6.f,  4.f/6.f,  1.f/6.f,  0.f,
    0.f,      4.f/6.f,  2.f/6.f,  0.f,
    0.f,      2.f/6.f,  4.f/6.f,  0.f,
    0.f,      1.f/6.f,  4.f/6.f,  1.f/6.f
);

void main() {

    int i = gl_InvocationID%4;
    int j = gl_InvocationID/4;

    vec3 H[4];
    for (int l=0; l<4; ++l) {
        H[l] = vec3(0,0,0);
        for (int k=0; k<4; ++k) {
            H[l] += Q[i][k] * inpt[l*4 + k].v.position.xyz;
        }
    }

    vec3 pos = vec3(0,0,0);
    for (int k=0; k<4; ++k) {
        pos += Q[j][k]*H[k];
    }

    output[gl_InvocationID].v.position = vec4(pos, 1.0);

    gl_TessLevelInner[0] = GetTessLevel(patchLevel);
    gl_TessLevelInner[1] = GetTessLevel(patchLevel);
    gl_TessLevelOuter[0] = GetTessLevel(patchLevel);
    gl_TessLevelOuter[1] = GetTessLevel(patchLevel);
    gl_TessLevelOuter[2] = GetTessLevel(patchLevel);
    gl_TessLevelOuter[3] = GetTessLevel(patchLevel);
}
```

Listing 7.8: Tessellation control stage for regular patches.

7.11.1.1 Handling Surface Boundaries

Most surface models tend to represent enclosed volumes, but their topology is rarely simple enough that regular patches alone can be used. One of the topological features that we need to account for is the existence of surface boundaries. An edge with only a single incident face is a *"boundary edge,"* and a face with two consecutive boundary edges is a *"corner."* All the boundaries around a surface can eventually be expressed with just these two types, although we may have to subdivide some faces to reduce the number of corners (ex: a single quad face).

By selecting preset boundary interpolation rules, users can control whether corner vertices and boundary edges are to be either smoothed or kept sharp. We apply these rulesets during the adaptive feature isolation stage of our topological analysis, but the process generates special boundary and corner patches. These patches require dedicated tessellation shader programs.

Figure 7.29 shows that the main difference between a regular and a boundary patch is that four control vertices from the 1-ring are undefined, being on the other side of the boundary. These vertices can be very easily obtained though, simply by mirroring the control vertex that is inside the boundary against the control vertex that straddles the boundary. Similarly, a corner patch mirrors six vertices along its edges, then mirrors the diagonal vertex. The interpolation of boundary patches is the same as that of regular patches, but we can account for the "mirroring" simply by modifying the coefficients of the interpolation matrix, which saves some cycles.

```
// Regular patch tess-eval stage
void main() {

    vec2 UV = gl_TessCoord.xy;

    float B[4], D[4];
    vec3 BUCP[4], DUCP[4];
    Univar4x4(UV.x, B, D);

    for (int i=0; i<4; ++i) {
        BUCP[i] = vec3(0);
        DUCP[i] = vec3(0);
        for (int j=0; j<4; ++j) {
            vec3 A = inpt[4*i + j].v.position.xyz;
            BUCP[i] += A * B[j];
            DUCP[i] += A * D[j];
        }
    }

    vec3 WorldPos  = vec3(0);
    vec3 Tangent   = vec3(0);
    vec3 BiTangent = vec3(0);

    Univar4x4(UV.y, B, D);

    for (int k=0; k<4; ++k) {
        WorldPos  += B[k] * BUCP[k];
        Tangent   += B[k] * DUCP[k];
        BiTangent += D[k] * BUCP[k];
    }
    int level = int(inpt[0].v.ptexInfo.z);
    Tangent *= 3 * level;
    BiTangent *= 3 * level;

    vec3 normal = normalize(cross(Tangent, BiTangent));

    outpt.v.position = vec4(WorldPos, 1.0f);
    outpt.v.normal = normal;

    gl_Position = (OsdProjectionMatrix() * vec4(WorldPos, 1.0f));
}
```

Listing 7.9: Tessellation evaluation stage for regular patches.

There is one additional problem: we have to rotate the control vertices of the patch so that the boundary or the corner is lined up with the mirroring encoded in the matrix. This correction is applied early on during the feature analysis stage, thus fully amortizing the cost of the rotation.

7.11.1.2 Handling Patch Transitions

Aside from surface boundaries, we also have to manage a problem that is a by-product of our patch nesting strategy: we need to prevent *"cracks"* from forming at the boundaries between patches.

Figure 7.30 shows a typical patch nesting pattern around an isolated extraordinary vertex. The darker patches in this figure indicate that at least one edge of the patch is bordered by two adjacent patches from a higher level of isolation. In Listing 7.8, we have seen that the hardware primitive generator only accommodates a single scalar (gl_tessLevelOuter) to describe the number of vertices that need to be generated along a given edge of the patch.

In order to be able to match a fractional rate of tessellation along the outer edge, we need to split these patches so that we can transition the rates of tessellation with vertices matching on each side of the boundary.

FIGURE 7.28: Wireframe showing the triangles generated by the GPU tessellation unit. Fractional patch tessellation allows for a continuous screen-space level of detail without cracks at the patch boundaries. **(See Color Insert.)**

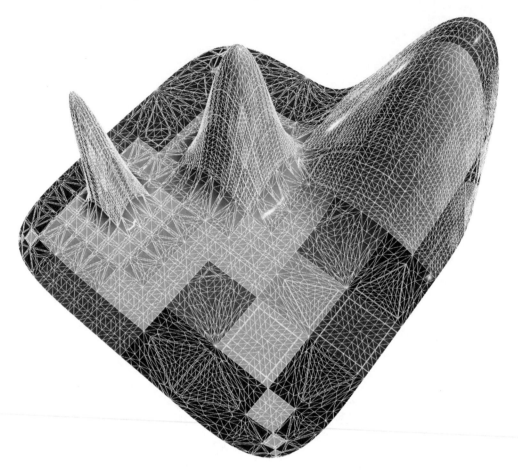

Figure 7.31 shows the five transition constellation patterns connecting patches and sub-patches. The central square patch is split into triangular sub-patches, the corners of which are matched with the "T" junctions. Each constellation is also associated a rotation component, in order to describe all the possible topological configurations. We also have to apply these constellation patterns to the boundary and corner patches. Between the special types of patches and transition patterns, we are indeed generating a growing number of combinations that each require dedicated shader codes, and so on.

7.11.1.3 "End" Patches

One aspect of feature-adaptive isolation that we have put aside until now is what happens in the close neighborhood of an extraordinary vertex. Since we cannot afford to nest a literal infinity of patches, eventually we are going to have to approximate the limit surface around that area.

One possible solution is to use Gregory patches, as described in by Loop et al. [44]. If we set an arbitrary limit level to our feature isolation algorithm, we can use these bicubic patches to fill the remaining gaps in the surface. The patches provide a very close

FIGURE 7.29: Boundary patch and corner patch with mirrored vertices.

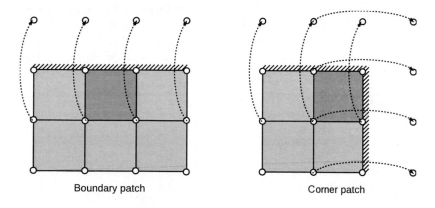

FIGURE 7.30: Matching tessellation across isolation levels.

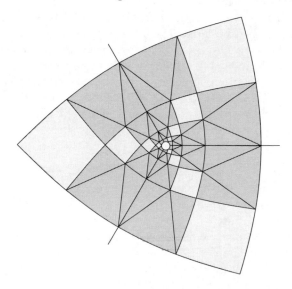

FIGURE 7.31: All five possible transition patterns.

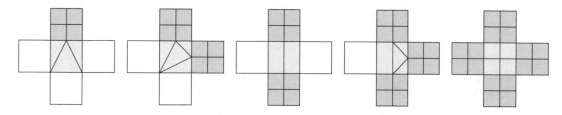

approximation to the limit surface and with tessellation, they hold up fairly well, even in extreme close-ups. The downside, however, is that the mathematics are significantly more complex, require more computations as well as dedicated data tables. For many applications though, the high precision afforded by Gregory patches is unlikely to justify these hefty trade-offs.

Another possible solution is to simply use bilinear quads as "end patches." Assuming that we can make sure that the area they cover is either very close to flat or tiny in screen-space, this would be a much more lightweight solution. We could isolate extraordinary features to a very high level during our precomputation pass, but we do not necessarily have to use all these levels when displaying a given frame. We could dynamically switch the level of isolation based on the distance of the object to the camera. Bilinear quads are a very crude approximation of the limit surface, but they are much cheaper than Gregory patches. Within a dynamic isolation system, we believe that they can offer a more attractive compromise between precision and performance.

7.11.2 Mitigating Drawing Overheads

While the various bi-cubic types of patches are relatively simple to implement within the programmable tessellation control and evaluation shaders, an efficient implementation of the feature-adaptive scheme still presents some challenges. With our goal of fully representing the limit surface, we have created a fairly large collection of distinct combinations of patches that each require separate shading programs.

Unfortunately, with the current generation of graphics APIs (OpenGL 4.1), each shading program can only be switched by launching separate individual draw instructions; one for each sequence of patches of each type. Even though we are sorting all the patches to be drawn by type, we are still incurring a substantially large number of driver state changes, along with the attending execution launches. In practice, while a typical mesh only contains a fraction of all the possible patterns, we are still queuing many driver calls from the CPU. Moreover, as the number of surfaces to be drawn increases, this eventually leads to very noticeable performance overheads. We are investigating several avenues to help mitigate this problem:

- Our first approach has been the implementation of a batching system in OpenSubdiv: we provide factory classes that can combine the arrays of patches from several meshes. Considering that a typical feature film character is often composed of a couple hundred distinct primitives (eyeballs, teeth, nails), this technique can considerably mitigate driver overheads. It does, however, add some complexity when access to individual primitives is required (e.g., highlighting a selected eyeball on selection), so this approach is not entirely satisfactory.

- We can also try to address the fragmentation of patch types more directly by simplifying transition patch patterns. Currently, the outer tessellation rate can only be specified with a single fractional value along a given edge. This situation is forcing our implementation to resort to multiple draw calls in order to render each of the five transition patterns with several triangular sub-patches (see Figure 7.32). Even though this limitation is embedded within the hardware tessellation unit of the current generation of GPUs, we are proposing an extension to the existing tessellation standard for future generations of chips.

  In order to achieve crack-free tessellation, the outer tessellation levels of adjacent patches must generate the same vertex locations along the edge. The proposed extension would give us the flexibility of drawing transition patches within a single draw call, by allowing the tessellation of an outer edge to be first split in half exactly at the 0.5 domain location, and then use two fractional tessellation rates: one for each half of the edge. This extension would greatly simplify not only the tessellation shader code required for crack-free transition patches, but also the host application's drawing code.

FIGURE 7.32: Comparing an example transition pattern drawn with sub-patches against our proposed extension.

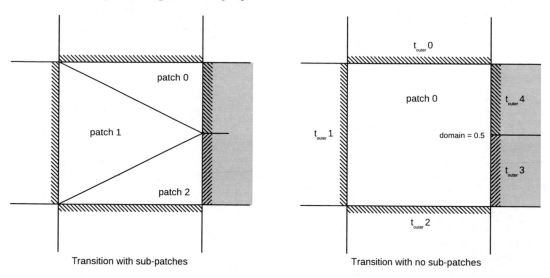

7.12 Texturing

Thus far, this chapter has been focusing on limit surface representation, at the cost of neglecting texturing tasks, which are equally critical in producing compelling imagery. Since subdivision surfaces are controlled by a coarse polygonal mesh, most of the usual mapping and painting techniques can be applied successfully.

However, since our underlying representation is a bi-cubic patch, we are not constrained to a bilinear interpolation of the texture coordinates. Instead, we can opt to use a smoother bi-cubic texture coordinate interpolation scheme, although this comes at a hefty cost both for performance and code complexity. A more detailed description of face-varying interpolation falls, unfortunately, beyond the scope of this book.

There is, however, another texturing technique that has been developed specifically for subdivision surfaces: Ptex [10]. Originally developed by Walt Disney Studios for their own feature production rendering, this particular texturing system has since been open-sourced, and support for its file format has been incorporated into most of the leading DCC applications. The key feature of Ptex is that the system assigns a unique texture to each face of a given mesh, thereby alleviating the need for labor intensive UV assignments. The file format is very efficient and can store hundred of thousands of textures in a single file. A topological adjacency table is also stored in the file, which allows filters to blend texels across face boundaries.

Although direct graphics hardware support for Ptex is still a work in progress, Open-Subdiv does offer an interactive GPU implementation. Upon reading the file, an optimizing algorithm packs each face texture, including mip-maps, into a 3D texture bank. The shader code then simply uses the parameterization of each bi-cubic patch as an implicit coordinate frame to access each texel. By comparison, a UV layout would require mapping coordinates to be associated with each vertex of the mesh, and the shaders would then need to interpolate these coordinates to locate the texels.

Unlike off-line renderers that can use the built-in adjacency table, interactive filtering across patch boundaries is achieved by guttering the face textures with a single row of redundant texels. Using a single row of texels is a compromise that allows us to render seamless textures, but prevents us from using the higher quality hardware-backed anisotropic texture filters. Anisotropic filtering would require each texture to be guttered with at least half the number of texels of the filter size (eight usually), which would cause an unreasonable increase of the texture size in GPU memory. This opens up some high-frequency aliasing problems that we have yet to address in OpenSubdiv, but we should be able to borrow from the many techniques already implemented in off-line rendering software.

7.12.1   Displacement Mapping

One of the benefits of using a geometrically continuous surface over polygons is that we can use differential calculus to integrate gradient functions. Practically, this allows us to establish robust local tangent spaces and smooth surface normals. By extension, we can also analytically integrate arbitrary surface displacement functions, which produces displaced normals (see Nießner and Loop [51]) that remain continuous under deformation.

In conjunction with the ability of tessellating meshes with very high densities of triangles, we have all the ingredients necessary to render high-quality articulated surfaces with displacement mapping in real time. Displacement mapping is becoming particularly relevant with the emergence of digital sculpting tools such as Autodesk's Mudbox or Pixologic's ZBrush. These tools empower artists to produce extremely detailed sculptures and manipulate interactive shapes that use upward of a billion quad faces. Obviously, the computing power required to pose and articulate this kind of geometry in real time is prohibitive, which is why digital sculpting has been limited to static artwork so far.

However, it is fairly easy to extract a displacement texture by differencing the high resolution sculpture and a much lower resolution smooth skin shape. The low resolution mesh can be posed and articulated, but it also retains all the visual quality and detail of the original sculpture thanks to the application of displacement mapping. With adaptive fractional tessellation we can effectively decouple the visual complexity of a model from the amount of static geometry required to produce an image on screen: using simple screen-space metrics, we can smoothly reduce the tessellation rate on regions that are far from the point of view. By comparison, applying similar geometry culling techniques to polygonal meshes produce very complex algorithms that are prone to "popping" and "cracking" artifacts.

Figure 7.33 shows a sculpture from artist Jesse Sandifer (`www.chickwalker.com`), originally executed in Autodesk's Mudbox. The full resolution model uses over half-a-billion quads. Once converted to Ptex textures though, the entire set of geometric and shading information fits within the texture memory of a \$300 GPU, and his Turtle Barbarian character can be posed in real time. The tessellation metric applied to produce these figures (also see the Color Insert for Figure 7.34) generates between 5 and 10 million triangles for each frame, at a consistent 30 Hz. This allows us to interact with a visualization of the model rendered with nearly sub-pixel shading rate, at full-screen resolution. This is the level of visual feedback that our animators require in order to make informed creative decisions that will not be invalidated later against the "ground truth" produced by the off-line renderer.

FIGURE 7.33: Interactive render using GPU hardware tessellation and Ptex displacement textures showing the extremely high density of geometric detail.

7.13 Conclusion

With subdivision surfaces we have tackled a problem that has been extremely resistant to parallel execution. We were eventually able to break from the constraints imposed by the exponential growth of the subdivision algorithm through leveraging the bi-cubic patch nature of the surface. This paradigm shift has resulted in the implementation of our feature-adaptive algorithm.

This fortunate turn of the situation opens up several powerful avenues to exploit many-core parallelism. During the refinement step, we can use either CPU or GP-GPU methods to apply the subdivision scheme to the vertices of the coarse mesh. If the data is intended for interactive display, we can then feed our patch control vertices to the built-in hardware tessellation generator, which can render up to half-a-billion vertices per second (Kepler generation hardware). While not all problems will be amenable to such fortuitous solutions, in this particular case, we were able to achieve an overall speed-up of about four orders of magnitude, compared to the legacy CPU-based implementations.

FIGURE 7.34: Mudbox sculpture showing analytical displacement with GPU hardware tessellation for interactive animation. Color and displacement textures are stored in the Ptex format. **(See Color Insert.)**

The massive performance gain is only one of several equally important benefits though: switching to a bi-cubic patch representation means that all the sampled vertices are now situated immediately on the limit surface instead of being discrete approximations. The resulting surfaces are watertight, with robust analytical normals, from which we derive the ability to apply displacements that remain consistent under deformation. The geometrically continuous normals also contribute to improved illumination, with smoother specular reflections. Finally, by applying fractional tessellation factors derived from screen-space metrics, we can dynamically adjust the amount of geometry that the GPU needs to sample for each individual frame, thus decoupling the computational load from the geometric density of the shape.

By efficiently leveraging all the features of the GPU architecture, we are now able to achieve interactive sub-pixel sampling densities that can rival the micro-polygon shading rates applied in off-line renders. We believe that the benefits from our implementation will prove to be a vital step toward increasing the realism and visual quality of interactive computer generated imagery.

Bibliography

[1] *Intel® 64 and IA-32 Architectures Optimization Reference Manual.* Intel Corporation, April 2012. URL: `http://www.intel.com/content/dam/doc/manual/64-ia-32-architectures-optimization-manual.pdf`.

[2] John C. Adams. *MUDPACK: Multigrid software for elliptic partial differential equations.* NCAR, 1999. Version 5.0.1.

[3] David Beazley. Python GIL, presented at PyCON 2010. 2010. URL: `http://www.dabeaz.com/python/UnderstandingGIL.pdf`.

[4] G. Bergen and D. Gregorius. *Game Physics Pearls.* A.K. Peters, 2010. URL: `http://books.google.com/books?id=8vIpAQAAMAAJ`.

[5] J. U. Brackbill and H. M. Ruppel. FLIP: A method for adaptively zoned, particle-in-cell calculations of fluid flows in two dimensions. *J. Comput. Phys.*, 65(2):314–343, August 1986. URL: `http://dx.doi.org/10.1016/0021-9991(86)90211-1`, `http://dx.doi.org/10.1016/0021-9991(86)90211-1` `doi:10.1016/0021-9991(86)90211-1`.

[6] Robert Bridson. *Fluid Simulation for Computer Graphics.* A. K. Peters, Wellesley, MA, 2008.

[7] Robert Bridson, Jim Houriham, and Marcus Nordenstam. Curl-noise for procedural fluid flow. *ACM Trans. Graph.*, 26, 2007. `http://dx.doi.org/10.1145/1276377.1276435` `doi:10.1145/1276377.1276435`.

[8] William L. Briggs, Van Emden Henson, and S. F. McCormick. *A multigrid tutorial.* Society for Industrial and Applied Mathematics, Philadelphia, PA, 2nd edition, 2000.

[9] J. Budsberg, M. Losure, K. Museth, and M. Baer. Liquids in *The Croods.* In *ACM Digital Production Symposium (DigiPro 2013)*, 2013.

[10] Brent Burley and Dylan Lacewell. Ptex: Per-face texture mapping for production rendering. In *Proceedings of the 19th Eurographics Conference on Rendering*, EGSR'08, pages 1155–1164, Aire-la-Ville, Switzerland, 2008. Eurographics Association. URL: `http://dx.doi.org/10.1111/j.1467-8659.2008.01253.x`, `http://dx.doi.org/10.1111/j.1467-8659.2008.01253.x` `doi:10.1111/j.1467-8659.2008.01253.x`.

[11] C. Loop Smooth subdivision surfaces based on triangles. Master's thesis, University of Utah, 1987.

[12] E. Catmull and J. Clark. Recursively generated B-spline surfaces on arbitrary topological meshes. *Computer-Aided Design*, 10(6):350–355, November 1978.

[13] Shannon Cepeda. *Vectorization — Find out What It Is, Find out More!* Intel Corp., 2013. URL: `http://software.intel.com/en-us/blogs/2012/01/31/vectorization-find-out-what-it-is-find-out-more`.

[14] Stuart Cheshire. Latency and the quest for interactivity. November 1996. URL: http://www.stuartcheshire.org/papers/LatencyQuest.html.

[15] Intel Corp. *Intel Cilk Plus Language Extension Specification Version 1.2.* Intel Corp., 2013. URL: http://cilkplus.org.

[16] J. Demmel. Applications of parallel computers. Retrieved from U.C. Berkeley CS267 Web site: http://www.cs.berkeley.edu/ demmel/cs267/, 1996.

[17] Tony DeRose, Michael Kass, and Tien Truong. Subdivision surfaces in character animation. In *SIGGRAPH*, pages 85–94, 1998.

[18] E. Dijkstra. Go To statement considered harmful. *Communications of the ACM*, 11(3):147–148, March 1968.

[19] D. Doo and M. Sabin. Behavior of recursive division surfaces near extraordinary points. *Computer-Aided Design*, 10(6):356–360, 1978.

[20] T. F. Dupont and Y. Liu. Back and forth error compensation and correction methods for removing errors induced by uneven gradients of the level set function. *J. Comput. Phys.*, 190(1):311–324, 2003.

[21] W. F. Engel. *ShaderX5: Advanced Rendering Techniques.* ShaderX series. Charles River Media, 2007. URL: http://books.google.com/books?id=isu_QgAACAAJ.

[22] Wolfgang Engel. *GPU Pro 5.* A. K. Peters/CRC Press, 2014. URL: http://www.crcpress.com/product/isbn/9781482208634.

[23] Christer Ericson. *Real-Time Collision Detection.* Morgan Kaufmann Publishers Inc., San Francisco, CA, 2004.

[24] Jason Evans. Scalable memory allocation using jemalloc. January 2011. URL: https://www.facebook.com/notes/facebook-engineering/scalable-memory-allocation-using-jemalloc/480222803919.

[25] N. Foster and D. Metaxas. Realistic animation of liquids. *Graph. Models and Image Processing*, 58:471–483, 1996.

[26] Nick Foster and Ronald Fedkiw. Practical animation of liquids. In *Proceedings of the 28th Annual Conference on Computer Graphics and Interactive Techniques*, SIGGRAPH '01, pages 23–30, New York, NY, 2001. ACM. URL: http://doi.acm.org/10.1145/383259.383261, http://dx.doi.org/10.1145/383259.383261 doi:10.1145/383259.383261.

[27] Khronos OpenCL Working Group. SPIR: The standard portable intermediate representation for device programs, 2014. URL: https://www.khronos.org/spir.

[28] Kronos Group. *The OpenCL 2.0 Specification.* Kronos Group, 2013. URL: https://www.khronos.org/opencl.

[29] Takahiro Harada. A parallel constraint solver for a rigid body simulation. In *SIGGRAPH Asia 2011 Sketches*, SA '11, pages 22:1–22:2, New York, NY, 2011. ACM. URL: http://doi.acm.org/10.1145/2077378.2077406, http://dx.doi.org/10.1145/2077378.2077406 doi:10.1145/2077378.2077406.

[30] F. Harlow and J. Welch. Numerical calculations of time-dependent viscous incompressible flow of fluid with free surface. *Phys. Fluids*, pages 2182–2189, 1965.

[31] F. H. Harlow. The particle-in-cell method for numerical solution of problems in fluid dynamics. *Experimental arithmetic, high-speed computations and mathematics*, 1963.

[32] R. D. Henderson. Scalable fluid simulation in linear time on shared memory multiprocessors. In *ACM SIGGRAPH Digital Production Symposium (DigiPro 2012)*, 2012.

[33] Hugues Hoppe. Optimization of mesh locality for transparent vertex caching. In *Proceedings of the 26th Annual Conference on Computer Graphics and Interactive Techniques*, SIGGRAPH '99, pages 269–276, New York, NY, 1999. ACM Press/Addison-Wesley Publishing Co. URL: `http://dx.doi.org/10.1145/311535.311565`, `http://dx.doi.org/10.1145/311535.311565 doi:10.1145/311535.311565`.

[34] Intel. *Intel Math Kernal Library Reference Manual*. Intel Coproration, 2011. Document number 630813-041US.

[35] S. Jacobs. *Game Programming Gems Seven*. Charles River Media/Course Technology, 2008. URL: `http://books.google.com/books?id=5mDwGgAACAAJ`.

[36] J. Jeffers and J. Reinders. *Intel Xeon Phi Coprocessor High Performance Programming*, 1st edition. Morgan Kaufmann, Waltham, MA, 2013.

[37] F. Ghorbel and K. Mamou. A simple and efficient approach for 3D mesh approximate convex decomposition, 2009. URL: `http://sourceforge.net/projects/hacd`.

[38] George Em Karniadakis, Moshe Israeli, and Steven A Orszag. High-order splitting methods for the incompressible Navier-Stokes equations. *J. Comput. Phys.*, 97(2):414–443, 1991. `http://dx.doi.org/10.1016/0021-9991(91)90007-8 doi:10.1016/0021-9991(91)90007-8`.

[39] B. Kim, Y. Liu, I. Llamas, and J. Rossignac. Flowfixer: Using BFECC for fluid simulation. In *Eurographics Workshop on Natural Phenomena*, 2005.

[40] J. Kim and P. Moin. Application of a fractional step method to incompressible Navier-Stokes equations. *J. Comput. Phys.*, 59:308–323, 1985.

[41] E. A. Lee. The problem with threads. Technical Report UCB/EECS-2006-1, EECS Department, University of California, Berkeley, January 2006. A published version of this paper is in IEEE Computer 39(5):33-42, May 2006. URL: `http://www.eecs.berkeley.edu/Pubs/TechRpts/2006/EECS-2006-1.html`.

[42] Fuchang Liu, Takahiro Harada, Youngeun Lee, and Young J. Kim. GSAP: Real-time collision culling of a million bodies on graphics processing units. In *ACM SIGGRAPH Asia 2010 Papers*, SIGGRAPH ASIA '10, pages 154:1–154:8, New York, NY, 2010. ACM. URL: `http://graphics.ewha.ac.kr/gSaP`, `http://dx.doi.org/10.1145/1866158.1866180 doi:10.1145/1866158.1866180`.

[43] Charles Loop and Scott Schaefer. Approximating Catmull-Clark subdivision surfaces with bicubic patches. *ACM Trans. Graph.*, 27(1):8:1–8:11, March 2008. URL: `http://doi.acm.org/10.1145/1330511.1330519`, `http://dx.doi.org/10.1145/1330511.1330519 doi:10.1145/1330511.1330519`.

[44] Charles T. Loop, Scott Schaefer, Tianyun Ni, and Ignacio Castaño. Approximating subdivision surfaces with Gregory patches for hardware tessellation. *ACM Trans. Graph.*, 28(5), 2009.

[45] A. McAdams, E. Sifakis, and J. Teran. A parallel multigrid Poisson solver for fluids simulation on large grids. In *Proceedings of the 2010 ACM SIGGRAPH/Eurographics Symposium on Computer Animation*, SCA '10, pages 65–74, Aire-la-Ville, Switzerland, Switzerland, 2010. Eurographics Association.

[46] M. McCool, A. Robison, and J. Reinders. *Structured Parallel Programming*. Morgan Kaufmann, 2012.

[47] J. J. Monaghan. Extrapolating B-splines for interpolation. *J. Comput. Phys.*, 60(2):253–262, 1985.

[48] Ken Museth. VDB: High-resolution sparse volumes with dynamic topology. *ACM Trans. Graph.*, 32(3):27:1–27:22, July 2013. URL: http://doi.acm.org/10.1145/2487228.2487235, http://dx.doi.org/10.1145/2487228.2487235 doi:10.1145/2487228.2487235.

[49] Ken Museth, Jeff Lait, John Johanson, Jeff Budsberg, Ron Henderson, Mihai Alden, Peter Cucka, and David Hill. OpenVDB: An open-source data structure and toolkit for high-resolution volumes. In *ACM SIGGRAPH 2013 Courses*, SIGGRAPH '13, pages 19:1–19:1, New York, NY, 2013. ACM. URL: http://doi.acm.org/10.1145/2504435.2504454, http://dx.doi.org/10.1145/2504435.2504454 doi:10.1145/2504435.2504454.

[50] Jakob Nielsen. *Usability Engineering*. Morgan Kaufmann Publishers Inc., San Francisco, CA, 1993.

[51] M. Nießner and C. Loop. Analytic displacement mapping using hardware tessellation. *ACM Transactions on Graphics (TOG)*, 32(3):26, 2013.

[52] M. Nießner, C. Loop, M. Meyer, and T. DeRose. Feature-adaptive GPU rendering of Catmull-Clark subdivision surfaces. *ACM Transactions on Graphics (TOG)*, 31(1):6, 2012.

[53] OpenMP. *The OpenMP API Specification for Parallel Programming*. OpenMP, 2011. Version 3.1.

[54] OpenMP. *OpenMP 4.0 Specifications*. OpenMP, 2013. URL: http://openmp.org.

[55] David Ott. Optimizing applications for NUMA. *Intel Corporation*, 2011. URL: http://software.intel.com/en-us/articles/optimizing-applications-for-numa.

[56] W. Press, S. Teukolsky, W. Vetterling, and B. Flannery. *Numerical Recipes in C: The Art of Scientific Computing*, 2nd edition. Cambridge University Press, 1996.

[57] J. Reinders. *Intel Threading Building Blocks: Outfitting C++ for Multi-Core Processor Parallelism*, 1st edition. O'Reilly & Associates, Inc., Sebastopol, CA, 2007.

[58] Steve Scott. No free lunch for Intel MIC (or GPU's). URL: http://blogs.nvidia.com/blog/2012/04/03/no-free-lunch-for-intel-mic-or-gpus/, April 2012.

[59] Andrew Selle, Ronald Fedkiw, ByungMoon Kim, Yingjie Liu, and Jarek Rossignac. An unconditionally stable MacCormack method. *J. Sci. Comput.*, 35:350–371, 2008. URL: http://dx.doi.org/10.1007/s10915-007-9166-4 doi:10.1007/s10915-007-9166-4.

[60] Jos Stam. Exact evaluation of Catmull-Clark subdivision surfaces at arbitrary parameter values. In *Proceedings of the 25th Annual Conference on Computer Graphics and Interactive Techniques*, SIGGRAPH '98, pages 395–404, New York, NY, 1998. ACM. URL: http://doi.acm.org/10.1145/280814.280945, http://dx.doi.org/10.1145/280814.280945 doi:10.1145/280814.280945.

[61] Jos Stam. Stable fluids. In *Proceedings of the 26th Annual Conference on Computer Graphics and Interactive Techniques*, SIGGRAPH '99, pages 121–128, New York, NY, 1999. ACM Press/Addison-Wesley Publishing Co. URL: http://dx.doi.org/10.1145/311535.311548 doi:10.1145/311535.311548.

[62] Herb Sutter. The free lunch is over: A fundamental turn toward concurrency in software. *Dr. Dobbs Journal*, 30(3):202–210, 2005. URL: http://www.gotw.ca/publications/concurrency-ddj.htm.

[63] Herb Sutter. Use lock hierarchies to avoid deadlock. *Dr. Dobb's Journal*, 2007. URL: http://www.drdobbs.com/parallel/use-lock-hierarchies-to-avoid-deadlock/204801163.

[64] Herb Sutter. Interrupt politely. *Dr. Dobb's Journal*, 2008. URL: http://www.drdobbs.com/parallel/interrupt-politely/207100682.

[65] Koen Vroeijenstijn and Ronald D. Henderson. Simulating massive dust in *Megamind*. In *ACM SIGGRAPH 2011 Talks*, SIGGRAPH '11, New York, NY, 2011. ACM. URL: http://dx.doi.org/10.1145/2037826.2037915 doi:10.1145/2037826.2037915.

[66] M. Wrenninge. *Production Volume Rendering: Design and Implementation*. CRC Press, Boca Raton, FL, 2013.

[67] Yongning Zhu and Robert Bridson. Animating sand as a fluid. *ACM Trans. Graph.*, 24(3):965–972, July 2005. URL: http://doi.acm.org/10.1145/1073204.1073298, http://dx.doi.org/10.1145/1073204.1073298 doi:10.1145/1073204.1073298.

Index

A

ACC Patches; *See* Approximate
      Catmull-Clark Patches
Advection solvers, 124–126
Aliasing
    high-frequency, 198
    pointer, 40
Amdahl's law, 104, 119
AMD CodeXL tool, 144, 161
Approximate Catmull-Clark (ACC)
      Patches, 188
Arithmetic Logic Units (ALU), 173
Array of Structures (AoS), 17
Autodesk's Mudbox, 198

B

Back and Forth Error Compensation and
      Correction (BFECC), 145
Background Execution, 64–69
    constant data, 67
      memory consumption, 67
      multiple-reader scenario, 67
      starter thread, 67
    frame scheduling, 65–66
    interruption, 66–67
      common edits, 67
      constant source of bugs, 66
      in-flight threads, 67
      repetitive strain injury, 66
      resource cleanup problems, 66
    problematic data structures, 67–69
      assumption, 68
      code reorganization, 68
      pseudocode, 67
    user interaction, 65
      debugging, 65
      feedback, 65
      performance surprises, 65
Bézier interpolation, 191
BFECC; *See* Back and Forth Error
      Compensation and Correction

Bounding volume hierarchy (BVH) query,
      150
Bspline patches with GLSL (bi-cubic),
      191–196
    Bézier interpolation, 191
    boundary edge, 192
    corner, 192
    crack prevention, 193
    end patches, 194–196
    Gregory patches, 194
    handling patch transitions, 193–194
    handling surface boundaries, 192–193
    hardware tessellation engine, 191
    mirroring, 193
    real-time render, 191, 194
    REYES rendering algorithm, 191
    up-front cost, 191
Bullet Physics (simulation with OpenCL),
      137–161
    GPU constraint solving, 155–181
      batch creation and two-stage
        batching, 157–158
      contact and friction constraint setup,
        155–156
      equations of motion, 155
      Euler extension, 155
      flood fill algorithm, 157
      future work, 159
      GPU deterministic simulation, 159
      kernel enqueue operations, 156
      Newton's second law, 155
      non-contact constraints, 158–159
      parallel projected Gauss-Seidel
        method, 156–157
      projected Gauss-Seidel algorithm,
        159
    GPU contact point generation, 151–154
      collision detection queries, 152
      collision shape representation,
        151–152
      contact clipping algorithm, 154

contact reduction, 154
convex decomposition, 151
convex 3D height field using cube maps, 152–153
HACD library, 151, 152
Minkowski Portal Refinement, 154
NP hard problem, 151
separating axis test, 153
Sutherland Hodgeman clipping, 153–154
GPU spatial acceleration structures, 145–151
bottleneck, 147
bounding volume hierarchy query, 150
brute-force algorithm, 146
hybrid approaches, 150
parallel 1-axis sort and sweep, 148
parallel 3-axis sweep and prune, 149–150
reference all pairs overlap test, 146–147
static local space AABB tree, 150–151
Sweep and Prune algorithm, 149
uniform grid, 147–148
workgroup, 148
refactoring before the full rewrite, 139–140
benchmark tests, 139
single-threaded performance, 139
rewriting from scratch using OpenCL, 140–145
algorithms, 143
AMD CodeXL tool suite, 144
AMD terminology, 142
brief OpenCL introduction, 140–141
clipContacts stage, 144
code conversion, 141
Compute Units, 142, 143
CPU math library, 144
dealing with branchy code/thread divergence, 143–144
debugging, 141, 144
exploiting the GPU, 142–143
Global Device Memory, 142
kernel, 141
OpenCL kernel source code, 145
precompiled kernel caching, 145
Private Memory, 142

serializing data to contiguous memory, 144
sharing CPU and GPU code, 144–145
Standard Portable Intermediate Representation specification, 145
wavefront, 142
Work Groups, 142
Work Item, 142
wrapper, 141
rigid body dynamics simulation, 138–139
Newton laws, 138
object–object interactions, 138
Visual Effects industry, 138
BVH query; *See* Bounding volume hierarchy query

C
Catmull-Clark terminology, 187
regular face, 187
regular vertex, 187
surfaces, 168
valence, 187
Character rigs; *See* LibEE (parallel evaluation of character rigs)
Cilk Plus (Intel), 10, 12
Collision detection queries, 152
Convex decomposition, 151
Critical path, 96
CUDA kernel execution overheads, 179
Cycle-suckers, 31

D
DCC platforms; *See* Digital Content Creation platforms
Debugging, 16
Background Execution, 65
Houdini, 23
OpenCL, 141, 144
Presto, 52, 70–71
TBB, 16
Dependency graph, 76
Designing for multithreading; *See* Presto execution system
Digital Content Creation (DCC) platforms, 118
Displacement mapping, 198
DreamWorks Animation (DWA), 2, 74, 75, 111, 136

E

Eigen space transform, 188
Elliptic solvers, 126–128
End patches, 194–196
Equations of motion, 155
Euler extension, 155
Existing software, multithreading of; *See* Houdini
External readers, 37

F

Face-varying primitive variable data, 167
Fast Fourier Transforms (FFTs), 113
Floating point (FP) number operations, 6
Flood fill algorithm, 157
Fluid Implicit Particle (FLIP), 129
Fluids (simulation on the CPU), 111–136
    data structures, 120–122
      particles, 120
      root node, 120
      sparse grids, 120
      volumes, 120
    fluid simulation, 120–136
      data structures, 120–122
      liquids, 128–136
      smoke, fire, and explosions, 122–128
    liquids, 128–136
      benchmark problem, 135, 136
      built-in reduction method, 135–136
      Fluid Implicit Particle, 129
      Incomplete Cholesky preconditioner, 132
      memory bandwidth, 135
      parallel point rasterization, 132–136
      parallel scalability, 135
      particle-in-cell approaches, 129
      pseudocode, 133
      scatter approach, 133
      smoothing kernel, 131
      sparse grids, 129
    motivation, 111–112
    performance, 119
      Amdahl's law, 119
      arithmetic intensity, 119
      asymptotic complexity, 119
      efficiency, 119
      Gustafson-Barsis' law, 119
      speedup, 119
    programming models, 112–119
      binary tree, 116

Digital Content Creation platforms, 118
    dynamic load balancing, 112
    everything you need to get started, 114
    example (dot product), 115–116
    example (maximum absolute value), 117–118
    example (over), 114–115
    Fast Fourier Transforms, 113
    Houdini Development Kit, 118
    Intel Math Kernel Library, 113
    library code, 118
    nested parallelism, 112
    OpenMP, 113
    performance, 119
    platform considerations, 118
    Threading Building Blocks, 113
    smoke, fire, and explosions, 122–128
      advection solvers, 124–126
      Back and Forth Error Compensation and Correction, 125
      benchmark problem, 128
      diffusion, 124
      Dirichlet boundary conditions, 128
      divergence control term, 123
      elliptic solvers, 126–128
      FFT-based solver, 128
      Helmholtz equation, 126
      Navier-Stokes equations, 122
      Poisson equation, 124
      scalar fields, 123
      speedup measurements, 126
Fork–join data parallelism, 13
Fortran, 12, 128
FP number operations; *See* Floating point number operations

G

Gauss-Seidel algorithm, 156–157
Global Device Memory, 142
Global Interpreter Lock (GIL), 58–59, 78
GOTO statements, 10
GPU compute and drawing; *See* OpenSubdiv (interoperating GPU compute and drawing)
GPU constraint solving, 155–181
    batch creation and two-stage batching, 157–158
    contact and friction constraint setup, 155–156

equations of motion, 155
Euler extension, 155
flood fill algorithm, 157
future work, 159
GPU deterministic simulation, 159
kernel enqueue operations, 156
Newton's second law, 155
non-contact constraints, 158–159
parallel projected Gauss-Seidel
    method, 156–157
projected Gauss-Seidel algorithm, 159
GPU contact point generation, 151–154
collision detection queries, 152
collision shape representation,
    151–152
contact clipping algorithm, 154
contact reduction, 154
convex decomposition, 151
convex 3D height field using cube
    maps, 152–153
HACD library, 151, 152
Minkowski Portal Refinement, 154
NP hard problem, 151
separating axis test, 153
Sutherland Hodgeman clipping,
    153–154
GPU exploitation (OpenCL), 142–143
AMD terminology, 142
Compute Units, 142
Global Device Memory, 142
Private Memory, 142
wavefront, 142
Work Groups, 142
Work Item, 142
GPU rendering engine, 190–196
assembly pipeline, 190, 191
bi-cubic Bspline patches with GLSL,
    191–196
Fragment Shader, 190
Geometry Shader, 190
mitigating drawing overheads, 196–197
Vertex Shader, 190
GPU spatial acceleration structures,
    145–151
bottleneck, 147
bounding volume hierarchy query, 150
brute-force algorithm, 146
hybrid approaches, 150
parallel 1-axis sort and sweep, 148
parallel 3-axis sweep and prune,
    149–150

reference all pairs overlap test, 146–147
static local space AABB tree, 150–151
Sweep and Prune algorithm, 149
uniform grid, 147–148
workgroup, 148
Gregory patches, 188, 194
Gustafson-Barsis' law, 119

H
HACD library, 151, 152
HbrVertex vertices, 169
Helmholtz equation, 126
Hierarchical Boundary Representation, 167
High performance computing (HPC), 12
Houdini (multithreading existing software),
    19–46
cleaning statics, 22–27
    callback functions, 25
    debugging, 23
    function signatures, 24
    global variables, 22
    hue-saturation-value color, 23
    member data, 25
    NURBS library, 24
    parameter problems, 24
    premature optimization, 26
    red-green-blue color, 23
    static keyword, 22
copy on write, 34–40
    const correctness, 35
    external readers, 37
    failure modes of this system, 38–40
    Java, 36, 39
    memory leaks, 38
    ownership contract, 38
    ownership is important, 36–37
    pitfalls, 38
    pointer aliasing, 40
    reader/writer locks, 35–36
    Resource Acquisition Is
        Initialization, 36
    safe write operation, 34
    sole ownership is a writer lock, 37–38
    usage scenarios, 34
dependencies, 40–44
    Mantra, 43–44
    task locks, 41–43
    upstream geometry, 40
    VEX programming language, 41
description, 19–21
    computer generated art, 19

Houdini Development Kit, 21
physically based rendering, 21
Renderman Shading Language, 21
screenshot, 20
Single Instruction, Multiple Data implementation, 21
Vector Expression language, 21
OpenCL, 44–46
bandwidth problem, 45
unified memory, 45
patterns, 30–34
admonition, 31
always be reentrant, 30–31
atomics are slow, 31–32
bucketed particles, 34
command line control, 33
constant memory versus number of cores, 33–34
cycle-suckers, 31
debugging, 33
destination object, 33
lock-based algorithms, 31
locks, 33
memory allocation, 34
never blindly thread, 32–33
never lock, 31
recursive locks, 30
rewrite or refactor, 21–30
cleaning statics, 22–27
threading the simple cases, 27–30
task locks, 41–43
deadlocks, 41
efficiency, 41
threading the simple cases, 27–30
blocked matrix algorithm, 29
debugging, 28
embarrassingly parallel algorithm, 27
lambdas, 29
load balancing problem, 29
synchronization, 29
thread pool paradigm, advantages, 29
VEX code, 29
Houdini Development Kit, 21, 118
HPC; *See* High performance computing
Hue-saturation-value (HSV) color, 23
Hyperthreading (HT), 93–95

I
Incomplete Cholesky preconditioner, 132
In-flight threads, 67

Instruction level parallelism (ILP), 4
Intel
Cilk Plus, 12
Compiler, 22
Core Duo platform, 21
IvyBridge configuration, 183
Math Kernel Library, 88, 113
Parallel Inspector tool, 82
Threading Building Blocks, 13–16
algorithm templates, 13
allocator, 88
binary tree, 116
case studies, 2
C++ programming, 11, 13
debugging, 16
fork–join data parallelism, 13
GPL licensing, 14
grain size, 15
learning more about TBB, 16
MySQL, 14
parallel_for, 14–15
parallel_invoke, 16
parallel_reduce, 15–16
recursive range, 15
reduction operation, 15
simple cases, 27
sub-vectors, 15
team responsible for developing, 8
threading engine, 79
vertex stencils, 180
VTune Amplifier XE, 31
Xeon Phi Coprocessor, 7, 61
Xeon Processors E5-2687W, 127, 136
Xeon Processors X5670, 128, 129
Ivy Bridge machines, 104

J
Java, 36, 39

K
Kill switch (threadsafety), 84

L
Lambdas, 29
Lattice deformations, 52
LibEE (parallel evaluation of character rigs), 73–109
graph, 79–80
graph evaluation mechanism, 80
switch nodes, 80
task list, 80

TBB task scheduler, 79
threading engine, 79–80
graph threadsafety, 84–85
   Globally Unsafe node, 85
   Group Unsafe node, 85
   reentrant, 85
   threadsafe, 85
   Type Unsafe node, 85
heavily multithreaded graph, 75
limits of scalability, 104–106
   Amdahl's law, 104
   hardware limitations, 104
   memory bandwidth, 106
   multiple graphs, evaluation of in
      parallel, 106
motivation, 76
   benefits, 76
   parallelism visualization tool, 76
   retrofitting, 76
overall performance results, 104, 105
   fps benchmarks, 104
   Ivy Bridge machines, 104
production considerations, 95–97
   character systems restructure, 96
   critical path, 96
   no more scripted nodes, 96
   optimizing for maximum parallelism,
      96–97
rig optimization case studies,
    100–104
   case study (free clothes), 100, 103
   case study (hair solver), 100, 102
   case study (quadruped critical path
      optimization), 100, 101
   claw deformation system, 100
   performance bottlenecks, 104
scalability (hardware considerations),
    92–95
   CPU affinity, 94
   CPU power modes, 92
   hyperthreading, 93–95
   many-core architectures, 94–95
   NUMA, 92
   turbo clock, 92
   vectorization, 94
scalability (software considerations),
    85–92
   authoring parallel loops, 86–87
   cache reuse (chains of nodes), 89
   cache reuse (scheduling nodes to
      maximize sharing), 89

   failed approaches discussion, 91–92
   graph partitioning, 89–91
   Intel Math Kernel Library, 88
   memory wall, 91
   other processes running on system,
      91
   oversubscription due to multiple
      threading models, 88
   overthreading, 87
   task priorities, 89
   TBB grain size concept, 86
   thread-friendly memory allocators,
      88
   threading fatigue, 87
specific requirements for character
    animation, 76–79
   animation graph constraints, 78–79
   animation graph features, 77–78
   animation graph goals, 77
   animation rigs have implicit
      parallelism, 78
   dependency graph, 76
   expensive nodes which can be
      internally parallel, 78
   few unique traversed paths through
      graph, 77–78
   Global Interpreter Lock, 78
   no graph editing, 78
   no scripting languages in operators,
      78–79
   Python, 78
threading visualization tool, 97–99
   concurrency metric, 97
   optimization approaches, 97
   statistics, 97
   strategies, 97
threadsafety, 80–85
   API layer, 81
   compiler flags, 82–83
   graph threadsafety, 84–85
   Inspector, 82
   kill switch, 84
   LD_PRELOAD, 83
   node threadsafety, 81–84
   OpenMP environment, 81
   parallel unit tests, 81–82
   threading bugs, 82
   threading checker tools, 82
Linux, 22, 34, 83, 161
Lock-based algorithms, 31

M

Mantra, 43–44
Math Kernel Library (MKL), 88, 113
Maya, 76, 79, 118, 165
Memory
    access patterns (Presto), 59–60
    command line control, 33
    consumption (Background Execution),
        67
    fragmentation, 34
    leaks, 38
    unified, 45
Memory Wall, 4
Microsoft
    D3D APIs, 190
    DirectX11 Direct Compute, 138
    partnership with Pixar, 166
    Visual Studio, 145, 161
Minkowski Portal Refinement (MPR), 153,
    154
MKL; *See* Math Kernel Library
Moore's Law, 4
Mudbox (Autodesk), 198
Multithreading; *See* Houdini
        (multithreading existing software);
        Presto execution system
        (designing for multithreading)
Multithreading, introduction and overview,
    1–18
    advancing programming languages for
        parallel programming, 10–11
        abstraction, 10
        Cilk Plus project, 10
        GOTO statements, 10
        new keywords, 10
        parallel programming needs, 10
        relaxed sequential semantics, 11
        template library, 10
    data movement and layout, 16–17
        Array of Structures, 17
        Structures of Arrays, 17
        vectorization, 16
    Intel Threading Building Blocks, 13–16
        algorithm templates, 13
        debugging, 16
        fork–join data parallelism, 13
        GPL licensing, 14
        grain size, 15
        learning more about TBB, 16
        MySQL, 14

parallel_for, 14–15
parallel_invoke, 16
parallel_reduce, 15–16
recursive range, 15
reduction operation, 15
sub-vectors, 15
    motivation, 3–7
    auto-vectorization, 6
    floating point number operations, 6
    free lunch, 5
    highly threaded hardware, 7, 8
    hyperthreaded cores, 5
    instruction level parallelism, 4
    Memory Wall, 4
    Moore's Law, 4
    move to multicore, 4–6
    Power Wall, 4
    quickly increasing clock speeds ended
        by 2005, 3
    serial processor illusion, 4
    SIMD is parallelism too, 6–7
    vector arithmetic, 6
    vectorization, 6
overview of case studies, 2–3
    memory allocation routines, 2
    paradigm shift, 3
parallel programming in C and C++,
    11–16
    brief survey of key parallelism
        options, 12–13
    Bullet Physics, 13
    Cilk Plus, 12
    GPU specific models, 13
    high performance computing, 12
    Intel Threading Building Blocks,
        13–16
    NVIDIA graphics processors, 13
    OpenCL, 13
    OpenMP, 12
    TBB, 12
program in tasks, not threads, 7–8
    Cilk project, 8
    multiple tasks, 8
    programmer's role, 7
    TBB library, 8
scaling and vectorization, 9
value of abstraction, 8–9
    algorithm design, 9
    forms of parallelism, 9
    motivations, 9

nested parallelism, 9
portability of functionality, 9
MySQL, 14

N

Nested parallelism, 9, 112
Newton laws of motion, 138, 155
Non-uniform rational B-splines (NURBS),
164
library, 24
tools, 167
No-op elision, 54
NUMA (LibEE), 92
NVIDIA
Dynamic Parallelism, 179–180
graphics processors, 13

O

OpenCL, rewriting from scratch using,
140–145
branchy code/thread divergence,
143–144
algorithms, 143
clipContacts stage, 144
Compute Unit, 143
brief OpenCL introduction, 140–141
code conversion, 141
debugging, 141
kernel, 141
wrapper, 141
exploiting the GPU, 142–143
AMD terminology, 142
Compute Units, 142
Global Device Memory, 142
Private Memory, 142
wavefront, 142
Work Groups, 142
Work Item, 142
precompiled kernel caching, 145
OpenCL kernel source code, 145
Standard Portable Intermediate
Representation specification, 145
serializing data to contiguous memory,
144
sharing CPU and GPU code, 144–145
AMD CodeXL tool suite, 144
CPU math library, 144
debugging, 144
OpenMP, 12
OpenSubdiv (interoperating GPU compute
and drawing), 163–201

bi-cubic Bspline patches with GLSL,
191–196
Bézier interpolation, 191
boundary edge, 192
corner, 192
crack prevention, 193
end patches, 194–196
Gregory patches, 194
handling patch transitions, 193–194
handling surface boundaries,
192–193
hardware tessellation engine, 191
mirroring, 193
real-time render, 191, 194
REYES rendering algorithm, 191
up-front cost, 191
control cage, 166–168
Catmull-Clark limit surfaces, 168
face-varying primitive variable data,
167
Hierarchical Boundary
Representation, 167
limit surface, 168
manifold surfaces, 167–168
NURBS tools, 167
patches and arbitrary topology,
166–167
topological data structures, 167
evaluating our progress, 182–183
clock frequency, 183
core over-subscription, 183
cross-platform support, 182
ease of portability, 182
interactive display, 183
performance comparison, 182
total frame execution time, 183
feature adaptive subdivision, 186–190
adaptive feature isolation, 188
adaptive topological feature
isolation, 188, 189
Approximate Catmull-Clark Patches,
188
bi-cubic patch representation, 188
Catmull-Clark terminology, 187
discontinuous topological features,
188
eigen space transform, 188
feature-adaptive subdivision,
189–190
GPU hardware tessellation, 186–187
Gregory patches, 188

regular face, 187
regular vertex, 187
tessellation units, advantage of, 186
topological hierarchical edits, 188
triangulaton process, 186
valence, 187
fundamental limitations of uniform
    subdivision, 183–185
    animating subdivision surfaces, 185
    better, faster, different, 185
    comparison of off-line and interactive
        assets, 185
    core occupancy readings, 183
    exponential growth, 184
    feature film characters, 185
    geometric fidelity, 184
    geometric progression of subdivided
        polygons, 184
    MMORPG, 185
    unreliable surface normals, 184
implementing the GPU rendering
    engine, 190–196
    assembly pipeline, 190, 191
    bi-cubic Bspline patches with GLSL,
        191–196
    Fragment Shader, 190
    Geometry Shader, 190
    mitigating drawing overheads,
        196–197
    Vertex Shader, 190
mitigating drawing overheads, 196–197
    batching system, 196
    crack-free tessellation, 196
    fragmentation of patch types, 196
    sub-patches, 197
optimization trade-offs, 179–182
    alternative strategy (NVIDIA
        Dynamic Parallelism), 179–180
    alternative strategy (vertex stencils),
        180–181
    coalesced global memory access, 181
    CUDA kernel execution overheads,
        179
    memory bottlenecks, 181–182
    mesh striping techniques, 181
    set of factories, 180
    worst case scenario, 179
reducing branching divergence,
    175–178
    Catmull-Clark subdivision schema,
        176, 177

further vertex sorting, 176–178
HbrVertex, 176
OsdCompute kernels, 175
SIMD execution, 176
sorting vertices by type, 176
vertex ranking system, 177
Warp, 175
worst case scenario, 177
representing shapes, 164–166
    Catmull-Clark scheme, 164
    fast subdivision, 165
    feature-adaptive subdivision
        algorithm, 166
    flexibility, 164
    legacy, 165–166
    non-uniform rational B-splines, 164
    OpenSubdiv, 166
    subdivision meshes, 164
serializing the mesh representation,
    170–172
    case study (subdividing a pyramid),
        170
    face-vertices, 172
    generating indexing tables, 170–172
    preparing for parallel execution, 172
    subdivision tables, 171
texturing, 197–200
    displacement mapping, 198
    ground truth, 198
    high-frequency aliasing problems,
        198
    Ptex, 197, 199
transition from multicores to
    many-cores, 173–175
    arithmetic and logic units, 173
    comparison of CPU and GPU
        architecture, 173
    object oriented programming, 174
    practical implementation with
        OpenCL, 174–175
    streaming multiprocessors and
        SIMT, 173–174
    weighted data, 175
uniform subdivision, 169–170
    HbrVertex vertices, 169
    implementing subdivision schemata,
        169–170

P

Particle-in-cell (PIC) approaches, 129
PhotoRealistic Renderman, 165, 186

Physically based rendering (PBR), 21
Pixar, 2, 49, 165; *See also* Presto execution
    system (designing for
    multithreading)
Pixologic's ZBrush, 198
Plugin code, 57
Pointer aliasing, 40
Power Wall, 4
Presto execution system (designing for
    multithreading), 47–71, 165
  Background Execution, 64–69
    assumption, 68
    code reorganization, 68
    common edits, 67
    constant data, 67
    constant source of bugs, 66
    debugging, 65
    feedback, 65
    frame scheduling, 65–66
    in-flight threads, 67
    interruption, 66–67
    memory consumption, 67
    multiple-reader scenario, 67
    performance surprises, 65
    problematic data structures, 67–69
    pseudocode, 67
    repetitive strain injury, 66
    resource cleanup problems, 66
    starter thread, 67
    user interaction, 65
  debugging and profiling tools, 70–71
  flexibility to experiment, 60–61
    example, 60
    modular design, 60
    targeting other platforms, 60–61
    VRAM data manager, 61
  interactivity, 48–49
    approach, 48
    bare minimum, 48
    playback rate, 48
  memory access patterns, 59–60
    bulk data, 60
    hardware prefetchers, 60
    major guiding principle, 59
    optimizing memory access patterns,
      59
    structure-of-arrays, 60
  multithreading strategies, 61–64
    fast nodes, 61
    per-branch multithreading, 62, 63
    per-frame multithreading, 64

    per-model multithreading, 62–64
    per-node multithreading, 61
    slow nodes, 61
    time budget, 61
  predictive computations, 70
Presto, 49–52
  animation, 52
  attributes, 50
  connections, 50
  constraints, 52
  examples, 52
  execution structures, 52
  geometry topology, 52
  hard-to-debug problems, 52
  human-readable objects, 51
  lattice deformations, 52
  objects, 50–51
  prims, 50
  rigging, 51–52
  scene objects, 51
  screenshot, 49
  weight object, 51
Presto's execution system, 52–56
  abstraction data managers, 56
  animation workflows, 54
  Background Execution, 56
  client code, 55
  common computations, 52
  compilation, 53–54
  data managers, 56
  engine architecture, 54–56
  evaluation, 54
  execution engine components, 54
  executors, 56
  expensive operation, 55
  hierarchy, 56
  network, 55
  no-op elision, 54
  phases of execution, 53–54
  point posing, 55
  request, 54
  schedulers, 55–56
  scheduling, 54
  simplest data manager, 56
  vectorization, 53, 55
strip mining, 69–70
user extensions, 57–59
  client callbacks are static functions,
    57
  dependencies declared *a priori*, 57
  Global Interpreter Lock, 58–59

iterators, 58
plugin code, 57
Presto singletons are protected, 58
Python, 58–59
Projected Gauss-Seidel algorithm, 159
Ptex, 197, 199
Python, 58–59, 78
Global Interpreter Lock, 58–59
performance, 59

R
Recursive locks, 30
Red-green-blue (RGB) color, 23
Reentrant locks, 30
Reference all pairs overlap test, 146–147
Relaxed sequential semantics, 11
Renderman Shading Language (RSL), 21
Repetitive strain injury, 66
Resource Acquisition Is Initialization
(RAII), 36
REYES rendering algorithm, 191

S
SAP algorithm; *See* Sweep and Prune
algorithm
Side Effects Software, 19; *See also* Houdini
(multithreading existing software)
Single Instruction, Multiple Data (SIMD),
21
Standard Portable Intermediate
Representation (SPIR)
specification, 145
Strip mining, 69–70
Structures of Arrays (SoA), 17
Sutherland Hodgeman clipping, 153–154
Sweep and Prune (SAP) algorithm, 149
Switch nodes, 80

V
Vector Expression (VEX) language, 21, 41,
29
Vectorization, 6, 16
auto-, 12
C++ programming, 11
data layout, 16
data movement and layout, 16
many-core architectures, 94
network, 55
Presto, 53
scaling and, 9
SIMD, 6
TBB, 13
Vertex stencils, 180–181
Vertex-vertex kernel, 176
VEX language; *See* Vector Expression
language
Voxels, 120
VRAM data manager, 61
VTune Amplifier XE (Intel), 31

W
Walt Disney Studios, 197
Weighted data, 175
Work Groups, 142
Worst case scenario (OpenSubdiv), 177, 179

X
Xeon (Intel)
Phi Coprocessor, 7, 61, 94
Processors E5-2687W, 127
Processors X5670, 128, 129

Y
YouTube windows, 31

Z
ZBrush (Pixologic), 198